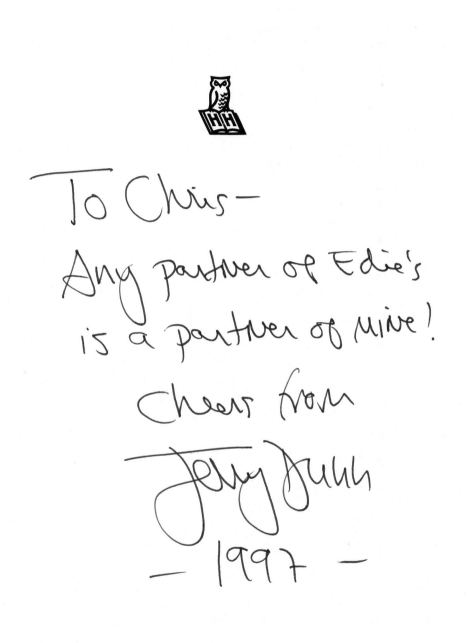

To Chris —
Any partner of Edie's
is a partner of mine!
Cheers from
Jerry Dunk
— 1997 —

IDIOM SAVANT

IDIOM SAVANT

SLANG AS IT IS SLUNG

Jerry Dunn

HENRY HOLT AND COMPANY
NEW YORK

Henry Holt and Company, Inc.
Publishers since 1866
115 West 18th Street
New York, New York 10011

Henry Holt® is a registered
trademark of Henry Holt and Company, Inc.

Published in Canada by Fitzhenry & Whiteside Ltd.,
195 Allstate Parkway, Markham, Ontario L3R 4T8.

Library of Congress Cataloging-in-Publication Data

Dunn, Jerry Camarillo.
Idiom savant: slang as it is slung / Jerry Dunn.—1st ed.
p.   cm.
1. English language—United States—Slang—Glossaries, vocabularies, etc.
2. Americanisms.   I. Title.
PE2846.D86   1997   96-52529
427′.09—dc21   CIP

ISBN 0-8050-5094-9

Henry Holt books are available for special promotions and
premiums. For details contact: Director, Special Markets.

First Edition—1997

Designed by Kate Nichols

Printed in the United States of America
All first editions are printed on acid-free paper. ∞

1   3   5   7   9   10   8   6   4   2

**WITH LOVE TO
JEAN WEBB VAUGHAN SMITH**

*My word-loving mother-in-law,
who always helps
with life's crossword puzzles*

CONTENTS

SHOW BUSINESS

CRIME AND PUNISHMENT

SPORTS AND RECREATION

AMUSEMENTS AND LIFESTYLES   221

A SLANG MISCELLANY 273

ACKNOWLEDGMENTS 287

INTRODUCTION

W hen skiers talk about a *yard sale,* they don't mean selling used household belongings on the front lawn. They mean taking a fall so spectacular that skis, goggles, and articles of clothing end up scattered across the snow as if laid out for sale to the neighbors.

When a lawyer says, "There's a witness missing, your Honor. I'm waiting for *Mr. Green* to appear," it carries a coded meaning: The attorney isn't ready to try the case because the client hasn't paid any cash yet.

How do such terms come into being?

Basically, you need a subculture. In any social group, lingo offers a shorthand way to communicate and, just as important, a way to identify yourself as a member. We all belong to groups, whether we're jazz fans, truck drivers, bartenders, or people with tattoos. As members, we need new words to express our group's shared experiences, to describe its equipment and ideas, and to prove that we belong.

The exuberance that leads human beings to create and enjoy new language is part of our nature. Since lingo is pithy and often funny, it adds freshness and zest to life. A story: Humorist S. J. Perelman once got in a traffic accident that wrecked his car. He quickly forgot being upset when a mechanic at the repair garage described the car as "totaled." Perelman, who had never heard this term, was nearly ecstatic. "Totaled!" he went around repeating. "Totaled!" The word was perfect.

Slang? Or What?

Linguistics experts debate the precise definitions of slang, jargon, argot, cant, vernacular, patois, and lingo. I happily leave this dispute to the experts. The book you're holding has the word "slang" in its subtitle basically because using "cant" or "patois" might sorely confuse people browsing at the bookstore. And I don't wish to confuse any potential customers, thank you very much.

One thing is clear: A subculture's lingo often escapes into the general population as slang. When this happens, it meets one of two fates: The term takes root in popular language (the 1967 hippie's *hassle*), or it dies out (the 1982 Valley Girl's *gag me with a spoon*).

Another observation: A person who is professionally or socially ambitious nowadays may get ahead faster by forgetting the "proper English" learned in school from Miss Grundy, and instead using the target group's slanguage. This rule applies equally at an advertising agency and on a surfing beach.

Researching via the Internet

You're holding a reference book, but not a dusty tome. It cradles living language, borne direct from people who use it every day. In fact, *Idiom Savant* is the world's first book to be largely researched "live" on the Internet.

Out there in cyberspace a remarkable mix of people share their common interests through what are called newsgroups. Each is an electronic clubhouse with ever-changing members, who use the newsgroup as a bulletin board for posting messages, queries, comments, and rants. I contacted dozens of newsgroups whose pet subjects range from collecting antiques to skydiving. I asked people to send me their group's lingo, and in return I got an avalanche of e-mail. Some correspondents offered a few well-chosen words; others sent long, articulate essays. The kindness of strangers!

As the words poured into my bowl, I savored the snap-crackle-and-pop of American lingo. It emphasizes wordplay, wit, and, of course, derogatory terms for things and people you don't much like.

At times lingo springs from black humor, often a defense mechanism against the stress and sometimes the pain of one's job or situation. For instance, to a nurse, a patient close to death is *circling the drain,* while a person in an oxygen tent has *gone camping.* A policeman having emotional problems is assigned to the *rubber gun detail.* Prison inmates refer to mystery meat served in the mess hall as *Mr. Ed.*

Some subcultures were wary of my poking into their private languages. Science fiction fans, for example, use the slang of "fandom" as a yardstick of insider status, judging others by how they use (or misuse) the lingo. I had to walk on eggs.

Other groups view their closed worlds with even more seriousness. Most folks at the Harley-Davidson motorcycle newsgroup were friendly, but one woman chewed me out for defining *bitch pegs* as "short foot pegs for the female rider'' (a definition provided by other members of her newsgroup). She wrote:

> Jerry, Jerry, Jerry. Haven't you paid attention? There are many fe-males who *ride* a Harley, not just pack. The paragraph above should say passenger, not female rider. The rider is the one at the controls, and it is NOT always a man. You'd be pinned down and pummeled for saying this in a real biker bar.

About other definitions, she observed: "You'd be killed for this state-ment if this were not cyberspace," and "FIX this, or you'll have women on your doorstep who will rip your arms off. I'll be one of them." For some reason I was reminded of the famous cantina scene in *Star Wars*—a rowdy-ass saloon out there somewhere in space, filled with possibly threatening life forms.

A few newsgroups shielded their lingo behind humor. When I made contact with a skateboarding group, I pictured a street-corner clot of teen-age guys in baggy T-shirts, mumbling ''Rad, dude.'' Instead:

> Dear sir,
>   What slang is it to which you refer? We skateboarders use only the purest forms of verbal communication to convey our views and to make known our thoughts. . . . For example, when my skating companion performs a trick which is beyond my expectation or scope of understanding, I might say, ''That's the way, Jason. You executed that three-hundred-and-sixty-degree flip with grace and quickness surpassing belief. The altitude you achieved was also quite impressive.'' As you can see, there is nothing interesting about our verbal communication.

Later I did receive some actual skateboarding lingo. My first draft in-cluded these terms:

> **huphtur** *n.*   a non-skater (pejorative).
> **Lloyd Bentsen** *n.*   a strange handstand on a skateboard.
> **Murray** *n.*   a non-skater (non-pejorative).
> **shaq** *v.*   to fall down while trying a trick. Syn. *blag, skik, svif.*

I posted my list to the entire newsgroup—as I always did, partly as a courtesy and partly for double-checking—and got back this reply:

I think someone's been pulling your leg, Jerry. Did you get all your info from one guy, 'cause if you did, then that shoulda been a hint. People are gonna be protective of their slang, 'cause as soon as you print it, we'll feel like twits saying it. See my logic?

I did, indeed. Soon I received another e-mail message:

Hmm . . . Let me see if I've got this straight: "Dooooood, you're such a huphtur. You can't even Lloyd Bentsen the right way. Man, you TOTALLY blagged yerself. Try not to shaq next time. Maybe you should go back to being a Murray." Whew!

After this instructive encounter with bogus lingo, I doubled my vigilance. And I was doubly grateful to people who trusted me enough to open the doors of their private clubs.

Of course, I also spoke to a great many people in person—dentists, magicians, lawyers, a *National Enquirer* reporter, baseball fans, a fake psychic reader, waiters, pilots, a veteran FBI agent, surfers, and many others. More than seven hundred names are listed in the Acknowledgments.

Opening Windows

Aside from the interesting company and the laughs, there's another reason why writing *Idiom Savant* has been rewarding. The slang of a group opens a window into their world. Social walls are penetrated to let in light and fresh air. I feel I understand the stage actors, used car salesmen, airline flight attendants, funeral directors, pool hustlers, emergency room nurses, and others whose slang fills this book.

I hope you find these open windows to be illuminating.

Finally, a few words of caution. I'm aware that some people see sexism in terms like "fisherman." Sexism is neither my intention nor my attitude. Yet, "fisherwoman" isn't in the dictionary, and I hate to strain for words such as "fisherfolk" (formerly restricted to Hans Christian Andersen tales). In referring to individuals, moreover, I often write the conventional "he" to represent people in general. To me, the manufactured usage "he/ she" is irredeemably clunky.

A really attentive reader will notice that the same slang occasionally pops up in more than one subculture. Among terms mentioned earlier, "yard sale" is common to skiers, snowboarders, and mountain bikers, while "circling the drain" is shared by nurses and police officers. Some terms, however, have various meanings depending on the group. To truckers a "bambi" is a deer; to television game show staffers it's a contestant who freezes in front of the camera lens like a deer caught in the headlights. To funeral directors a "shake and bake" is a simple cremation without services; to beach volleyball players it's what happens when someone dives for a ball and gets covered with sand. "Paper" to a crooked gambler indicates marked cards, but means traffic tickets to a police officer.

As you browse through the lingo of groups to which you belong, you may find unfamiliar words. This makes perfect sense, since no one person can be everywhere and hear it all. Lingo reflects regional differences (East Coast vs. West Coast), as well as age differences (twentysomethings vs. fiftysomethings). Also, most of the lingo in this book has never appeared in print before. If it's unfamiliar, that's the whole point of discovering it here.

IDIOM SAVANT

WORK

MEDICAL WORKERS

Nurses,* Doctors, and Hospital Staff

achieve his/her therapeutic goal *v.*   to die. "I saw Mr. Berman in the obits this morning. I guess he *achieved his therapeutic goal* in spite of us." Syn. **achieve room temperature.**

anal-olecranon confusion *n.*   a condition afflicting people who don't know their ass from their elbow.

Bard-Parker *n.*   a scalpel blade. This brand name is mentioned by the surgical team if the patient is awake for surgery.

beached whale *n.*   an extremely obese patient unable to do much but lie there with flailing arms and legs. Usually at least three nurses are needed to give such a patient a bedpan, pull him up in bed, and so on. "Can two of you help me turn the *beached whale* in Room 203?"

the big one *n.*   a heart attack.

---

* Nurses comment on their profession's slang: "As a group, we have a lexicon that is colorful, sometimes in poor taste, frequently witty, and quite intelligent. Whenever we say something really derogatory (always far from the public's ears), it's a way of dealing with the stress and frustration of the job, and it helps us to be pleasant and professional around those who may be driving us bonkers. One can only hope the public will see it from our side of the bed. . . . Yes, some expressions seem rather callous, but this is a defense mechanism that protects us from being overwhelmed by a sea of pain and suffering that we are witness to and at times participate in. This is not to say that nurses are not also caring. We are, or we wouldn't be in the business."

blade *n.* a surgeon. "I've been divorced from two *blades*. They just can't love anyone else as much as they love themselves." Rel. **neuro-blade:** neurosurgeon.

blow *v.* when a vein ruptures at the start of an intravenous procedure. "I stuck him three times for his IV, but they all *blew*."

blower *n.* a mechanical respirator. "The patient is still on the *blower*." Syn. **vent.**

bobbing for apples *v.* unblocking a badly constipated patient with one's finger.

BOHICA *v.* Bend Over, Here It Comes Again. Can refer to the next onslaught of patients in the emergency room or operating room, or the next pronouncement from hospital administration about raises, staffing, the budget, etc.

boogie *n.* a tumor or mass. "This patient has a serious *boogie* in his abdomen." Syn. **goober, goombah.**

Bordeaux *n.* blood in the urine.

bottle return *v.* removing a bottle stuck (by vacuum suction) in the anal canal of a patient, often a gay man.

BRAT diet *n.* bananas, rice, applesauce, and toast—a remedy for diarrhea in infants.

bug juice *n.* antibiotics administered intravenously.

bugs in the rug *n.* pubic lice.

bull in the ring *n.* a blockage in the large intestine.

bungee jumper *n.* a patient who pulls on his catheter tube.

bury the hatchet *v.* to sew up a patient with a surgical instrument mistakenly left inside.

CABG *n.* pronounced "cabbage." A Coronary Artery Bypass Graft, commonly called a coronary bypass. Rel. **cabbage patch kids:** patients having coronary bypass surgery.

Captain Kangaroo *n.*   the head of the pediatrics department.

celestial discharge/transfer *n.*   death. "We've had two *celestial discharges* on this shift."

chartomegaly *n.*   the condition of a patient whose many hospital admissions have generated voluminous records. Derived from "chart" (medical record) and "megaly" (enlargement). "He's got *chartomegaly.*"

circling the drain/CTD *adj.*   close to death, lingering. "We thought Mrs. Manning was *circling the drain,* but she pulled through." Syn. **FTD:** Fixin' To Die; **STBD:** Soon To Be Dead.

code/code blue *n.*   a life-endangering medical emergency. "Dr. Smyth, *code blue,* room 445A." Also, a patient who stops breathing or whose heart stops beating, necessitating resuscitation. "We have a *code blue!* Bring the crash cart." Also, *v.*   "He's *coded* on us."

code brown *n.*   when a patient has a major stool event in the bed. Sometimes requires several people to clean up, especially in the case of dementia patients who throw or smear their stool. "We have a *code brown.* Better bring rubber gloves and a mop."

code yellow *n.*   when a catheter breaks and the patient is covered in urine.

cranium rectumitis *n.*   having one's head up one's posterior. "I'm afraid the new patient has a severe case of *cranium rectumitis.*"

crappacardia *n.*   cardiac dysrhythmia, involving several types of aberrant heartbeat. "Mrs. Linden has had runs of PAT, VT, and AIVR. In short, she is in *crappacardia.*"

crash *v.*   when a critically ill patient has a major negative event. "My patient *crashed* last night and ended up back on a ventilator." Also, when a patient begins a possibly deadly collapse. "He's *crashed!* Start CPR and life support."

crash cart *n.*   a wheeled unit carrying a defibrillator (for cardiac arrest), medications, and other life-sustaining items for a "crash" emergency.

crispy critter *n.*   a badly burned patient. "In the bad old days when patients could smoke in their rooms, I warned the ones on oxygen not to light up or they might become *crispy critters.*"

crock *n.* a malingerer, often with silly or spurious complaints. Derived from "crock of shit." "That *crock* has come back six times for tests, but they never find anything." Rel. **have a high porcelain level** *adj.* to be a crock.

crump *v.* to collapse physically or psychologically. Short for crumple. "Mr. Baker in 4471 *crumped* on us last night."

cut and paste *v.* to surgically open a patient, find that there is no hope for treatment, and sew him up again without delay.

dandruff on wheels *n.* scabies or any other personal protein that moves and can be transferred to other people. "Careful with the homeless guy in the ER! We're talking *dandruff on wheels* here."

dash for cash *n.* helicopter transportation for desperately ill or injured patients, often provided by private air services charging high fees.

DFO *v.* Done Fell Out. Passed out cold. "This patient was at the state fair when all of a sudden he *DFO'd* right outside the cow barns."

discharged downstairs *v.* when a deceased patient is transferred to the hospital's morgue.

Doc-in-a-Box *n.* a doctor who works in a private, drive-in emergency room facility.

donorcycle *n.* a motorcycle. An emergency room term recognizing that many people in serious motorcycle accidents become organ donors. "Here comes another *donorcycle* victim."

DOV *adj.* pronounced "dove." Dead On a Ventilator. Refers to a comatose patient on a mechanical respirator. Also, *n.* "I took care of two *DOVs* last night."

drooler *n.* a catatonic patient.

DSB *n.* Drug Seeking Behavior. Refers to the actions of people who come to the hospital and angle to be given narcotics for their counterfeit complaints.

dump *v.* when nurses shuttle a problem patient to another unsuspecting floor. Also *n.* the patient who is dumped.

the dwindles *n.* weaknesses of old age; a failure to thrive.

eating in *v.* having intravenous feeding.

eat the bill *v.* when a hospital or doctor absorbs the cost of treating a poor or uninsured patient.

eternal care unit *n.* death.

expensive care *n.* Intensive Care.

family plan *n.* when parents bring all the children to the emergency room for free checkups when only one child actually has a cold or flu. "Ah, the Greens seem to be here on the *family plan* again."

fascinoma *n.* a fascinating disease or a patient of unusual clinical interest.

fireman-in-a-box *n.* a mechanical compression device for performing CPR (cardiopulmonary resuscitation).

flea *n.* an internist who orders numerous blood withdrawals to test for possible diseases, with no gain for the patient.

float a swan *v.* to place a Swan-Ganz catheter in a patient.

FLK *n.* Funny Looking Kid. A child suspected of having some sort of syndrome or genetic disorder that is difficult to identify immediately. Rel. **FLP:** Funny Looking Parents of an FLK.

flog *v.* to attempt to resuscitate an emergency room arrival who is already near death.

fluorescent light therapy *n.* a long stint in the ER waiting room under the bright fluorescent lights, a treatment prescribed by the admitting nurse when a nasty patient has annoyed her.

FOOBA *n.* Found On Orthopod, Barely Alive. A darkly humorous reference to a patient treated by an orthopedic doctor (orthopod) who hasn't kept up in general medicine, focuses only on his specialty, and disregards other ailments. Such a patient is belatedly referred to another doctor when a more life-threatening problem develops. "Dr. Robinson gave this *FOOBA* a hip replacement, and now she's got pneumonia. Hmm . . ."

FOS *adj.* Full of Shit/Stool. Constipated, with abdominal pain. "The X ray shows that he's *FOS* and needs a laxative."

frequent flyer *n.* a patient who has stayed in the hospital many times previously. "That *frequent flyer* comes in so often, she tells you what room she wants."

fry his beans *v.* to cause death of the kidneys, as when overly high doses of medication lead to renal failure. "God, all that dopamine really *fried his beans.*" Syn. **killed the kids.**

FUBAR *adj.* Fucked Up Beyond All Repair/Recognition. Refers to a patient, such as an auto accident victim, who has many complex problems. Also, a derogatory term describing the outcome of bad care. Can also refer to the caregiver. "That intern is so *FUBAR*, I wouldn't trust him to put on a Band-Aid." Also, *v.* "The resident got hold of this poor patient and *FUBAR'd* him."

gas passer *n.* an anesthesiologist.

GOK *adj.* God Only Knows. Refers to baffling symptoms that defy diagnosis.

gomer *n.* an older patient with chronic, debilitating health problems that have no easy cures. May be senile, messy, or highly unpleasant. From the expression "Get out of my emergency room," first appearing in *The House of God,* by Dr. Samuel Shem. Rel. **gome from the home:** a gomer sent in from a nursing home.

gomergram *n.* an array of all possible lab tests, ordered for a gomer unable to communicate his or her symptoms because of senility. Rel. **troll the labs** *v.* to order a broad set of tests.

gone camping *adj.* in an oxygen tent.

gork *n.* a patient who has severe mental impairment, is comatose, or possibly brain-dead. "I have three *gorks* on my shift." Rel. **gorked out** *adj.* semi-comatose or comatose. "The patient in 321 is completely *gorked out.*"

go to ground *v.* to fall out of a bed or chair. "No matter how careful you are, gomers will *go to ground.*" A Dr. Shem-ism. (*See* **gomer.**)

GSW *n.* gunshot wound.

happy feet *n.* a symptom of a grand mal epileptic seizure. "Get some IV Dilantin. He's got *happy feet!*"

head *n.* a patient with trauma to the brain.

hole in one *n.* a bullet through the mouth or other orifice.

horrendoplasty *n.* someone who has been returned to the operating room for one procedure after another, in order to correct complications.

hot *adj.* infected with a deadly, communicable bacteria or virus. "Put on full isolation protection gear. The patient was exposed to Ebola Zaire, and he's *hot.*" Also, about to explode; for example, referring to an aneurysm or an organ. "Get this patient up to surgery. He's got a *hot* gallbladder!"

impending social disaster *n.* a dark pattern in an abdominal X ray indicating a major gas buildup. Radiologist looking at film: "I'd say we have an *impending social disaster.*"

jump start *v.* to defibrillate, or restore normal contractions of the heart through electric shock or drugs. "Get the crash cart. We've got to *jump start* this guy!"

lead poisoning *n.* the problem afflicting someone who has been shot. "What a shift in the ER. We had three cases of *lead poisoning* before midnight."

Leave-'em-dead *n.* Levophed. A medication used as an often last-ditch effort to raise a patient's blood pressure from an extremely low level. "Here's the basic therapy plan for *Leave-'em-dead:* Increase it until the blood pressure goes up or the toes fall off."

liver rounds *n.* an outing to a cocktail bar after a tough case or a good job, taken for the purpose of drinking, debriefing, and decompressing. "The new intern did a really fine job. Let's take her on *liver rounds.*"

LOL *n.* Little Old Lady.

loose change *n.* a nearly severed limb that will require amputation.

LPN *n.*   Let's Play Nurse. Referring to a Licensed Practical Nurse. Ant. **RN:** Real Nurse. Referring to a Registered Nurse.

microdeckia *adj.*   mentally off, loony, "not playing with a full deck" in pseudo-Latin: "micro" (small) and "deck" (of cards).

Milk of Amnesia *n.*   Propofol. A milky white drug used to put patients to sleep.

MO'FAT *n.*   Minimum Operating [Room] Fucking Around Time. The time required to get an operation started once the patient has entered the room; i.e., finding the X rays, getting the lab results, locating the surgeon or getting him/her off the phone, and so forth.

NAD *adj.*   No Apparent Distress. "We have an LOL in *NAD.*"

negative wallet biopsy *n.*   the condition afflicting a patient with insufficient funds or insurance to cover treatment. Syn. **MI:** monetary insufficiency.

nose hose *n.*   a nasogastric tube, inserted through the nose in order to drain the stomach.

OOB *adj.*   Out Of Bed.

organ recital *n.*   the medical history of a hypochondriac.

O sign *n.*   when an unresponsive patient's mouth is hanging open. Usually indicates a poor prognosis. "He's showing the *O sign.*"

OTD *adj.*   Out The Door. Discharged from the hospital. Rel. **OTD—AMF:** Out The Door—Adiós Mother Fucker. Phrase used when discharging an obnoxious or unruly patient.

party package *n.*   group of medications given to an intoxicated patient; usually thiamine, multivitamins, and magnesium, plus IV fluids.

PB@B *adj.*   Pine Box at Bedside. A chart notation when the patient is so terminal that this would seem to be in order. Rel. **PPTB—LLO:** Pine Box To Bedside—Leave Lid Open.

personality transplant *n.* recommended treatment for any physician or nurse who hasn't learned to be a decent or caring human being or has other annoying characteristics. "That surgeon needs a *personality transplant.*"

PIA *n.* Pain In the Ass. "My patient has a serious case of *PIA.*"

PID *n.* officially, Pelvic Inflammatory Disease, a condition that involves infection and discharge from the vagina; unofficially, Pussy in Distress, or Pus in 'Dere.

piggyback *v.* to add a second IV bottle that runs in tandem with the main intravenous fluid. "We have a train wreck coming from the ER. I'll *piggyback* this antibiotic."

pit *n.* the emergency room.

POF *n.* Pillow On Face. A jocular reference to what will happen to a patient who doesn't stop complaining excessively. "If Mrs. Jones doesn't get off that call bell and go to sleep, she's gonna get *POF.*"

pop drop *n.* when a family parks their elderly, incapacitated father at the hospital so they can have a vacation.

positive chandelier *n.* when a doctor inadvertently causes a patient severe pain while performing an exam or procedure. The expression implies that the patient must be retrieved from an agonized leap onto the ceiling lights. "When I palpated his right lower quadrant, I got a *positive chandelier.*"

positive suitcase sign *n.* denotes a person who arrives at the hospital with an already packed suitcase, hoping to be admitted; may simply need a place to stay.

Q sign *n.* when an unresponsive patient's mouth is hanging open with the tongue hanging out. "He has the positive *Q sign.*" Rel. **dotted Q sign:** the Q sign with a fly on the tongue.

rafting on the Rio Caca *adj.* when someone has massive diarrhea. "The Lomotil just didn't work. He kept *rafting on the Rio Caca.*"

rear admiral *n.* a proctologist.

riding the squirrel train *adj.* when a patient has awakened in a confused state and is trying to get out of bed, pulling at his tubes, etc.

rocket room *n.* a room in the nursing unit where a high number of patients die, thus soaring to heaven. "Looks like he's going to die anyway. Better put him in the *rocket room*."

rock garden *n.* an emergency room filled with patients who aren't sick enough to admit to the hospital but who can't be moved out. They may be debilitated or senile, have relatives who insist on leaving them, or have no insurance or cash, making them impossible to admit.

rollerskate shift *n.* a busy shift during which a nurse never stops moving.

rooters *n.* people (often indigents) who hang around emergency rooms in big cities to observe and be entertained by the arriving patients.

round up the usual suspects *v.* to order all the routine tests for the patient's condition; often a gomergram.

sauce *n.* any disgusting bodily secretion, including vomit. "We were splashing in the *sauce*."

scratch and sniff *n.* a gynecological examination.

scut monkey *n.* a medical student who does the most menial jobs in the hospital, such as carrying samples to labs.

shooter *n.* an intravenous drug addict.

sick *adj.* extremely sick, possibly close to death.

sidewalk soufflé *n.* a person who has fallen from a building.

slug *n.* a patient (usually post-surgical) who should be getting out of bed and moving in order to prevent complications and regain independence, but who needs lots of encouragement and assistance to do so. "That post-op gall bladder inching his way down the hall is a real *slug*."

smoking a White Owl *v.* using an oral endotracheal tube. "No food for him. He's still *smoking a White Owl*."

snowed *adj.*   under heavy sedation and unable to respond; often occurs by mistake. "We gave that confused little man Haldol because he was pulling out all his tubes. Now he's *snowed.*" Also, **snow** *v.*   to administer large quantities of morphine or Demerol when a patient is suffering severe pain.

SOB *adj.*   Short Of Breath.

squash *n.*   brain. Rel. **cooked squash:** a brain-dead patient.

stick *n.*   a skin puncture made to draw blood or insert an IV. "It took three *sticks* before I could find a good vein." Also, *v.*

sundowner *n.*   a usually older patient who is alert and oriented during the day, but gets confused after dark. "The patient in 102 is a *sundowner.* Be sure to keep plenty of lights on, and watch her closely."

TBF *n.*   Total Body Failure. When the major organ systems begin shutting down and the patient has a very poor prognosis. "Mr. Schwartz is an end-stage alcoholic and practically in *TBF.*"

technicolor burp *n.*   vomit.

terrasphere *n.*   dirtball. An assessment of a certain type of emergency room patient. From Latin "terra" (earth) and "sphaera" (ball).

Thorazine shuffle *n.*   a shambling step often seen in psychiatric patients who are sedated with Thorazine, an antipsychotic drug.

three hots and a cot *n.*   three meals and a bed. Refers to the goal of a person trying to get admitted for bogus complaints or by faking psychiatric symptoms, such as hearing voices. Often the person has run out of money and is waiting for a disability check.

thumper protocol *n.*   initiation of CPR. "Let's put this guy on the *thumper protocol.*"

tough stick *n.*   a patient who requires a blood draw but whose veins prove elusive.

train wreck *n.*   a patient who is badly injured or has many medical problems. "This guy's a *train wreck.* His sugar is off the charts, he's got gastrointestinal bleeding, a bedsore, and dropping blood pressure. It also looks like he's been in a fight, since he's bleeding from a gash on his head.''

treat 'em and street 'em *v.* to deal rapidly with patients in the emergency room.

TSTL *adj.* Too Stupid To Live.

turf *v.* to get a gomer out of your department by finding a problem that another department must take care of. ''Ha! The patient now has chest pain—why don't we *turf* him to the Cardiac Care Unit?'' Also, *n.* a troublesome patient who is transferred because the sending nurse doesn't want to be bothered. ''We just got a *turf* from the surgical unit.'' Rel. **buff** *v.* to overstate a patient's recovery, thereby making him seem more attractive, in order to turf him. ''Mr. White is gone; I *buffed* him and turfed him to Internal Medicine.''

vah spa *n.* a Veterans' Administration hospital. ''This patient usually goes to the *vah spa.*''

vampire *n.* a nurse able to draw blood successfully from tough sticks. Also, **Dracula.**

vitamin P(ee) *n.* a small dose of the diuretic Lasixa, given to stimulate urination in post-operative patients. ''It was getting close to eight hours post-op, but once we gave her some *vitamin P,* the floodgates opened.''

vitamin V *n.* a dose of the tranquilizer Valium or Versed, given to calm a patient with pre-operative anxiety.

waiting for the train to Chicago *v.* close to death, in spite of the best medical efforts. ''He has his bags packed and is *waiting for the train to Chicago,* but I'll hold his hand while he waits.'' Syn. **waiting for the bus.**

walkie-talkie *n.* a patient who is able to get out of bed, walk around by himself, and speak coherently. ''Only one of my patients is a *walkie-talkie.*''

WNL *adj.* Within Normal Limits. Notation on a medical chart. For questionable doctors it means We Never Looked.

wouldn't do well in a sandstorm *adj.* refers to a patient who has no blink reflex. May be brain-dead or have severe neurological damage.

Dentists

Chiclets *n.*   bad caps on front teeth; commonly too white and too wide. "I love seeing the movie stars flashing their *Chiclets* on Oscar night." Syn. **Frigidaires.**

clickers *n.*   dentures and porcelain teeth. "You should see Mr. Edwards with his new *clickers*. He looks more like Mr. Ed."

drilling, filling, and billing *n.*   the dental business in a somewhat cynical nutshell. "It's all *drilling, filling, and billing*. No wonder we have such a high suicide rate."

flipper *n.*   a temporary denture replacing the upper front teeth. Often worn by hockey players. "The Detroit forward just got a *flipper*."

four-on-the-floor ortho *n.*   the outdated technique of removing four bicuspids to make room before putting in braces.

garbage dump *n.*   the mouth of a dental patient with unbelievably bad oral hygiene. "My poor hygienist—she's going to need oxygen after detoxing that *garbage dump*. Syn. **grungemouth.**

gum gardener *n.*   a periodontist.

happy gas *n.*   nitrous oxide.

"If it gets past the lip, it fits" *exp.*   the philosophy of a lazy dentist who will seat anything the lab sends.

"If it's bright, it's right" *exp.*   the hopeful motto of a dental student trying to get the instructor's approval of a gold inlay or crown by giving it a high polish that distracts from defects in fit.

pluggin' pewter *v.*   replacing silver fillings.

pulp popper *n.*   an endodontist, a specialist in dental pulp and tooth roots.

red-eye *v.*   to strike a tooth nerve while drilling. "It's a shame Mr. Nuñez was so unforgiving. After all, I didn't *red-eye* him on purpose."

robomouth *n.* a person with implanted false teeth.

rodeo dentistry *n.* treating an uncooperative child. "Get out the lasso for little Donna; it's *rodeo dentistry* time."

shovel jaw *n.* a patient with a protruding lower jaw.

shuck 'em *exp.* a diagnosis for multiple extractions.

slappin' plastic *v.* placing tooth-colored composite fillings. " 'I'm worn out!' cried Dr. Bloomquist. 'I spent the whole afternoon *slappin' plastic.*' "

sleepy juice *n.* Novocain.

spin the tooth down *v.* to reduce the tooth for capping with a crown.

squirt 'em and jerk 'em *v.* to give a Novocain injection, then extract teeth.

tin grin *n.* braces. Syn. **railroad tracks.**

wire bender *n.* an orthodontist.

LAWYERS

bag lady *n.* a woman seeking a divorce who brings a bag full of her husband's financial papers to the attorney's office.

beaten with a bag of money *adj.* settled out of court. Rel. **greenback poultice** *n.* a large, soothing monetary settlement.

blue-hair case *n.* a slip-and-fall lawsuit involving a senior citizen. "I don't think we should represent Mrs. Jones. You know how hard it is to win a *blue-hair case.*"

bomber *n.* a divorce lawyer who tries to wipe out the other spouse by grabbing all the assets for his client.

burnt-toast jurisprudence *n.* what you get when a judge is having a bad day and is in a foul mood by the time you see him.

capper *n.* a person who recruits accident victims for a personal injury lawyer. "That tow-truck driver makes more money as a *capper* than on his paycheck."

come to Jesus meeting *n.* a meeting in which the attorney advises the client that his case is fatally weak, and that he should settle quickly for whatever he can get. "We need to have a *come to Jesus meeting* with Chem-Tech. Will you set it up for Tuesday?"

criminal lawyer *n.* a redundancy.

do the Big Shoe Dance *v.* when an attorney makes an elaborate but meaningless presentation because he has no good arguments. Derived from Pee Wee Herman. Example: "I can explain that, your Honor. Other than my client's three felony convictions, he has never had any contact with the criminal justice system. None!"

dump truck *n.* a criminal attorney or public defender who promises a strong defense but does nothing and pleads his clients guilty. "Some lawyer he turned out to be—this *dump truck* basically backed into court and unloaded me." Rel. **bleed 'em and plead 'em** *v.* when a defense attorney charges a fee for legal work but enters a guilty plea before trial.

Federal Sentencing Guidelines decoder ring *n.* what is needed when trying to navigate a particularly difficult statute. In commercial law this would be a **Uniform Commercial Code decoder ring.**

hallway hero *n.* a prosecutor who tells exaggerated tales of his brilliant maneuvers in the courtroom.

home run *n.* a sure-fire case against a defendant with sufficient finances to pay big damages. "I've got a *home run* against Frito-Lay. A plumber broke three teeth on a rusty nail in a bag of Fritos."

home-towned *adj.* when an out-of-town attorney loses a case because of local bias.

Mr. Green *n.* cash payment of a lawyer's fee or retainer. "There's a witness missing, your Honor. I'm waiting for *Mr. Green* to appear." Translation: The lawyer isn't ready to try the case because the client hasn't paid yet.

nail and mail *n.* when a subpoena or other legal papers are tacked onto someone's front door, while a support copy is sent through the post office. "We can't locate her ex-husband to serve him. Let's do a *nail and mail.*"

nastygram *n.* a letter sent to the opposition in a new case, explaining the reasons why your own side is going to win and stating a settlement demand. "McGrath, send a *nastygram* to X Corporation. Let's wake 'em up a little bit."

pass the gas *v.* to order a death sentence. Rel. **get-high-and-die sentence** *n.* execution by lethal injection.

piss backwards *v.* when a witness offers testimony inconsistent with what he told police earlier.

pound the table *v.* part of a litigator's maxim: "When the facts are on your side, pound the facts. When the law is on your side, pound the law. When neither are on your side, *pound the table.*"

rainmaker *n.* an attorney whose main role is bringing new clients to the firm. "Henry isn't much of a litigator, but he's an amazing *rainmaker.* That's why he made senior partner at age 42."

rambo litigators *n.* attorneys who create a fight at every step of litigation—raising specious objections throughout a deposition, responding to discovery requests with long laundry lists of hair-splitting objections, seeking continuances in bad faith, and generally making litigation long, expensive for both sides, and unfriendly. Rel. **rambo litigation:** "The Supreme Court is considering rules designed to reduce the amount of *rambo litigation* and thus streamline pre-trial proceedings."

retread *n.* a divorce lawyer's client who has already been divorced one or more times.

tar-baby case *n.* a case in which the attorney becomes progressively more mired with less satisfaction.

sandbag *v.* to hold back evidence or testimony, in order to surprise the opposition.

shopper *n.* a wife with no income, assets, or marketable skills, thus requiring alimony. "Mrs. Carmody is a *shopper,* so we better ask for big monthly payments." Also, a person who goes around talking to lots of attorneys simply to get free legal advice.

treasure maps *n.*   records used by a divorce lawyer to locate a spouse's assets (bank accounts, tax returns, financial statements, business ledgers, etc.).

unring the bell *v.*   refers to the impossible task of getting a jury to disregard testimony or evidence after the judge rules it inadmissible. "The jury heard the words 'wife beater.' No judge can *unring that bell.*"

walk the dog *v.*   when a prosecutor goes to trial with a sure loser of a case. "I offered the defendant reduced charges, but he said no. Guess I'll be *walking the dog.*"

wet reckless *n.*   a charge of "reckless driving, alcohol related"; a reduction from the more serious charge of drunk driving.

JOURNALISTS

Newspaper Reporters and Photographers

bang bang *n.*   a photo assignment during which guns are fired.

banner *n.*   a headline stretching across the page.

brite *n.*   a brief story that is amusing or heartwarming, usually with little news value. "There's a lot of doom and gloom on the Metro page. We need a *brite* to lighten things up."

bulldog *n.*   the first edition of the day, usually available on the street the night before. "When you see the Sunday paper at the supermarket on Saturday night, that's the *bulldog* edition."

bullet *n.*   a large dot to mark items in a list. "This list of diet foods is hard to read. Better add *bullets* to the main categories."

bulletproof *adj.*   film so overexposed and opaque that a slug couldn't penetrate it.

crash and burn *n.*   a car accident and/or fire, to a news photographer.

cutline *n.*   the caption beneath a photograph.

dingbat *n.*   a typographical ornament or symbol.

dummies *n.*   mock-ups of pages before they are actually produced.

flag *n.*   the publication's name, which flies above the banner.

gang bang *n.*   when lots of news photographers show up at a crime scene or event. "I hate covering celebrity trials. They're always *gang bangs.*"

gooney *n.*   a fluffy story used to fill space in a bulldog edition until a more important story comes along later. So called because a typical subject might be something inconsequential such as gooney birds.

graf *n.*   a paragraph. "Give me two more *grafs* on the city council meeting, will you?"

grip and grin *n.*   a photo of someone shaking hands with another person or accepting a check or award. "I've got to shoot a *grip and grin* at the Red Cross banquet. Maybe they'll feed me."

Hail Mary *n.*   a photo snapped without being composed, leaving the photographer to pray for a usable shot. "At the premiere Tom Cruise was mobbed by so many people that I held the camera above their heads and just did a *Hail Mary.*"

hot corner *n.*   the lower right corner of page one in *USA Today,* which regularly has an attention-grabbing color photo.

jump *n.*   the continuation of a news story on a later page.

kicker *n.*   a subhead, or smaller headline under the main one. "Chris, will you write me a *kicker* for the London hotels story?"

lede *n.*   a story's first paragraph.

nut graf *n.*   a paragraph that explains a story's wider significance. It usually falls within the first five paragraphs.

perp walk *n.* a photo taken as police walk a criminal from place to place.

piece *n.* a news or feature article. "Did you read the *piece* on diet scams?"

put to bed *v.* to finish an edition and send it for printing. "After we *put* the paper *to bed,* let's get a drink somewhere."

showing the flag *v.* attending a news event in order to make your paper's presence felt, even though photo possibilities are slim.

take *n.* a typed page. (This term is dying in the computer era.)

-30- *n.* signifies "the end"; typed at the end of a story.

thumbsucker *n.* a long, ponderous story examining a vast theme. "Man, do I not want to write this *thumbsucker* on the federal deficit. I don't even want to read it!"

tick-tock *n.* a story that retells events in chronological detail. "I've sent Reynolds out to get a *tick-tock* on the robbery and murder spree."

Tabloid Reporters and Editors

AA story *n.* a story with "amazing appeal." Example: "The *Amazing Appeal* of Robert Redford: Why Is He So Popular?"

back-of-the-book story *n.* an article that is not a celebrity scandal, diet breakthrough, or other category reserved for page one. Example: "A 20-Foot Shark Swallowed My Leg—And I Lived to Tell."

bombshell *n.* a story or revelation with major impact. "What's this week's *bombshell?*" "Roseanne is having a baby."

comikaze *n.* term for a self-destructive comedian. Example: Richard Pryor.

diet cop *n.* a person hired by a celebrity to oversee a weight-loss effort. A term invented by the tabloids. "Is Rosie Daley still Oprah's *diet cop?*"

diet-or-die *n.*   a standard story in which a too-fat star is told to lose weight or risk the health consequences. "I got a quote from Dom DeLuise's doctor for this week's *diet-or-die.*"

doorstep *v.*   to confront a celebrity face-to-face in order to ask questions. "I couldn't get Drew Barrymore for a phoner—her charming publicist hung up on me—so I *doorstepped* her at the Viper Club." Syn. **pop.**

end-around *v.*   to outmaneuver and bypass someone. "If you want to visit Arnold Schwarzenegger on the set, you'll have to do an *end-around* on his agent."

family feud *n.*   a standard story about strife among celebrity family members.

Freddie *n.*   a page-one picture that is chancy but sells a lot of issues. From a photo of Freddie Krueger that the *National Enquirer* once ran with surprising sales success. "I just knew Cher's newest tattoo would be a *Freddie.*"

Hey, Martha *n.*   the kind of story that will be talked about across the country. *"Hey, Martha,* did you read that story about Elvis's alien love child in the *Enquirer?"*

Hollyweirdo *n.*   any bizarre or eccentric Hollywood star. Coined in the 1950s. "Sterling Hayden was the original *Hollyweirdo.*"

infanticipating *adj.*   expecting a baby. A term used in headlines.

inhuman-interest story *n.*   a story about aliens from outer space.

marry-me-or-else *n.*   a standard story about a marriage ultimatum issued by a celebrity. "We need a *marry-me-or-else* this week. Who have we got?"

money quote *n.*   a quote that expresses the essence of the story. "Here's the *money quote:* 'Madonna made me lick her toes.' "

NC *v.*   to respond "no comment." "When I asked the assistant producer about the 'sex-on-the-set' rumors, she *nc'd* me."

phoner *n.*   a telephone interview.

pre-plot *n.*   an article about a TV show that lets the cat out of the bag about a big development or knockout episode. "Who's writing the *pre-plot* on *Seinfeld*? I need it ten minutes ago."

shocker *n.*   any really surprising revelation. A headline term. "The Latest Burt Reynolds *Shocker:* He's Broke and Gobbling Tranquilizers!"

slagging *n.*   the trashing of a celebrity's image or reputation. "If I have to do another story on *90210,* I'm going to give those Beverly Hills brats a complete *slagging.*"

take a flier *v.*   to publish a story without a believable source or solid evidence. "That story on Demi's boob job? I *took a flier.*"

trained seal *n.*   a questionable expert paid to substantiate a flaky story. "Okay, we're going with the 'Eat More Donuts and Raise Your I.Q.' piece. Get me a comment from the *trained seal.*"

trial marriage *n.*   an early tabloid euphemism for people living together.

undress-for-success story *n.*   an article about a woman who shows off her assets in *Playboy* or *Penthouse* or uses her charms in bed in order to snare a husband or win showbiz success. "That reporter is a legend. He wrote the *undress-for-success story* about Donna Rice."

up-front *n.*   an interview. "We need an *up-front* with Sharon Stone by Friday, so get on it!"

AVIATION PERSONNEL

Pilots

Commercial and Private

arrival *n.*   a hard landing. "That wasn't a landing, that was an *arrival!*"

barber pole *n.*   the top speed of an aircraft. "That's all there is; we're on the *barber pole.*"

bend *v.* to damage an airplane. "You can solo in my airplane, but just don't *bend* it."

bent aluminum *n.* a damaged airplane. Rel. **rolled-up aluminum:** a destroyed airplane.

blue ice *n.* a frozen block formed when a lavatory leaks its blue fluid at high altitude. As the plane descends into warmer air, the ice block melts enough to fall on the unsuspecting populace below. "In Brazil a chunk of *blue ice* crashed through a house while the family was watching TV. No one was hurt, but it left an impressive hole in the roof."

bottom feeders *n.* small, low-powered, piston-engine airplanes that usually fly at low altitudes—i.e., at the bottom of the atmosphere.

bung off *v.* when a glider releases from the tow-plane.

bust *v.* to enter controlled airspace without prior clearance. "She *busted* the Class B airspace, and they pulled her ticket."

buy the farm *v.* to crash and die. Possible derivations: (1) World War II pilots from the Midwest often took out life insurance that paid off the mortgages on their farms in case they died in combat. (2) When post-World War I barnstormers crashed in a field, they would pay the farmer for damaged crops. In a fatal crash, they were said to have paid for the whole farm. "Jim's crash injuries were so bad we thought he'd definitely *buy the farm.*" Syns. **auger in, punch a hole.**

carbon units *n.* passengers on a commercial airliner. "Time to go slop the *carbon units.*" Probably derived from a *Star Trek* movie. Syns. **dogs, geese.**

chop and drop *n.* a quick descent.

churning the butter *v.* when a student is over-controlling the plane with too much motion of the stick.

cob it *v.* to slam the throttle forward to full power in order to get out of trouble.

come to Jesus *adj.* to go through a really frightening experience. "I *came to Jesus* when I lost my engine in the clouds."

counting the rivets *v.* being too close to another aircraft. "We're *counting the rivets* on that Cessna."

crash and dash *n.* when a pilot touches down, keeps rolling, and takes off again. A student's first practice attempts are often more like controlled crashes. Syn. **hit and run, smash and dash.**

crow hopper *n.* a landing, usually too fast, in which the plane does ever-diminishing bounces as it loses speed.

cumulo-granite *n.* clouds that obscure tall mountains. Flying into this type of cloud is usually fatal.

deadhead *v.* when a pilot travels as a passenger or in the cockpit to the airport from which his assigned flight departs. "I'm *deadheading* to Kennedy at noon tomorrow."

Death Cruiser *n.* a DC-10.

Diesel 9 *n.* a DC-9. So called because of the cloud of black smoke it belches on takeoff.

dirty up *v.* to lower the landing gear and flaps, thus spoiling the clean lines of an aircraft. "You should *dirty up* prior to the outer marker on this approach." Ant. **clean up:** to raise the landing gear and flaps. "Let's *clean up* and depart the pattern."

doctor *n.* any bad pilot. Standard joke: "What's the difference between a doctor and a pilot?" Answer: "The pilot doesn't think he's a doctor."

doctor killer *n.* a Beechcraft Bonanza. Rel. **forked-tail doctor killer:** a V-tailed Bonanza. Often bought for its high price and prestige by flyers without sufficient pilot training, its use is associated with many flying fatalities. "My internist bought a *forked-tail doctor killer*. Like I always say, 'Bonanzas don't kill doctors; doctors kill Bonanzas.' "

doing a tap dance *v.* landing in gusty crosswinds that require many corrections with the rudder, so the pilot must repeatedly kick the pedals.

don't say "fuck" *exp.* what the captain tells the first officer when handing him the microphone to make a cabin announcement on the public-address system.

don't say shit *exp.* maintaining a code of silence to cover up mistakes.

drilling expensive holes in the sky *v.* flying airplanes just for the fun of it.

fat, dumb, and happy *adj.* everything is good, the plane is filled with fuel (fat), and the pilot has no worries. "I was flying along, *fat, dumb, and happy,* when I realized I had no idea where I was."

flip *v.* when a crew member has an overnight layover. "I'm *flipping* in Miami, then back to D.C."

flying milkstool *n.* a Piper Tri-Pacer.

fly west *v.* when a fellow pilot dies. "Yeah, old Bob *flew west* last month."

fod *n.* "foreign object damage" on the runway.

foldaway feet *n.* retractable landing gear.

food simulator *n.* an airport vending machine.

fright instructor *n.* a Certificated Flight Instructor.

George *n.* the autopilot. "Let *George* fly for a while."

gouge *n.* information useful to a pilot, especially about high landing fees. "Give me the *gouge* on landing at Nantucket."

grease *v.* to make a smooth landing. "I always *grease* my landings." Syn. **paint it on.**

Groundbus *n.* a British Airways Airbus 320, an aircraft that spent much time out of the air.

Gutless *n.* a Cutlass (Cessna 172RG), considered underpowered.

hangar flying *v.* talking with other pilots about flying.

hangar queen *n.* an aircraft that spends a lot of time in the shop.

hangar rash *n.* damage to an airplane while it is parked or being pushed by ground crew.

heavy Chevy *n.* a Boeing 747. "I've got the *heavy Chevy* in sight." Syn. **whale.**

heavy metal *n.* airliners, as viewed by light plane pilots. Also, the rest of the aviation community as seen by glider or ultralight pilots. Syn. **big iron.**

hot landing *n.* coming in too fast. Rel. **hot and high** *adj.* coming in fast and high, then quickly reducing altitude and airspeed. "I came in *hot and high* in Denver—talk about scary!"

hundred-dollar hamburger *n.* a meal at an airport restaurant or a fly-in, serving as an excuse to go flying. "Does anyone know of a good *hundred-dollar hamburger* in the Boston area?"

Incontinental *n.* Continental Airlines.

Indian country *n.* lower altitudes where private pilots fly, often in Piper aircraft named for Native American tribes (Cherokee, Comanche).

in the penalty box *adj.* when an arriving aircraft ends up waiting in an area such as an unused runway before going to the gate. Often happens when an airline doesn't plan ahead for an empty gate.

in the soup *adj.* flying in clouds. "I was *in the soup* when the radio died. That sure raised the pucker factor!"

Jesus nut *n.* the hardware that connects a helicopter's main rotor to its shaft. Without it, the rotor is free to detach, which can result in a marked decrease in the helicopter's airworthiness. Rel. **Moses pole:** the shaft itself.

lawn dart *n.* a Concorde.

Los Federales *n.* the FAA.

Louie *n.* Alitalia Airlines.

Mad Dog *n.* an MD-80 series aircraft. "Follow the Delta *Mad Dog* on Alpha runway." Syn. **Long Beach Lunch Bucket;** so called because Douglas aircraft makes the planes in Long Beach, California.

Mixmaster *n.* a Cessna Skymaster, which has propellers in front and back. Syns. **huff 'n' puff, Skythrasher.**

noisy glider *n.* an aircraft with a poorly running engine that won't maintain altitude.

November Bravo *exp.* Numb Butt. Description of a pilot's posterior after a particularly long flight. From the military phonetic alphabet.

numbers *n.* the approach end of the runway. "I'm heading for the *numbers*."

oil-canning *n.* the sound made by a plane's metal when it is contorted and popped back into shape.

on the beach *adj.* when a pilot has lost his or her flying status.

pit bull *n.* a Pittsburgh-based flight attendant.

pogo this freq *v.* pronounced "freak." To temporarily switch to another frequency, then bounce back to a controller's frequency. "I want to get a weather report, so I'll *pogo this freq*."

prang *v.* to damage an aircraft on landing.

pucker factor *n.* fear quotient, as measured by the reaction of one's sphincter muscle. It is the gauge of a flying situation that requires great skill or luck to survive—penetrating a thunderstorm, a near mid-air collision, ice build-up on the aircraft, instrument or engine failure. A pucker factor of 10 indicates closed shut. Pilot 1: "I flew into a thunderstorm that was so turbulent I could hear the wings oil-can." Pilot 2: "Wow, the *pucker factor* must have been about 8 on that one!"

pull his/her ticket *v.* when the FAA revokes a pilot's certificate.

The Queen *n.* a British Airways Boeing 767. Rel. **Queen Mother:** a British Airways 747.

quiche wagon *n.* a Boeing 737-200. So called because a quiche has a flaky crust and tends to fall apart—as did an Aloha Airlines 737-200 whose upper portion ripped off in flight, making it a convertible.

rabbit *n.* strobe lights that flash in sequence, leading toward a runway. Named after the mechanical rabbit that greyhounds chase around a racetrack. Rel. **kill the rabbit** *v.* a request to the controller to turn off the strobes when their brightness interferes with the pilot's night vision.

San Antonio sewer pipe *n.* a Fairchild Metroliner. The Metro is manufactured in San Antonio, Texas, and resembles a long, hollow tube with wings.

ScareBus *n.* an AirBus A-320.

screwed the pooch *v.* made a mistake (usually fatal).

Scud running *v.* flying very low to avoid clouds, or flying in a valley when hilltops are obscured by clouds. "Be careful about *scud running;* it often results in encounters with cumulo-granite."

severe clear *adj.* really good weather. More formally called CAVU (Ceiling And Visibility Unlimited), less formally CAFB (Clear As a Fucking Bell).

Skyrock *n.* a Cessna 172 Skyhawk, considered underpowered.

slam dunk *v.* when air traffic controllers keep an arriving plane at a high altitude, forcing a steep descent on final approach. "I got *slam dunked* again coming into Dulles."

sniffing for asphalt *v.* flying low to try to find the runway in bad weather.

souls on board *n.* the total number of passengers and crew on a flight. "How many *souls on board?*" A rather grim phrase, usually used by air traffic controllers after a pilot declares an emergency.

soup dragons *n.* turbulence in the clouds.

Spam cans *n.* generic, single-engine production aircraft, especially Cessnas.

squawk *v.* to set a code into a radar transponder (a device that allows air traffic controllers to identify individual aircraft) and turn it on. So called because early devices sent an audio signal that sounded like a parrot's cry. "Aircraft CF-22, *squawk* 4367" means to set the transponder code on 4367.

stationary traffic *n.* the Sun. Rel. **stationary traffic at night:** Mars, which can resemble an airplane in the night sky.

sterile cockpit *n.* a federal regulation requiring that all non-essential talk cease below ten thousand feet. "Will you tell the flight attendants that it's now *sterile cockpit?*"

stick time *n.* period during which one is at the controls. "My instructor let me tag along on a trip, and I got a lot of *stick time.*"

sucker hole *n.* a hole in the clouds large enough to ascend through, but small enough that it can cloud over again. This would leave the pilot above a cloud deck through which he would have to descend for landing, not a pleasant prospect for the average non-instrument-rated pilot. "You can get your ticket pulled if you go through a *sucker hole* and then have to ask an air traffic controller to get you back down through the clouds."

that's a Charley *exp.* that's correct.

three-holer *n.* a Boeing 727, the first jet with three engines. Syn. **hog.**

Traumahawk *n.* a Piper Tomahawk. So named for its stall behavior, which has caused palpitations in many a student and flight instructor. Syn. **Tomarock.**

Tri-Tanic *n.* a Lockheed L-1011. Syn. **pig boat.**

turn and burn *v.* to start a jet engine.

Useless Air *n.* USAir.

vacation fly-back *n.* when a pilot must return to work during his vacation because the company is short of staff.

vacuum cleaner *n.* a Boeing 737-300/400/500. A quiet aircraft with in-takes very close to ground, it has a reputation for creeping up behind ground crews and sucking them in. Syn. **Hoover.**

vampires *n.* crews who fly from sunset to sunrise.

vector to hector *exp.* a straight line clearance to Los Angeles from any-where east of the Mississippi River. Hector is an airport in the Southern California desert. A pilot might request a direct routing from air traffic control, "Could you give us a vector to hector?" A clever pilot once asked a controller for the area, "Is this the sector director for a vector to hector?" The deadpan reply was, "No, he went to lunch."

when the rubber band breaks *adv.* engine failure.

whiskey dick *exp.* no wind. Describes the look of a limp wind sock.

worm burner *n.* a too-low landing approach, especially by a jet, that requires a thrust of power at the end. Syn. **dragging it in.**

Military

ace face *n.* the look of a fighter pilot's face when a tight-fitting oxygen mask leaves red marks on his cheeks.

angel *n.* a measure of altitude in thousands of feet. "I'm at *angels* ten."

Bravo Sierra *n.* BS, or bullshit. Military phonetic code.

break *n.* a high-performance turn.

BUFF *n.* Big Ugly Fat Fucker. A B-52 bomber. One military air traffic controller to another: "You have an F-4 on downwind and a *BUFF* on final."

check your six *exp.* look behind you. Refers to the six o'clock position in the clock system.

holding hands *adj.* when aircraft are in close formation.

hot pickle *n.* a bomb release. Dates to World War II, when hitting a target precisely was called "putting it in the pickle barrel."

kick the tires and light the fires *v.* to quickly check the plane and get the engines going.

oh-dark thirty *n.* very early in the morning. From the 24-hour clock used by the military. Hours are numbered from 0100 (1:00 AM) to 2300 (11:00 PM). Thus, 9:30 AM is written 0930 and pronounced "oh-nine thirty." "Gotta hit the sack. I have to be up tomorrow at *oh-dark thirty.*"

on rails *adj.* maneuvering smoothly. "It flies like it's *on rails.*"

poopy suit *n.* a military pilot's overwater survival suit. Worn when crossing a cold water environment, it has no provision for bodily relief on a long mission.

popeye *adv.* flying in clouds or low-visibility conditions.

punch out *v.* to eject from a plane. Syns. **get rid of a misbehaving jet, go swimming** (Navy); **hit the silk** or **take the silk elevator** (use a parachute); **take a Martin-Baker ride** (refers to a manufacturer of ejection seats).

Sierra Hotel *adj.* Shit Hot, an expression of approval, derived from military phonetic alphabet. "Did you see him grease that landing in the crosswind? That guy is definitely *Sierra Hotel.*"

souped-up crowbar *n.* a jet fighter.

squirrel cage *n.* a dogfight. Rel. **fur ball:** the area in which a dogfight takes place.

swap paint *v.* to have a mid-air collision.

tally-ho *exp.* means there are other aircraft in sight. Derived from World War II British pilots' popular in-flight hunting call. Typical radio conversation: "Navy XD-03, this is Mugu Approach, do you have the Cessna 150 in your two o'clock, low?" "Mugu, Zero 3, *tally ho.*" Ant. **no joy:** when a pilot doesn't see traffic that the controller asked him to look for.

technicolor yawn *n.* vomit. Often aerobatics or evasive maneuvers instruction makes a student pilot sick. "I did several *technicolor yawns* this morning. My instructor was thrilled."

vomit comet *n.* a KC-135, which performs parabolic flight to simulate weightlessness and often induces motion sickness. "I have to ride in the *vomit comet* today, so don't let me smell that greasy pork sausage sandwich you're eating!"

yank and bank *v.* to do air combat maneuvers. Syn. **turn and burn.**

zoomer *n.* what ground crewmen call Air Force pilots. Also, **zoomie.**

Civil Air Patrol

These terms are used when locating downed aircraft.

four winds *n.*   an in-flight break-up of an aircraft.

hedge clipper *n.*   a plane that came down across trees or vegetation, taking out treetops and swaths of growth.

smear *n.*   a high-speed impact at a shallow angle. Syn. **scatter.**

smoking hole *n.*   a plane that came almost straight down.

Airline Flight Attendants

blue room *n.*   the lavatory. Derived from the blue toilet-flushing fluid.

cockpit queen *n.*   a flight attendant who spends a lot of time socializing with the pilots. Syn. **cockpit wife.** Rel. **galley queen:** a flight attendant who shirks her duties by staying in the galley out of sight.

Hawaii 5-0's *n.*   middle-aged flight attendants on Honolulu flights.

hockey pucks *n.*   the small sandwiches served to passengers. Also, the small round filet mignons often included in first-class meals.

irates *n.*   passengers who become visibly hysterical, threatening, and sometimes vulgar. "I had two *irates* who flipped their lids the whole way to Phoenix. Their seats were wrong. We didn't board their special meals. They'd already seen the movie. Blah blah blah!"

leather or feather *n.*   the choice of a steak or chicken entrée offered to pilots. "The captain decided to go for the *feather* this time."

mile-high club *n.*   membership includes anyone who has had sex on an airliner. Rel. **gettin' busy in back** *v.*   having sex during a flight, usually in a lavatory located at the rear of the airplane.

miracle flight *n.*   when a passenger requires a wheelchair to board the plane (in order to get on first), but walks off with all the other passengers on arrival. "It was a *miracle flight!*"

non-rev *n.* a passenger, usually someone who works for an airline, who is flying free ("non-revenue"). "I've got nothing but *non-revs* in First Class."

pilot pellets *n.* peanuts, of which pilots munch many.

Polish suitcase *n.* any large paper or plastic bag, stuffed full and used as carry-on luggage.

roach coach *n.* a cheap charter flight. Also, a flight to a tropical destination.

spinner *n.* a passenger who boards an airliner, can't find a seat, and keeps turning around in circles looking for one.

stew zoo *n.* a hotel where flight attendants stay on layovers.

walking the dog *v.* walking through an airport while pulling a suitcase on wheels. "I hate *walking the dog* at LAX; it's about a mile to the gates."

Air Traffic Controllers

bird cage *n.* the controlled air traffic space near an airport.

caca *n.* collision alert, indicated by a flashing signal on a controller's radar scope.

deal *n.* a formal sanction imposed on a controller for allowing two aircraft to get closer than the legal minimum separation. "He got a *deal* from the shift supervisor for his mistake."

FLIB *n.* Fucking Little Itinerant Bastard. Usually a single-engine, general-aviation type plane transiting through local airspace.

piss quiz *n.* a urine test for drug use.

shoot *v.* to send aircraft from runways. "This morning we're *shooting* them from runway 22 Right."

snitch patch *n.* an automatic alarm set off by the controller's terminal when two aircraft get closer together than the prescribed safe distance. "Whose *snitch patch* just went off?"

spin an airplane *v.* when controllers issue a holding clearance.

stationary traffic *n.* slow, single-engine aircraft that appear to be stationary on a controller's screen, especially compared to jet traffic.

swinging tin *v.* doing a superb job guiding aircraft (tin) through heavy traffic. "What a day! I was really *swinging tin.*"

tight *adj.* refers to two aircraft that may be hundreds of miles apart, but are predicted to pass close enough eventually to require intervention by Air Traffic Control. "Heads-up. I have a Delta that's *tight* with your Canadian. I'll slow mine down now, so you don't have to vector."

FIREFIGHTERS

bean pot *n.* a fire started by a cook in the kitchen. "You know that *bean pot* last night? It was the woman who gives gourmet cooking lessons on TV!"

build a parking lot *n.* to fight a blaze that nonetheless razes the entire building. "We went and *built a parking lot* downtown."

crowd-pleaser *n.* a large fire where the public gets to see firefighters at work.

don't yank my halyard! *exp.* don't pull my chain! Don't tease or try to fool me. A halyard is the pull rope used to extend a ground ladder.

garbage truck *n.* a pumper truck in a big city. So called because all such trucks seem to do is put out trash and garbage fires.

motor *n.* a fire engine. Syn. **piece.**

nauger *n.* a chief officer who spends his time sitting around in a Naugahyde chair or recliner, and in case of fire comes out and tells the firefighters how to do their jobs.

96 *n.* radio code meaning "we're headed to the fire." May be used as an everyday term: "Jim and I are *96* to McDonald's."

nozzlehead *n.* a firefighter assigned to an engine company. Syn. **hoser.**

overhaul *v.* to clean up dirt, rubbish, and water after the fire is out.

rice rocket *n.* any fast fire truck made in Japan.

roof rat *n.* a firefighter who likes to climb ladders to the upper stories of buildings.

staff infection *n.* when a firefighter is shifted from a platoon-style work schedule to a staff assignment and a five-day work week.

WALL STREETERS

alligator spread *n.* facetious term for a situation in which the broker's commissions gobble more than the client can possibly earn in profits on a transaction.

barefoot pilgrim *n.* an investor left without a shirt on his back or shoes on his feet (jocular); an investor whom a broker can sucker into any idiotic trade, thus generating easy commissions.

blue chip *n.* a stock whose stability makes it a low risk. "The university invests strictly in *blue chips.*"

bottom fishing *v.* seeking cheap stocks that haven't performed well lately but may go up.

bullpen *n.* brokerage office area used by retail brokers dialing for dollars.

cats and dogs *n.* speculative stocks of low price and probably no worth.

cut the melon *v.* when a company distributes a dividend that's unexpectedly high.

dialing for dollars *v.* making phone calls to prospective brokerage clients, seeking business. Syn. **dialing and smiling.**

elephants *n.* institutional investors (pension funds, mutual funds, etc.). "No question, the *elephants* are now the most powerful beasts on Wall Street."

flowers *n.*   bonds purchased for a client near death; bought at a discount, they are later redeemed for face value to pay estate taxes.

glamour *adj.*   characterized by a high price/earnings ratio and unpredictable performance in the market. "TechCo was a classic 1980s *glamour* stock."

golden parachute *n.*   an executive's contract clause guaranteeing his salary for a designated period in the event of takeover by corporate raiders.

go out the window *v.*   when a new stock offering sells fast.

go public *v.*   when a company offers its stock to the public for the first time.

greenmail *n.*   a kind of financial blackmail in which a corporate raider threatens management with continued attacks unless the company buys out his stock at a premium.

hemline theory *n.*   a market forecasting theorem stating that markets go up or down in tandem with women's hemlines. "Look at the miniskirt in the Sixties: Stocks went up! That proves the *hemline theory.*"

the little people *n.*   members of the public; people who trade in small amounts of stock.

lobby lizards *n.*   people who hang around in brokerage office lobbies to watch the electronic ticker-tapes.

mullet *n.*   rich suckers; good targets for stockbrokers seeking commissions. "The American Medical Association convention is prime *mullet* territory."

pin-striped pork bellies *n.*   stock market index futures. So called because they blend the stock market (pin-striped suits) and the commodities market (pork belly contracts).

plain vanilla *adj.*   describes a bond offering with no extra features to lure investors. Rel. **sweetener:** an alluring extra feature.

quack *n.*   a stock price change of a quarter point. "GE's down a *quack.*" Rel. **laugh:** a half; **fried eggs:** five eighths.

rocket scientists *n.* research analysts for financial markets.

sex without marriage *n.* when friendly negotiations for a corporate merger don't work out. Rel. **brought to the altar** *adj.* successfully merged.

sleeping beauty *n.* a cash-rich and undervalued company with slumbering management that is ripe for takeover by corporate raiders. Syn. **maiden.** Rel. **damsel in distress:** a sleeping beauty that calls for help from a "white knight" of Wall Street.

take a flutter *v.* when a market novice makes a small speculative investment. "My dentist client decided to *take a flutter* on that high-tech stock."

tombstone *n.* a broker's announcement of a new stock issue, which runs in a newspaper with a hairline box around it.

white knight *n.* a friendly buyer aiming to outbid a corporate raider and fend off a hostile takeover.

widows and orphans *n.* conservative small stockholders whose income relies on blue-chip stock dividends. Rel. **Aunt Jane:** proverbial little old lady in tennis shoes who owns a few shares of a company's stock but often appears at shareholders' meetings.

window dressing *n.* appealing stocks purchased by money managers just before their performances are judged at the end of a quarter. The goal is to make managers look good and to catch the eyes of potential investors.

ADVERTISING AGENCY PEOPLE

attitude *n.* what used to be called image or identity. "Whatever theme we give to this campaign, it's got to sell the company's hip, in-your-face *attitude.*"

bleed *n.* when a photo runs off the edge(s) of a page. "Let's run this shot as a full-page *bleed.*"

book *n.* a magazine. "Who's the ad director at that *book?*"

brainstorm *v.*   to generate a whirlwind of concepts, headlines, copy ideas, and visuals for an advertisement or commercial. "Let's do some *brainstorming* on the beer account at two-thirty. Make sure the whole team is here." Syn. **paper the walls.**

bullet *n.*   a brief, punchy copy line that sells a product's features. Also, a heavy typographical dot used to draw attention to items in a list.

copy *n.*   text.

creative *n.*   the copywriting and/or artwork for an ad. "Hey, Bill—great *creative!* The client should fall on his knees and worship you as a god."

double truck *n.*   two adjacent pages in a magazine. "A *double truck* gives the creative department a lot more room to play in." Also, *adj.*   "Let's run the ad *double-truck.*"

face *n.*   typeface. "I think Bodoni is the right *face* for the headline."

greek *n.*   nonsense text that holds a place for headlines and copy still to be written.

ink *n.*   a mention in the press. "That PR firm is so lame it couldn't get *ink* for Madonna."

matchmaker *n.*   a firm that links marketers with special events to sponsor, in order to connect with their target audiences. "We used a *matchmaker* and found a surfing contest for our BagRays sunblock account."

price point *n.*   a product's position on the price spectrum. "Don't you think the *price point* for this wine is too low? It's supposed to be elegant and classy, not Hobo Red."

psychographics *n.*   a personality profile of target customers for a product.

put the pants on it *v.*   to flesh out a basic concept for presentation to the client. "I like your idea for the coffee account. *Put the pants on it,* and we'll present it at Wednesday's meeting."

rights-free music *n.*   prerecorded music available at low cost for radio spots and commercials.

shop *n.*   an advertising agency. "Colin was a star at that *shop* for 6 years, until it lost the Chrysler account and let everybody go."

space *n.*   what an advertiser buys in a magazine.

unit price *n.*   the cost of a 30-second television commercial.

visual *n.*   the graphic content or look of any kind of advertising. "What kind of *visual* do you have in mind for this teabag ad?"

FASHION INDUSTRY PEOPLE

AIDS brigade *n.*   male window dressers and display riggers, particularly when they travel from store to store together. "Tuesday we'll move the shirt fixtures. And Wednesday the *AIDS brigade* is here."

bridge *n.*   the share of the fashion market between prestigious designer names and unknown names.

butt soup *n.*   a retail customer wearing a hideous or grotesque outfit.

catwalk *n.*   the runway where fashion models parade during a show.

cherry pick *v.*   when a retail buyer selects only the obvious best items from a line without "supporting the name" by buying peripheral items, which would give the manufacturer or designer a more conspicuous presence in the store. "I *cherry picked* the line for three fabulous blouses; the rest of the line was drech."

ditzy print *n.*   a print with small flowers. "Jumpers in a *ditzy print* are really big with the pre-teens this season."

done *adj.*   high-fashion. Ant. **undone:** casual.

drop *n.*   the difference between the chest measurement of a suit coat and the waist measurement of the accompanying trousers. A size 40 regular suit carries size 34 trousers, and thus has a six-inch drop.

editorial *adj.*   having the sleek, stylized appearance of photographs in fashion magazines. "These catalog shots won't work for us, Brian. You've gone too *editorial.* Think homespun: We're selling clothes to middle-aged women here.''

essemmellex *adj.* small, medium, large, extra-large. Clerk: "Did those striped shirts come exact size or *essemmellex?*"

fast *adj.* refers to styling that is exaggerated, high-fashion, fringe. "I like the black and white tweed. But the green and red is a little *fast* for our customer." Rel. **fast fashion** *n.* a fad, usually directed at kids, that is expected to last less than a season.

flairful *adj.* adventurous, having pizzazz. Stylist: "It's a great dress, but something's missing. What can we do to make it more *flairful?*"

garanimals *n.* an outfit assembled around the simple-minded matching of colors. From the color-coordinated children's line. "The matching purse, belt, and shoes were sooo *garanimals.*"

garmento *n.* someone in the "rag trade," especially a person who is canny, aggressive, and possibly unscrupulous. "Stan is such a *garmento,* I can't stand doing business with him anymore."

the girls *n.* the upper echelon of models.

going forward *adj.* in the future. "Spring will be pastels. Then, *going forward,* we'll transition into brights for summer."

gorge *n.* where the top collar of a coat joins the lapel. Often a "notch" marks the gorge.

knockoff artist *n.* a company that copies the designs of famous designers and sells them at lower cost.

leave paper *v.* to order after seeing a preview of the line. "Now here's a first: Rosie actually *left paper* for fall—and she didn't cherry pick."

maven *v.* to hold forth or lecture like an expert. "Stop *mavening* me like you know what you're talking, already." Also, *n.* Often used mockingly.

on wheels *adj.* on consignment. "I think Adrienne isn't getting many orders; she's got most of her clothes out *on wheels.*"

pissovers *n.* men's briefs that have no fly.

The Pope *n.* either Giorgio Armani or Ralph Lauren, depending on the orientation of the store. Their fashion judgment is thought to be infallible. "Have you seen the new white shirt from *The Pope*? It's fabulous!"

put on weight *v.* for a model to have a breast augmentation. "Is it my imagination, or has Cindy *put on weight* since the spring show?"

schlepper *n.* a salesman who carries his wares from appointment to appointment. Yiddish origin. Rel. **schlep** *v.* to carry the wares. One buyer to another: "I made that jerk *schlep* the whole line back here so I could take a note on one sweater. And now I'm not going to book it! Ha!"

schmatte *n.* derogatory term for merchandise. Yiddish origin. Syns. **drech, schade.** "I wouldn't buy this *drech* if it was free." (Words of disapproval seem to outnumber words of approbation in the fashion business. Even words that apparently express profuse praise—"Fabulous!" "Stunning!"—are often undermined by a brassy note of irony.)

scye *n.* the hole in the shoulder of a coat where the sleeve is attached.

such good goods *exp.* uttered under their breath by retail salesmen when a customer, particularly an elderly one, is inspecting, say, a coat sleeve as if it were a gem under a jeweler's loupe.

there *adj.* complete, all the way. "That pulls the whole look together. It's *there.*"

REAL ESTATE AGENTS

been around the block *adj.* when a potential homeowner has sought a loan at numerous banks.

birdbath *n.* an area by a house where water accumulates, although it wasn't designed to be that way.

bottom feeder *n.* a buyer who doesn't move until the market hits a low.

caravan *n.* parties of real estate agents driving to inspect newly listed properties. "I saw a wonderful Colonial on *caravan* today, and I think it's just what you're looking for." Syn. **broker's open.**

choke point *n.* the level of mortgage interest rates that drives buyers away from the market.

fizzbo *adj.* "For Sale By Owner"; derogatory, reflecting agents' dislike of sales that don't involve them.

garbage fees *n.* various lender's fees that are extremely high or padded, but legal.

handyman special *n.* a house so dilapidated it is all but condemned.

kennel *n.* a dog of a house.

monkey *n.* mortgage.

POS *n.* Piece Of Shit. Rel. **OPPOS:** Over-Priced POS.

puffing *n.* enticing comments about a property; may be deceptive but not utterly false. Example: "Close to Transportation" may translate as "There's a freeway overpass at the back door."

teardown *n.* a house that a new buyer will demolish in order to build on its desirable lot. "A Beverly Hills agent told me nobody actually moves into a house there anymore. Every sale is a *teardown.*"

upside down *adj.* a homeowner's situation when his outstanding loan balance is greater than the market value of his house, because of falling prices in the real estate market. "They're *upside down* on the duplex, since they bought at the peak."

wonderful starter home *n.* a house the size of coat closet. Rel. **cozy.**

ANTIQUES DEALERS

as found *adj.* damaged or incomplete. Syn. **as is.** "The dealer wrote *as is* on the ticket, since the piece was in bad shape."

be-back *n.*   someone who looks at your merchandise and says, "I'll be back," though isn't likely to return. "Not much of a morning in the shop so far. Just two *be-backs.*" Also, **be-backer.**

bin diver *n.*   a dealer who goes through the bins at thrift shops looking for vintage or collectible clothing. Also, someone who goes through trash bins searching for treasures. Syn. **dumpster diver.**

fleabite *n.*   a small chip or notch. "I'll probably have to mark down this jug. Look at all the *fleabites.*" Syns. **bump, chigger, ding:** "This vase has a *chigger* on the lip."

hairline *n.*   a barely noticeable crack. "This pitcher has a *hairline,* but I don't think collectors are going to care."

harlequin *n.*   a collection of objects that look pretty much alike, but are from different sources. These items are usually sold in sets, but they may have members missing. Examples are dining room chairs and bedroom suites.

important *adj.*   expensive, prestigious. "If you're really in the market for quality, let me show you an *important* piece I acquired through Sotheby's."

instant ancestors *n.*   antique photographs of unidentified people. "The dealer had photos in a basket with a sign that said, '*Instant Ancestors,* Two for $5.'"

married *adj.*   when two pieces that didn't start out in life together are joined; usually refers to furniture. Considered less valuable than items in their original state. Rel. **marriage** *n.*   such a combination. "I wouldn't buy that desk with the hutch stuck on the top. It's a *marriage.*"

MIB *adj.*   Mint In Box. In untouched condition in its original packaging; generally commands a higher price. "The G.I. Joe doll was sold *MIB.*"

picker *n.*   someone who buys items at rummage sales, auctions, and flea markets for resale to antiques shops. "I sold a bunch of silver forks to a *picker* this morning. I'm sure he'll make a bundle on them from his dealers."

repop *n.*   a reproduction piece. "Your desk chair—that's a *repop,* isn't it?" Syn. **repro.**

salty *adj.*   expensive. "That's a nice rocker, but a little *salty* for my taste."

smalls *n.*   knickknacks, tchotchkes. These include salt and pepper shakers, knives, cigarette lighters, glass collectibles, badges, watches, fountain pens, and so forth. "I carry some furniture, but mostly a lot of *smalls*. That way my customers don't need a truck to get things home."

vulture *n.*   an antiques dealer with swooping tendencies, especially at an auction. "I couldn't get anything because of all the *vultures.*"

widow *n.*   an item without its mate (e.g., a salt shaker but no matching pepper shaker).

AUCTIONEERS

aggravation *n.*   defect, imperfection. "This Early American desk does have some *aggravation*. It's missing a leg." Syns. **agitation, distortion, infraction.**

all over the house *adj.*   when a number of people bid at once, creating a tie that must be broken. "We've got to move it up, folks. I've got $210 *all over the house.* Who'll go $225?"

Arizona Windsor *n.*   a chair whose style is strange or laughable.

black light *n.*   ultraviolet light, used on paintings to detect repairs or later additions that stand out clearly under such illumination.

boat anchor *n.*   a joking reference to a clunky item that draws few bids. "Folks, not only can you do laundry in this old washing machine; it also makes a lovely *boat anchor.*"

box lot *n.*   small items sold together in a cardboard carton; usually left-overs that wouldn't sell separately. "Now here's a *box lot,* I don't know where it came from. Maybe somebody missed the road to the county dump!" Syn. **flea market kit.**

burnt *adj.*   not sold, despite having been auctioned several times.

the choice *n.*   the right of the buyer of one item in a group to select which one. "If you're the winning bid on the side chairs, you'll have the *choice.*"

Rel. **the privilege:** the right to buy the rest of the lot at the same price per item.

fast knock *n.* a stratagem to spark the buyers' excitement by asking for a low opening bid, then lowering the price suddenly for the first bidder (who may be a friend).

feed *n.* the procession of items brought up front for sale. "I think the California Plein Air paintings are going to be hot items, so save them for later in the *feed.*"

gone *adj.* lost, missing. "How much am I bid for this fine baby carriage with a *gone* wheel?"

honeymoon kit *n.* a lot with a bit of everything. "The auctioneer introduced the cast iron kettle, rug beater, and bear trap, saying, 'Now, here's a real *honeymoon kit.* Who'll give me five dollars?' "

New Jersey tourist birds *n.* ordinary duck decoys, neither antique nor carved by celebrated craftsmen, and therefore of low value.

no's *n.* listed prohibitions at an auction (no two-party checks, no smoking, no pets, etc.).

off the chandelier *adv.* when an auctioneer "recognizes" a nonexistent bid in order to raise the price. "Hmm . . . I think that last bid came *off the chandelier.* I didn't see anybody raise his hand." Also, **off the wall.**

POS *n.* Piece of Shit.

puffing *n.* the overstatement and exaggeration with which auctioneers may promote goods. "You should take that 'fine early piece' stuff with a grain of salt. The auctioneer is famous for *puffing.*"

run-up *v.* causing a bidder to spend more than he planned, by bidding against him fairly, or unfairly through the use of shills, fake absentee bids, and other subterfuges.

salting *v.* an auctioneer's practice of placing a good item into a box lot, thus inducing people to bid on what is basically a bunch of rubbish. Also, when people at a pre-auction exhibition transfer items they'd like to bid on from one box lot to another.

shadow bidder *n.* a bidder who outmaneuvers a known dealer by remaining one step ahead of him on a valuable item. The goal is to avoid having to buy it later from the dealer for more money.

shill *n.* an employee of the auction house who improperly sits in the crowd and bids against legitimate bidders, thereby raising prices. Syn. **puffer.**

thunder jug *n.* jocular term for a chamber pot. Rel. **New York tureen:** a bedpan.

white goods *n.* major household appliances, such as stoves and refrigerators. "I just don't have the storage, so I don't auction *white goods* anymore."

CAR SALESMEN

barefoot *adj.* equipped with bad or bald tires. "His trade-in was *barefoot* and his kid had spilled a milkshake down the radio speaker. What a junker!"

base *n.* the price paid by the dealer.

be-back *n.* a car buyer who promises to "be back" later but clearly doesn't mean it; often used derisively. "My *be-back* walked after I spent all afternoon with him."

blow the brains out *v.* to install a sunroof. "The mayor is going to buy the red T-bird, but first he wants *the brains blown out.*"

bushing *n.* the deceptive practice of raising a car's price after the customer signs a sales contract. A common scenario is that the sales manager refuses to allow the high trade-in allowance promised to the customer, which makes the cost go up.

cream puff *n.* a good-looking, mechanically sound car that is attractive to buyers.

curbstoner *n.* a marginal dealer who gets by with a few used cars, a phone, and flashy newspaper ads.

desk a deal *v.* to move negotiations along to the point where the customer sits down at the salesman's desk for serious discussions—a big moment for the salesman.

detail *v.* to touch up and polish an auto to conceal flaws and make it more appealing to buyers. "Eddie, *detail* that Lumina and we'll get another $500 for it." Rel. **detail for delivery:** to clean up and remove the stickers from a car so the new owner can take possession.

dimples *n.* dents.

door whore *n.* a salesman who courts an excessive number of walk-in customers, but fails to close deals because he doesn't carry through.

doping *n.* any means of concealing a car's problems, not always legally.

down *adj.* refers to a salesman who has finished with a customer and moves to the bottom of the ups list. (*See* **ups list.**)

ether *n.* the unreasoning daze that comes over a shopper who is puzzled or overstimulated by the process of buying a car. "I could see she was under the *ether,* so I socked her for the extended warranty and undercoating."

executive car *n.* an auto driven by the dealer, then offered for sale as a swank or exclusive demonstrator. Syn. **factory demo.**

flea *n.* a customer shopping only for a steal of a deal.

gold ball *n.* a top credit rating, or a buyer who has one.

good up *n.* a customer ready to buy a car.

green pea *n.* a salesman with little experience. "I really cleaned up when I worked at that dealership. All the guys on the floor were *green peas.*"

grind *n.* a buyer who haggles unrelentingly over each detail. "That *grind* got me to throw in the premium stereo and power windows, all for only three hundred bucks over invoice." Syn. **mooch.**

happy man *n.* a finance company or loan officer.

jack *n.* a person who goes out looking at cars as a recreation, without intending to buy.

juice ticket *n.* gas voucher. "A guy is here to test drive the Miata, but the tank's empty. I'll need a *juice ticket.*"

kissed by the Santa Fe *adj.* in a bad crash and then repaired. "At first glance that '94 Jeep looks okay, but it's been *kissed by the Santa Fe.*"

laydown *n.* a pushover or dupe. "That *laydown* paid sticker half an hour after he walked in." Rel. **barefoot pilgrim:** a naively trusting auto buyer.

lick paint and suck chrome *v.* to fall in love with an automobile at the showroom. "The lawyer took a test drive in the 'Vette and spent the rest of the afternoon *licking paint and sucking chrome.*"

lipstick *n.* purely cosmetic changes in a new model, designed to disguise the fact that it's virtually identical to the old model.

lot *n.* the area where cars are parked.

low-ball *v.* to quote a remarkably low price in order to entice a customer. Once the buyer is hooked, the salesman finds a way (such as bushing) to raise the price.

pack *v.* to add various costs—finance charges, dealer preparation, document fees—to the base.

paperweight *n.* an unpopular make or model that is difficult for salesmen to move. Syns. **cold car, hangar queen.**

piece *n.* a battered trade-in of little value. Syn. **lump.** Rel. **sled:** large car, often a junker.

qualify *v.* to ascertain the reasons why a customer has come to the dealership and whether he is a serious buyer. This is done by asking the customer what model he is interested in, his budget limitations, whether he has a trade-in, and so on.

roach *n.* a buyer with poor or no credit. "I took him on a test drive, worked out a price, and then he turned out to be a *roach.*"

rode hard and put away wet *adj.*   not serviced and cared for properly. "His piece practically died in the driveway. It had been *rode hard and put away wet.*"

skate *v.*   to steal a deal or a buyer from a fellow salesman, often through deceit. "I *skated* that weasel, Jimmy. I told his buyer he'd gone home sick."

slam-dunk *v.*   to manipulate a customer into paying top dollar. "The guy wanted that Explorer so bad, I totally *slam-dunked* him." Syns. **kick him in the ditch, knock his head off, take his eyeballs out.**

sneakers *n.*   tires. "If we take the Mustang as a trade, it's going to need new *sneakers* before it'll sell."

spiff *n.*   extra money paid to salesmen as incentive. "If you sell five Explorers or Mustangs this month, I can promise you some great *spiffs.*"

sticker *n.*   the full retail price, as shown on a form pasted to the car window. "This is last year's model, so of course I don't expect you to pay *sticker.*" Syn. **Moroni,** named for the senator whose legislation required that auto prices be clearly displayed.

store *n.*   the dealership. Syn. **house.**

tourists *n.*   lookers who go to luxury dealerships and photograph fancy cars they'd like to own.

trip *n.*   a sale. "That 280Z is a *trip.* The buyer is coming back at noon with the check." Also, *v.*   to sell.

turn over *n.*   to hand over a customer to another salesman after exhausting all possibilities of selling him the car.

unhorse *v.*   to convince a customer to give over his car for a lengthy trade-in appraisal, thus gaining time to sell him a new car.

up *n.*   a customer. "Larry, that's your *up;* he wants to see the Taurus." Also, *v.*   to claim a prospective customer. "Hey, Red, I already *upped* that guy in the suit. You get the next one."

upside down *adj.* owing more on a prospective trade-in than the car is worth. "The schoolteacher is *upside down* on her Camaro, so it's got to be a cash deal." Syn. **buried.**

ups list *n.* the order in which salesmen are slated to take customers.

walk *v.* to leave the lot without buying anything. "Don't let that lady *walk*. She loves that teal Aerostar, and she's not leaving till she signs a frigging contract!"

whorehouse *n.* a dealership with a high sales volume and quick turnover of salesmen.

FUNERAL DIRECTORS

cosmetize *v.* to use make-up to restore the deceased to a lifelike appearance; one of the mortuary arts. "Once Phil *cosmetizes* their Aunt Edna, the family will say they've never seen her look better."

cremains *n.* bone fragments left after cremation. They resemble broken seashells and are generally pulverized by crematories.

desairology *n.* arranging the hair of the deceased. "Before Whoopi Goldberg made it as an actress, she worked at a mortuary where *desairology* was her area of expertise."

funeral director *n.* a person hired to handle preparations for a funeral and disposition of a dead body. Originally termed a coffin maker, the position later became undertaker, then mortician, and now the more genteel funeral director.

good and plenty *n.* a receptacle full of cremains. So called because when jiggled it sounds like a box of Good and Plenty candy.

loved one *n.* the deceased. This is used whether or not everyone in the family was on great terms.

minimum container *n.* an inexpensive box of cardboard or plywood for a body. Rel. **china:** simple wooden coffin, a type once used for burying Chinese laborers.

over-enrollment *n.* a greater number of body-part donations to a medical school than is needed at a given time. "Harvard and Dartmouth have an *over-enrollment* these days."

peekaboo *n.* a quick viewing of the body and brief funeral service, typically for the immediate family only. "The Davises are scheduled for a *peekaboo* at three o'clock."

perpetual care *n.* the maintenance of a cemetery in perpetuity, either through tax money or fees charged.

pre-need *n.* funeral arrangements made and often funded before death. "Grandma paid off her *pre-need* account before she died." Ant. **at-need:** funeral arrangements paid for after a person's death. "I'll need to get the check before the funeral; this is an *at-need* situation."

road kill *n.* a highway fatality. One funeral director to another: "I see you went out and picked up a *road kill* last night."

sealer *n.* a higher-priced casket with a rubber gasket that may slow the intake of ground water but actually has no other preservative qualities. "This *sealer* will give your husband's body extra protection! *(And increase my profit margin, too . . .)*" Rel. **coffin vault sealer:** a cement box sprayed with gold paint; it may perhaps keep out ground water, but will definitely add to the price.

shake 'n' bake *n.* a simple cremation, without services, at a funeral home. "We won't make much profit here—his family only wants a *shake 'n' bake.*" Syns. **crispy critter, deep-fry, dust in the wind, rattle in a can, roasty-toasty.**

shoot the juice *n.* to embalm by injection with chemicals that retard decomposition. "Answer the phone, will you? I'm going downstairs to *shoot the juice* before the family arrives."

slumber room *n.* the chamber at the funeral parlor where the deceased lies at rest.

tin can *n.* a metal casket made with the least expensive grade of steel.

RESTAURANT WORKERS

Waiters and Waitresses

Adam and Eve on a raft *n.*   two eggs on toast. A term from diners. Rel. **sink 'em** *v.*   break the yolks.

all the way *adj.*   served with everything (mayonnaise, mustard, lettuce, tomato, onion), referring to a sandwich. Syn. **full house.**

Blanche *n.*   a waitress who doesn't know what she's doing. "That *Blanche* is so absent-minded, all her tables keep asking *me* for refills on coffee." Rel. **shoemaker:** a novice waitperson.

blast *v.*   to heat up. *"Blast* that sirloin!"

burn one *v.*   to cook an order right away; done because the order is late, the waiter forgot it, or the customer is in a hurry. *"Burn one* swordfish platter, or I'm not getting a tip."

campers *n.*   customers who occupy a table too long. "The *campers* on table two have been there since five o'clock." Syn. **sitters.**

Clampetts *n.*   diners without rudimentary social graces. From the featured family on TV's *The Beverly Hillbillies.*

crumbs *n.*   children. So called because they often leave crumbs under their chairs.

damages *n.*   the bill. "Here are the *damages.*"

deep-six *v.*   to throw out. From Navy slang. "You better *deep-six* the rest of that lobster tail, even though I'd like to eat it myself."

deuce *n.*   two diners at a table. Rel. **four-top:** a four-person table.

drag *v.*   to lack part of an order from the kitchen, requiring a server to wait. "Jeannie's *dragging* two soups."

duke *n.*   a tough customer who thinks he knows everything. Syn. **John Wayne.**

eighty-six *v.* to throw someone out. "The drunk guy tossed a jelly container at me, so I had the manager *eighty-six* him."

fazed *adj.* not on the schedule for a work shift. "Billy's *fazed* both nights this weekend."

fluff and fold *v.* to handle with care. Can refer to either a regular patron or a difficult diner.

gummer *n.* an older person who takes forever to get through a meal.

in the weeds *adj.* swamped with work. May refer either to the kitchen or the waitperson. "The cook's *in the weeds,* and I've got eight tables screaming for their food." Syns. **under, treed, dusted.**

in the window *adj.* describes food that is cooked, wrapped, and ready to go. "Number 6, pork chop special, *in the window!*"

Julia Child *n.* a customer who analyzes the meal at length. "The *Julia Child* at table five just performed a chemical analysis of the vinaigrette."

Leona *n.* any difficult customer. From hotelier Leona Helmsley.

lungs *n.* smokers.

no commercials *exp.* no excuses why something wasn't done right. "Listen, that customer ordered the meatloaf special and you gave her the chicken. Make it right, and *no commercials.*"

red flag *n.* a coded alert to the manager about a patron who is intoxicated. "*Red flag* on the corner booth. Send over some coffee."

Romper Room *n.* a table with lots of children.

send-back *n.* an order that was messed up and must be returned to the kitchen.

setup *n.* a complete set of tableware and a napkin. "That girl's date showed up, so I need another *setup.*"

slammed *adj.* burdened by having many tables in your section filled at once. "It was only 6 o'clock, and I was already *slammed.*"

squat and gobble *n.*   a family-dining restaurant.

stiff *v.*   to fail to tip. "I did everything but chew the food for those ladies, and they *stiffed* me."

table from hell *n.*   a group of intoxicated, offensive patrons.

to travel *adj.*   indicates a take-out order. "Gimme a cheeseburger *to travel.*" Syns. **on wheels, with legs.** "Put the cheeseburger *on wheels.*"

VSOP *n.*   Very Selectively Opinionated Person. An abbreviation appended to a name in the reservations book to indicate a problem or finicky customer. "We've got a *VSOP* at 7:30. Fluff and fold him, okay?"

working *adj.*   on the grill. "I've got two burgers *working!*"

yesterday *adv.*   right away. "I need the chef's salad *yesterday.*"

Bartenders

bang *n.*   a jigger, shot. "Here's your *bang* of Cuervo Gold and a Lone Star long neck."

behind the stick *adj.*   operating the beer taps. "Brian, you'll be *behind the stick* tonight."

on scholarship *adj.*   when a bartender shirks work, choosing instead to flirt with pretty girls, chat with customers, etc. "Jim is apparently *on scholarship,* so I have to pick up the slack."

potatoed *adj.*   intoxicated. Syns. **blasted, blotto, bombed, canned, fried, loaded, polluted, wasted,** etc.

shrapnel *n.*   coins left as a tip.

Car Parkers

stack the deck *v.*   to park expensive or flashy cars out in front, in order to enhance the restaurant's image or flatter the owners.

teach Muhammad Ali how to fight *v.* when an arriving patron gives an experienced valet a long lesson in how to drive and lock a vehicle.

CARNIVAL WORKERS

agent *n.* the operator of a carnival game.

alibi agent *n.* the operator of a crooked game who keeps a customer playing by suggesting excuses for his losses and offering friendly tips for the next try.

anatomical wonder *n.* a performer of odd physical stunts in a sideshow. Examples: the Indian Rubber Man, who ties himself up like a pretzel; the Human Skeleton, who sucks in his stomach until his spine shows.

back end *n.* the section of the midway featuring rides and shows.

bally *n.* a free show staged outside an attraction to lure a crowd. Short for ballyhoo.

banner line *n.* a row of canvas pictorial banners hung in front of a midway show.

beef *n.* a complaint from a customer or police.

belly joint *n.* a crooked carnival game whose rigging mechanism is controlled by the operator leaning his stomach against the counter. "Nobody wins much at the wheel of fortune; it's a *belly joint.*"

blowoff *n.* an additional sideshow attraction, offered for an additional price.

break the ice *v.* to make the day's first sale.

bugs *n.* chameleons. The lizards are displayed by "bug board" salesmen on the midway and sold as pets.

bunkhouse *n.* a large trailer used for sleeping quarters.

burn the lot *v.* when a crooked carnival bilks people so severely that the town won't allow another carnival to visit. "We're skipping Odessa this year. Last fall another show *burned the lot.*"

carnies *n.* carnival workers.

chump heister *n.* ferris wheel.

cops *n.* small prizes given away to induce further interest.

doniker *n.* toilet.

doniker location *n.* a site on the midway where business isn't as good as in other spots.

First of May *n.* a person new to the carnival business. So called because May is the traditional beginning of the carnival season. "That kid called me a 'barker' instead of a 'talker,' so he must be a *First of May.*"

flash *n.* costly-looking merchandise and prizes exhibited at a game concession to lure players. Rel. **hard flash:** a prize so desirable that a customer will blow a lot of money trying to win it. "A full set of flatware was the *hard flash* at the ring-toss game."

flat store *n.* a crooked carnival game. Syns. **alibi store, G-joint;** G stands for gaffed or gimmicked. (*See* **gaffed.**)

floss wagon *n.* a purveyor of cotton candy. Rel. **flossie:** a person working a food concession.

forty miler *n.* a carnival trouper who never moves his ride or concession very far from home; often used derisively. "Oh, he's just a *forty miler,* never goes anywhere."

gaffed *adj.* when a game is mechanically rigged so wins and losses can be controlled. "The horse race game is *gaffed.*"

gazoonie *n.* a young working man.

girl-to-gorilla show *n.* a common sideshow illusion in which a pretty girl is transformed into a gorilla.

go to the barn *v.*   when a carnival outfit moves to winter quarters.

grab joint *n.*   a concession selling food to be eaten by carnival goers as they walk through the grounds.

green help *n.*   employees who work a single carnival booking.

grinder *n.*   a carnie who delivers a fixed spiel outside a midway attraction. The "grind" may be delivered continuously or between ballys.

half and half *n.*   a hermaphrodite attraction in a sideshow.

hanky-pank *n.*   a winnable game.

heat *n.*   trouble, either with police or with townspeople angry about losing at carnival games. "The church deacon dropped all his money at the wheel of fortune, and later there was a lot of *heat* from the town clowns."

Hey Rube *n.*   a fight between carnies and townspeople. "There was a *Hey Rube* our last night in Stockton, but we got out okay." Also, a call to arms for immediate help during such a fight.

iron *n.*   a carnival ride, especially a flat, heavy one. "Go unload the *iron* at the end of the right-hand side."

jennie *n.*   a merry-go-round.

joint *n.*   a game or concession stand. Rel: **jointee:** the person who operates a game.

juice *n.*   electrical current.

jump *n.*   the move from one town to the next.

lot *n.*   the carnival grounds.

marks *n.*   townspeople, especially those who play the carnival games.

mitt camp *n.*   a fortune-telling booth.

pickled punks *n.*   human fetuses, real or fake, displayed in glass jars. "My spiel went like this: 'Ladies and gentlemen, inside the tent you'll see Siamese twins! They're absolutely genuine, true marvels of nature!' But all they'd see were *pickled punks.*" Rel. **bouncer:** a rubber replica of a fetus.

pitch *n.* a concession in which a salesman gives a spiel while demonstrating an item that is for sale. Also, *v.* "Nobody can *pitch* Svengali Decks like Jimmy Swink. Once he sold 200 packs of trick cards in half an hour!"

plush *n.* big stuffed animals and other desirable prizes at a game booth.

popper *n.* the food trailer.

rehash *n.* a scam in which the ticket taker surreptitiously returns used tickets to the ticket seller for reselling; they split the profits later.

ride jocks *n.* employees who run the rides.

right-hand side *n.* the best midway site for early-opening shows aimed at families and children. So called because Americans tend to go to the right upon entering an establishment, a fact that carnival outfits use to their advantage.

signal 40 *n.* code for vomit. "Get over to the Tilt-A-Whirl with a mop; it's a *signal 40.*"

slough *v.* pronounced "slo." To take down a carnival.

slum *n.* shoddy prizes, worth less than the cost of playing the game. "We just got in a load of *slum* from Taiwan."

stick *n.* a carnival shill who plays games or buys tickets for midway attractions in order to induce marks to follow him. Carnies say "stick," never "shill." "After the *stick* won the plush panda, all the marks crowded in to try their luck." Also, *v.* to act as a shill.

Sunday school *n.* a carnival outfit with no gaffed games or raunchy shows.

talker *n.* someone who addresses the crowd outside an attraction. The term "barker" is never used by carnies. "He's the *talker* for the ten-in-one, and that man can really build a tip." Rel. **lecturer:** the emcee inside a show.

ten-in-one *n.* a midway show featuring multiple attractions, often including a magic or freak show.

tip *n.* the crowd that forms outside an attraction, lured by the talker and bally. Rel. **turn the tip** *v.* when a talker persuades a crowd to buy tickets to enter an attraction.

town clowns *n.* local police.

trailer joint *n.* a game mounted on a trailer or truck. Also, **truck joint.**

two-way store *n.* a game that an operator can run either straight or crooked.

water-hose ride *n.* a ride that frequently makes customers nauseated.

whoop-de-doo *n.* the most intense and exciting part of a carnival ride, such as when a roller coaster speeds down the tallest hill.

with it *adj.* a code term by which carnies communicate that they're in the know and in the same business.

TRUCKERS

alligator *n.* a tread or recap from a blown tire. Creates a road hazard. Rel. **alligator bait:** bits and pieces of a blown tire.

at your back door *adj.* behind a truck. "You got a bear *at your back door.*" Ant. **front door:** in front of a truck.

back row *n.* the area at some truck stops where prostitutes hang out.

Bambi *n.* a deer, whether dead or alive. Rel. **swamp donkey:** a moose.

bear *n.* a county or state cop. "Got a *bear* in the chicken coop at the 39 yardstick." (*See* **yardstick.**) Syn. **Smokey.** Rel. **she bear:** a female cop.

bear in the air *n.* a police airplane that monitors highway speeds.

bedbuggers *n.* household moving companies.

big rubber *n.* 24-inch tires. Also, **tall rubber.** Rel. **small rubber:** 22-inch tires.

bingo cards *n.*   paper cards that hold trucking permits from various states.

bobtail *adj.*   running without a trailer.

boogie *n.*   top gear. "I've got 'er up into *boogie* now."

brake check *n.*   a sudden slowdown in traffic, causing a driver to hit the brakes.

Bulldog *n.*   a Mack truck.

bumper sticker *n.*   an automobile following too closely. Syn. **hitchhiker.**

bundled out *adj.*   carrying a very full load.

cash register *n.*   a toll booth. "You're coming up on a *cash register* at yardstick 154."

chicken coop *n.*   a weigh station. Also, **coop.**

chicken lights *n.*   extra lights on the truck and trailer.

city kitty *n.*   a female city police officer.

comedian *n.*   the median strip.

county mountie *n.*   a sheriff. Syn. **local yokel.**

covered wagon *n.*   a flatbed or gravel trailer topped with a tarp.

crotch rocket *n.*   a motorcycle. Syn. **murdercycle.**

destruction *n.*   road construction.

diaper-wrap *v.*   when household movers swaddle furniture in pads. "Here's a full-length mirror for you to *diaper-wrap.*"

double nickel *n.*   55 miles per hour, the speed limit in many states.

down stroke *n.*   a steep descent. Ant. **up stroke:** a steep ascent.

dry box *n.*   a freight trailer. Syn. **van.**

18-wheeler *n.*   any articulated truck, even if it has fewer or more than 18 wheels.

4-wheeler *n.*   a passenger car.

free coffee *n.*   a whorehouse. So called because the coffee is usually free—although nothing else is.

FreightShaker *n.*   a Freightliner truck.

funny book *n.*   a Department of Transportation logbook, required by law. Syn. **comic book.**

Gay Bay *n.*   San Francisco.

gearjammer *n.*   a speeding truck driver, one known to accelerate and decelerate quickly. Syn. **gearslammer.**

General Mess of Crap *n.*   GMC truck by Volvo/White.

good buddy *n.*   a homosexual.

go to the Harley *v.*   to put your CB on channel 1. Rel. **go to double Harley:** to put your CB on channel 11.

got your ears on *exp.*   used when looking for someone on the CB. "Hey, J. T., you *got your ears on?*"

gouge on it *v.*   go fast; step on it.

granny gear *n.*   the lowest gear, usually used in a parking lot.

granny lane *n.*   the slow, right-hand lane on an interstate highway or freeway.

greasy side up *adj.*   when a car or truck has flipped over. "There's a 4-wheeler with the *greasy side up.*" Rel. **keep your greasy side down** *exp.*   stay safe, take care of yourself.

green stamps *n.*   money, usually tolls.

ground pressure *n.* weight. "The coop is just checking *ground pressure*. No sweat."

gumball machine *n.* lights on top of a police cruiser. "He's got his *gumball machine* going." Rel. **hit the jackpot** *v.* when police lights are flashing. "Looks like someone *hit the jackpot*."

hammer lane *n.* the fast, passing lane on an interstate highway or freeway. Syn. **bumper lane.**

haulin' dispatcher brains *v.* pulling an empty trailer. Syn. **haulin' sailboat fuel.**

have shutter trouble *v.* to fall asleep. "He ran off the road. Must have had *shutter trouble*."

Ho Chi Minh Trail *n.* California Highway 152, which has heavy traffic and is a "minefield" of accidents.

hood *n.* any conventional tractor, as opposed to a cab-over. Syn. **long-nose.**

hook *n.* a tow truck.

horse cock *n.* the kingpin that attaches a trailer to a tractor.

$100 lane *n.* the left lane of a highway or freeway that has more than two lanes in each direction.

in the big hole *adj.* in top gear.

Kenworthless *n.* a Kenworth truck. Syn. **K-Whopper.**

Kojak with a Kodak *n.* a police officer with a radar gun. "You got a *Kojak with a Kodak* behind the overpass."

large car *n.* a big, fancy truck.

Left Coast *n.* the West Coast.

lot lizard *n.* a truck-stop hooker. "Hey, get a load of the two *lot lizards* in the back row!"

meat wagon *n.* an ambulance.

mission *n.* a rush load. "I'm on a *mission* today."

motion lotion *n.* truck fuel.

parking lot *n.* a truck carrying automobiles. Also, a traffic back-up.

pickle park *n.* a rest area or roadside park, often a hangout for hookers.

plain white wrapper *n.* an unmarked police car.

reefer *n.* a refrigerated cargo trailer. "The sign at the front desk at Motel 6 says, 'No running *reefers* after nine P.M.' "

road pizza *n.* a badly mangled road kill.

rollerskate *n.* any small car. Originally referred to a Volkswagen.

sandbox *n.* a gravel trailer. Syn. **coal bucket.** Also, the escape ramp on a mountain grade.

Schneider eggs *n.* orange drums used by road-work crews to block off a lane. They are the same color as Schneider company trucks.

scoot *n.* a Harley-Davidson motorcycle.

seat cover *n.* an attractive female passenger in a car, often wearing a short skirt and showing some leg.

Sesame Street *n.* CB channel 19. This channel is often taken over by the "kiddies"—townies trying to listen in on the truckers, inexperienced truckers, and obnoxious folks who talk right over everyone else, making the channel useless.

sex lights *n.* when someone is getting a ticket—i.e., getting screwed—and the squad car's lights are flashing. "*Sex lights* on the 5 North, by the Castaic exit."

Shaky City *n.* Los Angeles. Syns. **Lost Angels, Lower Arkansas.**

shoot you in the back *v.* when a concealed highway cop uses a radar gun after you pass. "You got a bear settin' under the bridge who's gonna *shoot you in the back* when you go by."

skate board *n.* a flatbed trailer.

skins *n.* tires. Syn. **rubbers.**

smashing side *n.* the right side of a truck. "You got a 4-wheeler coming up your *smashing side.*" Ant. **passing side:** the left side of a truck.

smokin' scooter *n.* a motorcycle cop. Syn. **Evel Knievel.**

squirt the dirt *v.* to urinate. Syns. **check the tires, cool the brakes.**

step on *v.* to talk right over someone else on the CB radio, causing both parties to sound garbled.

sticks *n.* furniture. Used by van-line movers. Rel. **chowder:** miscellaneous items, tossed into boxes and hard to move.

Sure Wish I'd'a Faster Truck *n.* a SWIFT company's truck.

swinging *adj.* carrying a load of carcass beef.

taking pictures *v.* when a police officer is using radar equipment. "There's a smokin' scooter *taking pictures* at yardstick 25."

thermos bottle *n.* a tanker trailer. Syns. **pipeline, portable gas station.**

too many eggs in the basket *adj.* overweight.

toothpicks *n.* lumber. "I got a load of *toothpicks.*"

travel agent *n.* a dispatcher.

triple digit ride *n.* a truck that can exceed one hundred miles per hour.

VW *n.* a Volvo/White tractor.

West Coast turnarounds *n.*   benzedrine pills, speed. So called because a driver could theoretically drive from coast to coast and back without stopping to sleep.

wiggle wagons *n.*   double or triple trailers. Syns. **pups, rolling trouble, snakes, wasp-waists.**

yardstick *n.*   a mile marker alongside a highway.

SHOW BUSINESS

THEATER PEOPLE

Annie Oakley *n.* a free pass. Derived from Buffalo Bill's Wild West show, where free passes were punched (as if Annie Oakley had shot a bullet through them).

barn doors *n.* the adjustable shutters that help focus a spotlight.

blue-hair shows *n.* weekday matinees tending to attract ladies' groups.

break a leg! *exp.* good luck! Derived from Shakespearean times when a troupe of actors that got an ovation at the end of a play would bend (break) a leg and go down on one knee. Thus, the expression wishes an actor an ovation. Over time the phrase became a means for superstitious theater people to avoid bringing an actor bad luck by overtly wishing him good luck.

buck and wing *n.* a song and dance routine. One of many vaudeville terms still in active use in the legitimate theater.

bullets *n.* small sandbags used as weights in the fly system. (*See* **flies.**)

canary *n.* a singer.

cat *n.* catwalk, a gridwork of walkways above the stage.

cattle call *n.* an audition for actors.

deck *n.* the stage. Syn. **boards.**

dress *v.* to place props on the set. To put on a costume isn't to "dress" but to "get into wardrobe."

face *n.* a pretty girl or handsome young male. "We need a *face* for this part." Syn. **pretty boy:** a male face. Rel. **voice:** a person with a trained bass speaking voice that commands. "We need a *voice,* somebody like James Earl Jones."

fall on your face *v.* to utterly blow your performance or your lines, make a mess of it, fail.

flies *n.* the area above the stage into which curtains, set pieces, scrims, and other equipment can be raised and retrieved for set changes. Also, *fly* *v.* to raise or lower something from the flies. *"Fly* that scrim, will you?" Rel. **well** *n.* the top of the fly space. "Stick it in the *well"* means to haul a set piece as high as it will go.

give stage *v.* to let someone else be the focus of the audience. This is done by turning your back partially to the spectators and allowing the other actor to "upstage" you. Syn. **work in the trough.**

go up *v.* when an actor forgets lines on stage. "Sarah *went up* in the middle of Act One."

ham *n.* an actor who overacts.

hoofer *n.* a dancer.

house *n.* the audience. "Have you counted the *house* tonight?"

hum-heads *n.* theater soundmen. Syn. **noise boys.**

-ing *v.* present-tense verb form used by stagehands giving orders. Instead of telling someone to close the door, it's "closing the door." Some theater people joke by saying, "Thanking you."

looking for termites *v.* when an actor stands with head down, looking at the floorboards rather than at the audience. Not desirable. Director during rehearsals: "Umm . . . Alice, are you *looking for termites?"*

macguffin *n.* a disaster. "The night was a *macguffin."*

mount *v.* to do preproduction for a play—i.e., building and putting up sets, gathering props, hanging and focusing lights, working on the sound, etc.

paper the house *v.* to give away lots of free tickets so the theater will be filled. "We *paper the house* on opening nights for the press, so the critics will hear lots of audience reaction."

put it on its feet *v.* to mount and stage a play.

rag *n.* the heavy velvet main curtain.

run *n.* engagement. "We've got a three-week *run* at the Pantages."

schmooze *v.* to chat or engage in polite small talk. "Lesley Manning usually spends about half an hour *schmoozing* with her fans after the show."

the Scottish Play *n.* a certain Shakespeare play that has a one-word title which begins with the letter "M," involves a witch's curse, and is considered bad luck to mention in a theater.

scrim *n.* a transparent fabric curtain used to create special effects of light or atmosphere. "We backlight the *scrim* to make everything look ethereal for *A Midsummer Night's Dream.*"

shuffle off to Buffalo *v.* to make an exit. Stage manager: "Sharon—wake up, darling! That was your cue to *shuffle off to Buffalo.*"

spot *n.* a section of the script. From the notion that this portion will be in the spotlight. "This spot is a *buck and wing.*"

stage *v.* when a director assembles the cast, gives them their blocking (stage movements), conducts rehearsals, and so on. "He did a fabulous job of *staging* the play in New York."

strike *v.* to disassemble a production.

taking it on the road *v.* shipping the production from city to city.

third-row stare *n.* for an actor to fix his gaze at the third row of seats; this puts his head in a position such that every person in the house feels that he is looking at them.

whistling in the dressing room *v.* one of many things considered bad luck among theater people.

working off the walls *v.* when an actor is projecting his voice so it can be heard at the very back of the house.

MOVIE AND TELEVISION INDUSTRY WORKERS

Motion Picture People

Abby Singer *n.* the day's next-to-last shot. Named for an assistant director who habitually announced the day's last shot and then said: "No, wait! Just one more!"

back end *n.* a movie's total profits from theatrical release, video, and such marketing endeavors as novelizations, soundtracks, and toys.

baby spot *n.* a 500- or 750-watt lamp.

baffle blanket *n.* a portable barrier used to prevent reverberation on a sound stage.

banana *v.* when an actor walks a curved path in front of the camera so as to stay in focus.

bang *n.* an exclamation point on a movie advertising poster, appended to a tepid headline to lend excitement. Example: "A Movie For All Time!"

bazooka *n.* a lighting support, used on a catwalk.

BCU *n.* Big Close Up. A shot of a face that fills the screen.

blimp *n.* a soundproof cover that fits over a movie camera.

bloom *n.* a sudden bright glare reflected from an object on camera.

box office *n.* revenue from ticket sales for a movie. Also, an actor's potential to draw an audience and earn the studio a profit. "Paul Newman is good *box office.*"

the 'bu *n.*   Malibu, the Southern California beach community of the stars.

buck *n.* $100,000, in Hollywoodese. "My client will do the picture for five *bucks.*"

the business *n.*   the motion picture industry. "When you've been in *the business* as long as I have, you learn not to believe anything until the contract's signed." Syn. **the industry.**

callback *n.*   an invitation for an actor to return for a second audition.

C-47 *n.*   a clothespin used for attaching a colored gel to a spotlight. The term is used in order to sound highly technical and important. "Bring me a *C-47* on the double!"

creative differences *n.*   often cited as the reason why somebody was fired from a picture.

cucaloris *n.*   a screen with odd-shaped holes cut through it, placed before a light source to throw diverse shadows on an otherwise uniform surface. Syn. **kook.**

day for night *n.*   a night scene actually shot in daylight through filters.

deal memo *n.*   a brief memorandum outlining an agreement that will later be finalized in a full contract. "Bill Goldman's got a *deal memo* for the script. He's starting right away."

doily pushing *v.*   fussy adjustments of set decorations. "Okay, you've got exactly one more minute for the *doily pushing.* Then we shoot the scene."

dope sheet *n.*   a list of every shot and every take filmed.

dress *v.*   to decorate or arrange a set for filming. Rel. **dress the windows for night:** to redo what is seen through the windows to give the appearance of nighttime.

face approval *n.*   an actor's contractual right to okay any photo or illustration of him- or herself used in advertising or promoting the film.

favored nations *adj.*   a contract clause stating that a party will receive the best treatment offered to anyone on the project in terms of profits, theatrical billing, size of dressing room, etc. "One more thing, Sy. This contract has to be *favored nations,* or Uma doesn't want the work."

focus puller *n.* a cameraman's assistant who adjusts the focus of the lens.

fold and hold *v.* to dismantle a set and store the props for later use. "We need to *fold and hold* the police squad-room set. They're filming a Pepsi commercial on that stage tomorrow."

Foley *n.* the art of creating believable sounds to add to a film after it is shot. This includes simulating footsteps, punches (done by slugging a piece of beef), squeaking hinges, and many other sounds. "Have the *Foley* artist do the run across the gravel driveway, and give it lots of crunch."

four-wall *v.* to rent a theater and exhibit a motion picture in hopes of attracting an audience and a distributor. "It's an art film, so we'll have to *four-wall* it."

French hours *n.* a very long work day with no formal lunch break.

gobo *n.* a black-painted screen that blocks out extraneous light.

golden time *n.* overtime, with extra pay.

golden retrievers *n.* savvy studio executives.

green light *v.* to approve a project to go into production. Rel. **flashing green light:** when a project is close to approval.

green out *n.* to arrange plants and trees on a set or location, either for visual effect or to conceal undesired backgrounds. "Better *green out* those telephone poles, since we're supposed to be in the Jurassic Period."

gross player *n.* a star with enough clout to demand a percentage of a movie's gross income. (A percentage of the net is worth nothing if the studio somehow never declares a net profit on a picture.)

hair in the gate *n.* what a cameraman calls any foreign matter lodged in the camera. (The gate is the opening where the film is exposed.)

hand props *n.* small items that an actor handles during a scene, such as a magazine, dagger, or fountain pen. Syn. **smalls.**

heat *n.* what a "hot" actor has, reflected in audience appeal and box office revenues. Rel. **top spin:** an agent's effort to manufacture synthetic heat for an actor.

helm *v.* to direct a movie, in the lingo of Hollywood trade papers. "Ron Howard will *helm* the picture for Castle Rock."

hero *n.* any prop handled by a lead actor.

he's a/she's a *n.* a standard format for movie poster advertising. *"He's a* mad bomber. *She's a* munitions expert turned cop. Together they're *Pure Dynamite."*

honey wagon *n.* a trailer housing toilets for a crew on location.

hot set *n.* a set dressed and ready for shooting, not to be disturbed. "Don't walk in the living room! It's a *hot set."*

hummer *n.* a film score composer who hums a melodic theme and then assigns ghostwriters to orchestrate and develop it, rarely with credit.

inky dink *n.* a small incandescent light.

insert *n.* a brief detail shot, inserted to make a situation clear or provide continuity. Examples: a hand with a pen circling a name in the telephone book, broken glass on the floor.

in the can *adj.* finished. "The picture is *in the can,* and I'm going on a long vacation." Derived from the metal canister used to hold motion picture film.

jump cut *n.* an abrupt shift from the previous scene, used to speed up the story.

knife-o-suction *n.* removing excess flab from an actor's photograph in a movie poster via judicious cropping. Syn. **Slim Fast.**

lose *v.* to get rid of. "Let's *lose* that car in the background."

martini *n.* the last shot of the day; i.e., after that one, it's time to have a drink. "Okay, gang; this two-shot will be the *martini."*

Mickey Rooney *n.* a "short creep," referring to movement of the dolly, a wheeled vehicle that transports the camera. "As she steps over to get the gun from the desk drawer, we'll do a *Mickey Rooney.*"

moo print *n.* a film lab term for a perfect print.

murder-your-wife brick *n.* a fake brick, named after and first used in the 1965 Jack Lemmon film, *How to Murder Your Wife.*

nonpro *n.* a person outside the film industry. "For a *nonpro,* Jane Austen wrote some pretty good stuff."

numbers *n.* receipts. "I hear the new *Batman* had incredible *numbers* this weekend."

pay or play *n.* a contract clause guaranteeing payment to a star, director, or writer even if the film is not produced.

points *n.* the percentage points of a film's profits commanded by high-powered directors, actors, and writers as part of their deal. "Not many stars can get *points* on the gross."

positive word-of-mouth *n.* approving comments that a movie audience passes to friends and acquaintances. "The picture generated *positive word-of-mouth.*"

quote *n.* the fee that an actor received for his or her most recent film. "We see Steve Martin for the part. Do you know his *quote?*"

reaction shot *n.* a shot of a person responding to whatever happened in the previous shot.

reverse *n.* a shot repeating the same action from the opposite point of view. "Let's come around and get the *reverse* on their argument."

Salvador *n.* a camera dolly. A play on the name of painter Salvador Dali. "Bring in *Salvador* for this shot."

Sam Brown *n.* a police gun belt from the prop department.

shoot *n.* the filming of a movie. "Nevada in August! No town for 75 miles! That *shoot* was hell."

speed! *exp.* the soundman's cue to the director that the sound recorder has reached the proper speed to synchronize with the camera.

skin *n.* movie "make-up" for a vehicle, either a decal or a magnetic sign. Example: nondescript sedan + decal = county sheriff's patrol car.

star baggage *n.* a big budget set aside for perks for major talent working on a picture.

sweetening *n.* improvements in a soundtrack after filming is completed.

take a meeting *v.* to have a meeting, in Hollywood.

talent *n.* generic term for actors, actresses, singers, dancers, and other performers. "We need sandwiches and drinks for the *talent.*"

That's my Hitler! *exp.* used when a director finds just the right actor or actress for a role. From Mel Brooks's movie, *The Producers.*

topline *v.* to star, in Hollywood trade-ese.

two-shot *n.* a camera image of two people.

upfront exposure *n.* the amount paid for a film project, even if it is never produced. "Fox's *upfront exposure* on the alien movie is something like $2.5 million."

wallah *n.* background noise of people, indistinguishable voices, and various other sounds added to the soundtrack to make a scene more realistic.

whirly *n.* a lift used to hold the camera for high-angle shots.

wide *adj.* refers to broad distribution of a picture. "The Clint Eastwood movie is opening *wide*—something like 2,200 theaters."

wild sound *n.* sounds recorded without picture, such as wallah.

wrangler *n.* the animal handler on a movie set or location.

Television Industry Folk

B-roll *n.* footage that establishes the context of a news story. "I need *B-roll* of the protest march." Rel. **A-roll:** the interviews and stand-up portion of a news broadcast.

bumper *n.* a brief transition to a commercial. Example: *"Unsolved Mysteries* will be back in a moment!"

bye-bye *n.* a transitional phrase used on the air, such as, "Now let's go to Lana Lang, live on location . . ."

color commentary *n.* background information, analysis, and insider chat to add variety and interest to a play-by-play sports broadcast.

crawl *n.* credits moving down the screen at the start or end of a TV program. Syn. **creep.**

dead air *n.* an unintended period of silence or blank screen.

drooling *n.* unrehearsed chitchat used to fill out the remaining time on a broadcast segment.

eyeballs *n.* viewers, people watching a certain show. "For advertisers, city *eyeballs* are better than rural eyeballs. They spend more money."

foam the runways *exp.* used by a news producer when one of the show's segments isn't completed and the deadline is imminent.

gearhead *n.* an engineer. "Whoa! What happened to the audio on Katie's mike? We need a *gearhead* quick."

hammock *v.* to sandwich a low-rated program between two stronger programs, hoping the audience will carry over.

hiatus *n.* the period when production shuts down after all of the season's episodes have been shot.

HINT *n.* Happy Idiot News Team. A behind-the-scenes term for local newscasters who are encouraged to banter among themselves between story segments.

If it bleeds, it leads *exp.*   when local news programs feature gory crime and accident stories.

illustrated radio *n.*   a derogatory term for television that is all talk.

kicker *n.*   a cheery story that closes out a news broadcast.

meat puppet *n.*   a news anchor modestly endowed with intelligence. "That *meat puppet* couldn't say the name of the program without a tele-prompter." Rel. **meat with eyes:** actors and actresses.

nostril shot *n.*   an unflattering picture of someone caused by using a bad camera angle.

package *n.*   a finished story, ready for broadcasting. "Bob, I need your *package* by 3:30."

reversal *n.*   shots of the reporter reacting to an interviewee's statements. Often taped later and intercut with interview footage.

rundown *n.*   blow-by-blow outline of a news show, timed to the second.

stand-up *n.*   when a reporter stands facing the camera and gives a news report. "I want you to do a *stand-up* outside the White House right after the President vetoes the bill."

strip show *n.*   a program airing five days a week in the same time slot.

tag *n.*   a short scene tacked onto the end of a show. Often an after-thought, kicker, or joke. Also, final comments by a newscaster added to a taped news story.

walk and talk *n.*   a stand-up in which the reporter walks and the camera follows along.

wallpaper *n.*   video filler shots. "After we show him being interviewed a while, we better lay in some *wallpaper* of him playing with his kids, fooling around in the kitchen, that sort of stuff."

web *n.*   a television network, in the language of Hollywood trade papers. "The comedian was signed by the Alphabet *Web* [ABC] for a family sitcom."

yakker *n.* a talk show, in trade papers. "He's CBS's newest entry in the battle of the late-night *yakkers.*"

Screen and TV Writers

backstory *n.* a character's history that explains his current behavior. "Ned's *backstory* is that his father always told him he was a screw-up. So now Ned figures, well, why not screw up big-time?"

bananas on bananas *n.* a sitcom gag that overdoes it. "When Phoebe does a double take, it's funny. But having everybody else do takes is just *bananas on bananas.*"

beat *n.* an important plot point or emotional moment. "Okay, *beat* one, the husband says he's off to a business meeting in New York. *Beat* two, the wife unpacks his suitcase and finds a matchbook from a hotel in Miami." Rel. **beat sheet:** a summary listing a story's major developments.

between brads *adj.* complete. Refers to a script bound with metal fasteners. "I'll feel better about it when I see it *between brads.*"

coverage *n.* a written script assessment by a studio story analyst, whose recommendation (or lack thereof) determines whether studio executives ever bother to look at a script.

echo dialogue *n.* repetition of what another sitcom character just said. Example: "Kramer says, 'Jerry, why is your cereal hidden in the bathroom?' And Jerry says, 'Cereal? Bathroom?' "

ET *n.* Evil Twin. A soap opera character's friend who behaves abominably to him or her (stealing his big business deal, seducing her spouse, etc.). Why? To generate dramatic conflict.

exclusivity *n.* a contract term stating that no other writer will work on the screenplay. "Hey, it's only your second picture; we're not about to give you *exclusivity.*"

fix it in the pinks *n.* to rewrite a script's problem spots or weak dialogue in a later draft. Derives from the paper colors (pink, yellow, blue) used for successive rewrites.

gangbang *v.* to collaborate with other writers. "The scene with Frasier and his brother isn't working. We'll have to *gangbang* it before rehearsal."

hairball *n.* a sitcom scene that is thick with sticky sentiment. "After the wacky chase around the apartment, let's stick in a *hairball.*" Rel. **huggy tag:** a scene-concluding hairball. Ant. **treacle cutter:** a biting or acerbic neutralizer of a hairball.

hang a lantern on it *v.* to underline a plot point with a brief shot. "We'd better *hang a lantern on it* and show Ashley listening outside the door when Brad phones his new mistress."

high-concept *adj.* describes a story idea that is very commercial and can be expressed in a sentence or two. "I've been pitching a *high-concept* picture about a baseball-playing chimp. Sort of *Gorillas in the Mist* meets *Field of Dreams.*"

hit and run *n.* when a soap opera character appears just long enough to do something that stirs up other characters' emotions or reactions.

hook *n.* the "something special" that makes a story different; the sizzle that sells the steak. "The plot's pretty standard cop stuff, but there's a great *hook*—our hero was exposed to radiation that made him invisible."

in turnaround *adj.* when a script hasn't been produced by the studio that bought it and is now made available to others. "I understand the baseball-playing-chimp script is *in turnaround,* and Universal may look at it."

Iowa *adj.* laughably unprofessional. "Did you read this buddy-story script? Strictly *Iowa.*"

Irving the Explainer *n.* overmuch discourse on the action or characters. "Why have Indy blab about how a whip is better than a gun? What an *Irving the Explainer!* Just have him snap the pistol out of the Nazi's hand." Syn. **world expo.**

knowers telling knowers *n.* a writing flaw in which one character recites information that the other character already knows.

limbo *n.* vague surroundings with no set, a contrivance used on soap operas. "We'll show Barbara in *limbo,* apparently brushing her hair backstage at the theater."

log line *n.*   a one- or two-sentence summary of a script, rendered by a reader.

NTBSLT *adj.*   Not This, But Something Like This. A comment jotted on a sitcom script where a joke isn't working.

page-oner *n.*   a script so putrid it needs rewriting from the first page.

Pasadena *exp.*   let's pass on the script. "What shall we do with this girls-on-the-road script?" *"Pasadena!"*

pitch *v.*   to narrate and promote a story idea to studio bigwigs, hoping to sell the project. "I'll be in L.A. Monday to *pitch* the invisible cop script."

plot point *n.*   a turning point in the action.

polish *n.*   a refinement and smoothing of a script, but less than a revision. "I've got to do a *polish* by Monday."

PUC *n.*   pronounced "puke." Previously Unknown Child who is suddenly introduced into the life of a soap opera character.

reader *n.*   the person who first reads a script submitted to a studio, writing a summary and evaluation for executives. Syn. **story analyst.**

rec *v.*   when a reader recommends a script to the studio.

rhyme *v.*   to connect something from an early scene with something in a later scene. "When he was a kid his grandfather beat him with a cane, right? We can *rhyme* it to the crowbar he uses later as a serial killer."

spit take *n.*   a reaction shot in which a sitcom character spews his beverage for comic effect. "Let's lighten it up when Monica tells Chandler she got fired from her third job in a week. He can do a *spit take.*"

treatment *n.*   a detailed synopsis of a story, often with some dialogue.

Game Show Staffers

Bambi *n.*   a contestant who becomes immobile and speechless in front of the camera. From the image of a deer frozen with fear in auto headlights.

"That *Bambi* stood there with her mouth open for so long we had to go to a commercial."

Barney Fife *n.* a player who nervously pushes his buzzer before he actually thinks of the answer. Named for Don Knotts's nervous, shaky character on television's *The Andy Griffith Show.*

cheerleader *n.* a person who reacts in a lively fashion, energizing the rest of the contestant group. "Be sure to put her on first; she's a real *cheerleader.*"

civilian *n.* an ordinary contestant on a show that uses showbiz celebrities. "We'll need more *civilians* in December, so let's run an ad in the *L.A. Times.*"

clean sweep *n.* a series of correct answers from one player, without opponents even getting a chance to respond.

Cliff Claven *n.* a *Jeopardy!* contestant so far ahead that he can't lose, except by stupidly gambling all his winnings on Final Jeopardy—which he does, losing the game. Taken from the *Cheers* character who made this boneheaded error during a fictitious appearance on the show. "Did you see *Jeopardy!* last night? The Chicago schoolteacher really pulled a *Cliff Claven.*"

contestant phony *n.* a person who tries too hard to impress the producers during show tryouts and comes across as artificial. Actors and actresses often fall into this category.

corrective surgery *n.* the quiet elimination of a contestant from an audition or the contestant pool, usually due to obnoxious, superior, or strange behavior.

cue the Kleenex *exp.* used when a highly emotional contestant is on the brink of winning a large prize.

DAS *adj.* Dull As Shit. Utterly lacking personality. "That contestant is *DAS.* If you ask, 'Tell us about yourself,' he talks about cleaning out his garage."

dead wood *n.* a contestant who shows no energy or reactions.

dumb off *n.*   when none of the contestants gets the right answer, so the host must tell them.

elbow grabber *n.*   a model who escorts contestants on and off the set.

Forest Lawn *adj.*   lifeless. "I ran Monday's contestant tryout. They were strictly *Forest Lawn.*" Ant. **high-octane.**

god *n.*   the staffer who determines whether an answer is sufficient or admissible. "Can a koala be called a 'koala bear'? Let's let *god* decide."

hooker *n.*   a woman who appears for an audition or taping in cheap, gaudy clothes. "Will you gently tell the *hooker* that we've got a change of clothes for her in the dressing room?"

idiot *n.*   the game show host, to TV producers.

Judas *n.*   anyone in the audience who says an answer loudly enough for contestants to hear. "Sorry, but your answer won't count. *Judas* in the third row yelled it, too."

kiss-off *n.*   the host's words of farewell to a contestant leaving the program.

lovely parting gifts *n.*   consolation prizes given to contestants who didn't win anything. "On our show the *lovely parting gifts* include Lee Press-On Nails and Preparation H."

march of shame *n.*   escorting a loser off the platform. "I hate doing the *march of shame.* You know, 'Step right this way. We have some lovely parting gifts for you. . . .' "

Pasadena *n.*   a hopeful contestant whose boring personality or weird behavior prevents him or her from being chosen for the program. Derives from "pass on this one." "When that *Pasadena* started chatting about her collection of cookie jars, she was as good as gone."

PITA *n.*   Pain In The Ass. A contestant who is difficult or argumentative; often written on the file card that staffers keep for each player.

Poindexter *n.*   a contestant of remarkable intelligence. From the brainy boy in "Felix the Cat" cartoons.

read your rights *v.*   to recite the rules to contestants before the game begins. "Okay, people! Let me *read your rights,* and we'll start taping."

rock 'n' rollers *n.*   contestants who look as if they're in a rock band, or wish they were. "That *rock 'n' roller* plays the game pretty well, but tell him to lose the leather jacket for the taping."

Samoan *n.*   a contestant who jumps all over the host after a big win, possibly causing bodily harm. Reportedly, Bob Barker first used the term in reference to two Samoans who almost knocked him cold.

schlockmeister *n.*   one of the corporations or brokers that provides prizes to give away. "Can you believe the *schlockmeister* who keeps sending us depilatory cream? I'm sure our male contestants just treasure it."

star wrangler *n.*   a booker of celebrity guests for game shows. "Some *star wrangler!* That guy couldn't even deliver Troy Donahue."

thorazine *n.*   a total wacko. "We did a dozen tapings without a hitch. Then yesterday, in comes Miss *Thorazine.*"

tornado *n.*   a contestant who wins a great number of prizes. "What a *tornado!* She walked away with everything but the host's necktie."

uptown set *n.*   a showy stage set. "It's an *uptown set* with about a million blinking lights, deep-pile carpeting, a teak podium, the works." Ant. **downtown set:** a cheap stage set, often no more than the host's podium and some chairs.

Stunt Doubles

air ram *n.*   an air pressure–powered box with a lid that flips up and throws a stunt double about 30 feet through the air. "Keep your knee stiff when you step on the *air ram,* Buck. Otherwise, it will break your leg."

auger in *v.*   to make a hole, as if with a drill. "When I leaped off the motorcycle, I really *augered in!*"

blood capsule *n.*   a pill-sized container of theatrical blood, kept in the mouth during a stunt fight in order to "spit blood." Usually peppermint flavored.

breakaway table/chair *n.* a balsawood prop held together with slivers of wood and glue, but no nails. "First he punches you, Loren; then you smash the *breakaway chair* over his head. Peace and love!"

cable off *v.* to be attached to a safety cable. "I was *cabled off* in case I slipped off the roof."

candy glass *n.* sugar and other ingredients molded like glass. It shatters into bits, unlike plate glass, which breaks into big, jagged pieces that are dangerous. Used in breakaway bottles and small windowpanes.

come in hot *v.* to do a stunt very fast, perhaps too fast. "I *came in hot* on the dune-buggy jump."

double *n.* an actor who takes the place of another actor in scenes requiring special skills or preparation. Also, *v.* to function as a double.

double car *n.* a duplicate vehicle used in risky scenes or brought in after a wreck, so filming can continue. "Okay, people, we're going to shoot the big chase. Let's get the *double car.*" Ant. **cast car:** a vehicle driven by the star or actor.

fight choreographer *n.* a person who plans a big fight and teaches the routine to the stunt doubles.

fly *v.* to use cables for stunts in which a person appears to fly. "The script says you float above the streets of New York, so we'll *fly* you."

gag *n.* a stunt. "In this *gag* you get dragged under the stagecoach for 200 yards."

get air *v.* to have all the wheels of a car, motorcycle, bicycle, skates, etc., leave the ground. "When you ride the bike down the stairs, Steve, *get some air!*"

half tough *adj.* very strong, rough, and scrappy. "He's about *half tough*, so don't mess with him."

handy *adj.* having great ability at stunts. Rel. **hand** *n.* a skilled stuntman. "Rocco's a *hand.*"

heart-thumper *n.* a dangerous, hairy, or spooky stunt. "In *How the West Was Won,* I stood on top of a moving train, got shot, leaped off into cactus—and then fell over a cliff. What a *heart-thumper!*"

John Wayne punch *n.* a highly theatrical blow invented by the Duke. He would block a punch with his right arm, then bring the same fist down for a right cross.

loose horse *n.* when someone on horseback doesn't know how to ride. "There goes a *loose horse.*"

Michelin Man *n.* an overly padded stunt double.

no-brainer *n.* a stunt in which the stuntman is merely a passenger helplessly along for the ride—on a horse, train, wagon, etc.

over the shoulder *n.* a camera angle looking over a stuntman's shoulder from behind. When his fist crosses an imaginary line between the lens and the other stuntman's jaw, the camera "sees" a hit.

ratchet *n.* a system of pulleys and cords used to jerk a stuntman backward through the air up to twenty feet. It simulates the effect of being hit by a shotgun blast, explosion, etc.

rockers *n.* small explosive charges rigged around large panes of glass and detonated just before a stuntman dives through the window. Also, nails or ball bearings that are shot into the window to shatter it.

roll over *v.* to flip a car one or more times during a crash.

rubber cement *n.* a gasoline glue smeared on a stunt double's clothes, to make him appear to have caught fire. Just before the camera rolls, the director's last command is, "Glue him down, and light him!"

saddle fall *n.* a gag in which the stuntman falls off a horse. Rel. **horse fall:** when both horse and rider go down.

sell out *v.* to give a stunt the maximum effort, without holding back or being too cautious.

snap *n.* the jerk and recoil of an actor's head that makes a fake punch appear to have actually connected. "The Duke was a real pro. When a roundhouse punch knocked his head sideways, he always added a good *snap.*"

squib *n.* a device consisting of a small sack of stage blood and a tiny charge. It is attached to electric wires that detonate it, spattering the "blood" to simulate a bullet hit.

stick it *v.* to land precisely on a mark. From gymnastics.

stunt coordinator *n.* a highly experienced man or woman who plans and choreographs stunts, chooses locations, obtains vehicles for car chases, and so on.

trip *n.* a hand-held release mechanism used when a stuntman is being dragged by a horse. One type is released by pulling it, another by letting go. (The latter is a safer design in the event the stuntman gets knocked cold.)

Animators

antic *n.* pronounced "an-TIK." Anticipation; a technique for adding impact to an animation sequence. "In the frame just before the balloon bursts, implode the balloon a little. That gives it some *antic*, like the windup before the punch."

arc of action *n.* the curved lines traced by a body in motion. In good animation these curves are rendered smoothly. "Watch your *arc of action*, or the ice-skating hippo is going to look choppy and stiff."

cel *n.* a sheet of celluloid, the plastic on which images are drawn, painted, and then photographed in front of a background. Theatrical animation uses up to 24 cels per second. "I've got two original *cels* from *Alice in Wonderland* that I could sell for more than twenty thousand dollars as collectibles."

cha-cha (-cha) *n.* taking a few frames and playing them back and forth to make a person or animal look as if it's dancing or doing a double-take. Derived from a Purina Cat Chow commercial in which a cat appeared to dance. Syn. **rock-and-roll.**

cushy *adj.*   soft and smooth, without choppiness, like Disney animation. "Maybe your style would work for 'Beavis and Butt-head,' but it's not *cushy* enough for this studio."

Disney death *n.*   a character's "demise" staged to whip up the audience's emotions; however, before the film ends, the character is somehow wondrously resurrected, as in Disney features like *Snow White*. "The elf girl can have a *Disney death* in the black whirlpool. There won't be a dry eye in the house when the wizard brings her back out safely."

dope sheet *n.*   a frame-by-frame chart prepared by the animators as a cel timing guide for animation camera operators.

fanny gag *n.*   a visual joke showing a character's bottom. "Look, it's a tradition at this studio—at least one *fanny gag* in every cartoon. Let's have one of the characters slice Pegleg Pete's belt, so his pants fall down."

hero *n.*   a final, perfect shot. Supposedly first used on *Tron*.

in-betweens *n.*   drawings between major poses, overseen by an animator but actually rendered by assistants.

key drawings *n.*   a character's major poses during a scene. "Okay, in this sequence Roger Rabbit stands up from the table, turns, and walks out. The *key drawings* will be Roger in his chair, Roger standing up, the pivot on the heel, and the exit."

line of action *n.*   a character's movements as conceived in diagrammatic shorthand. The line of action shows what the character is thinking or doing, even without words. Example: Elmer Fudd says to Bugs Bunny, "You! Wascally wabbit! Get out of here!" The line of action: Elmer points to Bugs ("You!"), then jerks his thumb toward the door ("Get out . . . !").

Mickey Mousing *n.*   the practice of animating everything to a fixed beat. So called because early Mickey Mouse cartoons (and the hundreds of copycat non-Disney cartoons of the same period) would feature everything bouncing jauntily along in time to the music. The term came to describe any suffocatingly close synchronization of sound and image.

on twos *adj.*   when each drawing is photographed twice, which cuts the work in half. The action unfolds at 12 frames per second instead of 24, but in many situations the motion remains quite fluid. "Lots of Bugs Bunny footage was shot *on twos.*" Ant. **On ones:** when each drawing is photographed once, making the action look smoother. "Knowing which kinds of action require shooting *on ones* and which you can get away with shooting on twos was one of Disney's early trade secrets."

pencil mileage *n.*   the amount of work a drawing requires. "Boss, why do you always give me stuff like the crowd scene at the town hall? Do you know how much *pencil mileage* that'll take?"

pencil test *n.*   the photographing of animation drawings in sequence, in order to view the scene in "film time" and see if the motion looks correct.

personality animation *n.*   animation that creates believable characters, who are well developed and have distinct personalities. "People feel that the Little Mermaid really exists, that she's a being. That's great *personality animation.* The same thing can be said of Daffy Duck or Rocky and Bullwinkle."

skippy *n.*   a nut on animation trivia. "At the animation festival, two *skippies* almost came to blows over a scene in *Fantasia.*"

slugging *n.*   the process by which vocal tracks are broken down into timing sheets, so they can be animated.

squash and stretch *n.*   when a figure's mass is made to condense (squash) or elongate (stretch) under the stress of action. "In this scene do a *squash and stretch* with Wile E. Coyote. As he hits the canyon floor, flatten him down to a pancake, then have him go elastic and bounce like a ball."

stagger take *n.*   a vibrating movement, often accompanied by a bell, gong, or cymbal, that occurs when a character is struck a blow. The movement expands briefly, then decreases. "When Foghorn bonks the dog's head with the kettle, let's have a *stagger take.*"

storyboard *v.*   to blueprint a cartoon with a series of small sketches that tell the story. Also used in film and advertising. "Once we *storyboarded* it, we realized there were two scenes with animals dancing in the woods, so we cut one."

strobing *n.*   an animation problem in which a movement appears to stop. It occurs when drawings that express continued movement are too similar or close together. "Geez, I had a lot of *strobing* in that scene. It looked like an old western movie, where the wagon-wheel spokes freeze." Also, when the successive images that make up a progressive movement appear as staccato jumps, rather than being fused by the human eye's persistence of vision.

traceback *n.*   when a long-held pose is retraced over the entire figure, rather than drawing only the moving parts and maintaining the rest of the figure on a held cel. "Let's do a *traceback* on this character's legs; she looks dead from the waist down."

tree chopper *n.*   an animated sequence that undergoes repeated changes, thus requiring great quantities of drawing paper.

Yogi run *n.*   a gag device in which a character springs up and spins his feet in the air before actually running away. Derived from Yogi Bear. "When the dynamite goes BOOM, the duck can do a *Yogi run.*"

DISC JOCKEYS

bam-and-scram *n.*   a hit-and-run accident, as phrased by radio traffic reporters.

big-rig *n.*   a semi truck and trailer, to a traffic reporter. "We've got a *big rig* stalled in the number two lane on the Bayshore Freeway."

burnt *adj.*   when a record is overplayed until listeners can't stand hearing it. "Man, if ever a tune was *burnt,* it's the Supremes's 'Where Did Our Love Go.' "

contest pigs *n.*   people who try to hog prizes and giveaways on radio contests, often by using speed dialers and multiple telephones. "If the thirteenth caller is that Randy guy, just hang up on him. He's the worst *contest pig* I've ever seen."

hit the post *v.*   to talk during a song's musical lead-in, stopping precisely as the vocalist starts to sing. Ant. **step on it:** to talk on top of the singer's first few words; considered very clumsy.

maggot *n.*   a boring listener who phones radio talk shows and believes his every word is of riveting interest. "I had a *maggot* call me last night to report that he'd just installed a new garage-door opener."

morning personality *n.*   the deejay on a drive-time show.

on the beach *adj.*   unemployed. "Remember Charlie O'Soul? He's *on the beach* since the station went country western."

out of the box *adj.*   just released by the record company. "Playing a song *out of the box* is a great way to earn yourself some plugola."

plugola *n.*   gifts from record companies to deejays.

puker *n.*   a deejay whose vocal delivery—fast, smooth, artificial—is virtually a parody of disc jockeys.

shaggy dog *n.*   a listener who phones a radio show and chats earnestly with the deejay, creating an atmosphere of trust and rapport, then suddenly spews crude obscenities on live radio.

slow-and-go *n.*   rush-hour traffic that speeds up and slows down repeatedly, as phrased by radio traffic reporters. "We have plenty of *slow-and-go* right now, as the baseball game lets out."

MUSICIANS

Jazz Musicians

baby *n.*   affectionate term of address to both males and females.

bleat *v.*   to growl and grunt along with your playing. "During his piano solos, Errol Garner used to *bleat* a whole other tune."

blow *v.*   to play any instrument (not just a wind instrument).

blue notes *n.*   flatted third and seventh notes of the scale, which create the characteristic sound of the blues.

burn *v.*   to best another musician when trading solos. "I can't believe the way you *burned* Jimmy on that tune tonight, man." Syn. **cut.**

cat *n.*   a musician. Also, any man. "Who's that *cat* sitting next to the Pope?"

changes *n.*   a chord progression.

chops *n.*   extreme proficiency. "Branford has incredible *chops.*"

fake *v.*   to improvise.

head arrangement *n.*   a mental musical score that musicians work out together.

horn *n.*   any instrument.

riff *n.*   a short musical phrase.

wild *adj.*   amazing and surprising.

woodshed *v.*   to practice in an isolated place, such as a woodshed, so that nobody else has to endure hearing the repetitive exercises and drills. "The great saxophonist Charlie Parker stayed in Kansas City and did about eight years of *woodshedding* till he had enough chops to play with better ensembles."

Studio and Tour Rock Musicians

axe *n.*   guitar. "Let me get my *axe,* and I'll teach you that tune." Syn. **old lady.**

bus face *n.*   the tired, rumpled appearance of a musician who has slept on a tour bus overnight. "I better get rid of this *bus face* before the show!"

hum-heads *n.*   the audio crew.

lick *n.*   a riff. A musical phrase. "Can you show me that country *lick* of yours?"

road kill *n.*   a one-night gig during a tour.

studio tan *n.*   the pale and pasty look caused by working nights in a recording studio and sleeping during the day. Coined by Frank Zappa.

swag *n.* the goodies, such as tour jackets and posters, that are given as freebies to the tour crew.

Wedding Musicians

doubler *n.* a musician who plays more than one instrument. "He's a moderate violin *doubler*. The only problem is he holds the violin a little too close to his body. About another five feet should do it. Why doesn't he stick to saxophone?"

eating job *n.* when the party hiring the musicians also feeds them. "I have an afternoon gig at the Hilton and an evening in Brooklyn. Thank goodness the evening is an *eating job.*"

gig *n.* a job or booking.

noodler *n.* a musician who prefers to play lots of extra (usually fast) notes around the melody, rather than playing the song so the average listener would immediately recognize it. Some noodlers are very tasteful and add excitement to the music. Also, *v.* "Many musicians, unfortunately, choose to *noodle* because they don't actually know the song the rest of the group is playing."

preheat *n.* the portion of a wedding during which only part of the band plays, usually before the evening gets warmed up. "There was a trio for the *preheat.* After the ceremony the rest of the band joined them."

three flats, one sharp *adj.* shorthand to indicate the key in which to play a song (e.g., three flats is the key of E-flat major or C minor). "Okay, people. French waltzes, *three flats.* One, two, three. One, two, three . . ."

wedding mill *n.* a hotel, hall, or other facility with multiple weddings going on.

wide receiver *n.* the bridesmaid most determined to snag the bride's bouquet. "And she makes the catch! An incredible job by the *wide receiver!*"

STANDUP COMEDIANS

bit *n.* a part of an act based on one theme or premise.

bomb *v.* to have a bad set, and get a poor reaction. Syns. **eat it, eat my dick.** Rel. **eat a plate of dicks:** to bomb horribly. "What a show! About a hundred people, and two of them laughed. I *ate a plate of dicks.*" Also, **eat the midget:** "She didn't just *eat the midget.* She gobbled the midget with mustard and mayo."

brutal *adj.* what a bad audience is.

call-back *n.* a reference to an earlier bit or a point in a previous joke.

civilian *n.* anyone not in the comedy business.

comedy condo *n.* any housing where the club puts you up for the night.

dead mom shows *n.* television sitcoms starring male standups who play single parents.

feature *n.* the second act in a three-comic show; performs for half an hour. Syn. **middle.**

get the light *v.* to be signaled by the comedy club's stage manager that you have about a minute left to perform. The light insures that a show runs smoothly, but can also function as "the hook." "The stage manager at the Improv hates my guts. I always *get the light* just when I get on a roll."

guys in ties *n.* male monologuists in the vein of Jerry Seinfeld and Paul Reiser.

hack *n.* a comic who does obvious jokes on trite themes: New York vs. Los Angeles, cops in doughnut shops, dogs vs. cats, airplane trips, and so on. Also, a comic who has been doing the same act, verbatim, for years. Rel. **hacky** *adj.* describes a comic who sticks to the comedy clichés.

headliner *n.* the last act in a three-comic show; usually performs for 45 minutes.

hook *n.*   a special something that sets a comic apart and makes him or her memorable. "Let's see, you want a great *hook?* How about you're a single-parent lesbian Latina?"

kill *v.*   to do really well, perform a great set. "Man, I *killed* out there tonight!" Syns. **crush, murder, slay, smoke the room.**

magician *n.*   what comics become when all else fails, according to comics.

one-man show *n.*   what standup comics began doing with their routines once the comedy club scene was nearly dead. "Jimmie's *one-man show* is actually just his act, but longer and not as funny."

opener *n.*   the first act in a three-comic show; usually performs for 15 minutes. Syns. **emcee, host.**

papered *adj.*   describes a club filled with people because of promotional giveaways and free tickets.

passholes *n.*   bad audiences papered into comedy clubs so the owners can make money from drinks. "The club management says they're 'supporting comedy' by bringing in freebie audiences, but those *passholes* have no appreciation for what we're doing."

play to the back of the room *v.*   to use inside references that only the comics at the back of the club will get, leaving the rest of the audience clueless.

prop act *n.*   a comic who uses funny props as gimmicks. "Carrot Top is my favorite *prop act."*

punch *n.*   punch line, the climax that pays off the set-up.

riff *v.*   to take off on a theme, often improvising. "Did you see Jackie on *The Tonight Show, riffing* about his blind dog?"

set-up *n.*   the first part of a joke, establishing the premise. "The *set-up* is typically quiet. Then comes the punch."

slamming it shut *v.*   ending a comedy showcase.

tag *n.*   a funny line that follows and is related to the punch line. "I just love *tags,* because right away you're getting another laugh."

toilet *n.*   a second-rate comedy club.

voice *n.*   a comic's point of view about the world, as expressed in his or her material.

walk the room *v.*   to cause an audience to clear out. "He says nobody can follow him. And he's right—because he *walks the room.*"

MAGICIANS

Ambitious Card *n.*   a routine in which a chosen card is lost in the middle of the deck, but repeatedly comes to the top under increasingly impossible conditions.

back-palm *v.*   to hide something (card, coin) behind the hand by gripping it with the fingers. "The great magician T. Nelson Downs could *back-palm* ten coins. I tried one, and it fell on the floor."

beat *v.*   to fool, usually another magician. "I have to admit he *beat* me bad with his four-coin production. I have no idea."

black art *n.*   a technique using black items against a black background to make objects appear, vanish, float, or become animated.

book test *n.*   a standard effect of mentalism in which the performer divines words that spectators randomly choose from a book.

bottom *n.*   a card dealt from the bottom of the deck, while apparently dealing from the top. Rel. **second:** a card dealt from second-to-the-top position.

box act *n.*   a stage illusionist who uses various large boxes in which assistants appear, disappear, are sawed in half, and so on.

burn *v.*   for a spectator to focus intently on the hands of a close-up magician, trying to detect the secret. "Patrick baffles people with his borrowed-ring-off-string routine, even when they're *burning* his hands."

close-up magic *n.*   conjuring performed right under spectators' noses, rather than on a distant stage.

color change *n.*   when one card visibly changes to another.

crimp *n.*   a secret bend in a card for locating it in the deck. Also, *v.*   to place a bend in a card.

ditch *v.*   to get rid of something secretly. *"Ditch* the ball when you reach into your pocket to get the wand."

dropper *n.*   a gimmick that delivers balls, coins, or other objects into a magician's hand.

effect *n.*   a trick. "James Lewis's 'Visible Coins Through the Glass Table' is one of the prettiest *effects* in magic." Also, the central idea of a trick (a cut rope is restored, a dollar bill floats in midair). "That card trick involves so much counting, cutting, and other procedure that the audience has no idea what the *effect* is supposed to be."

Eight Kings *n.*   shorthand for a system of arranging a deck of cards in a prescribed order. ("Eight Kings Threatened to Save . . ." translates as eight, king, three, ten, two, seven, . . ."). Rel. **Si Stebbins:** another common stacking system.

equivoque *v.*   causing a spectator to choose a certain item among several, although it appears he has a free selection. The method relies on equivocally phrased instructions and clever psychology. Syn. **magician's choice.**

false count *n.*   a counting procedure by which objects (usually cards or currency) appear to be more or fewer than the actual number.

finger flinger *n.*   a magician who is interested in flashy sleight-of-hand moves, perhaps more than in entertaining people. "At the magic convention the *finger flingers* sat in the corner showing each other moves." Syn. **move monkey.**

flash *v.*   to give spectators an unintended glimpse of a palmed object or secret action. "The ball vanish would have beat me, except it *flashed."*

force *v.*   to make a spectator choose a certain card (number, suit, etc.), despite an apparently free choice. *"Force* the queen of hearts on the spectator." Also, *n.*   "Use your favorite *force."*

French drop *n.*   a move in which one hand appears to take a coin or other small object from the other. Actually, the coin falls behind the fingers of the hand holding it. Syn. **tourniquet.**

gaff *n.*   something apparently ordinary but secretly modified to create a magical effect. Also, *adj.*   "He's got that deck *gaffed* to the hilt."

gimmick *n.*   a hidden device used to accomplish a trick.

go south *v.*   to palm a card or other object and hold it secretly or dispose of it. "Larry Jennings can *go south* with a card three times in the same routine, and you'll never know it."

handwashing *v.*   when a magician who is palming something makes choreographed and usually unnatural hand gestures to "prove" that his hands are empty. "That guy stinks. He does one second of magic and ten seconds of *handwashing.*"

jog *v.*   to position a card during an overhand shuffle so it protrudes from the deck, thus marking a location in the pack.

key card *n.*   a glimpsed card adjacent to the chosen card, used as a locator.

lap *v.*   to secretly drop an object into your lap while performing at a table.

layman *n.*   a non-magician. "This effect totally fries *laymen.*"

leak *v.*   for an item concealed in the hand to reveal itself between the magician's fingers. "He palmed the card well, but it *leaked.* You could see its red back like a neon sign."

living and dead test *n.*   a traditional mentalism effect in which a spectator writes the name of one deceased person and several others living. The mentalist divines which person is dead. Nowadays, this effect more often uses names of favorite movie stars, cities, cereals, cartoon characters, etc.

load *n.*   a hidden item for production during a trick. "In his cups and balls routine, the final *load* is a live chick."

misdirection *n.*   the techniques of conducting attention toward the false facade of a trick and away from its secret architecture. This is accomplished through psychology, gestures, patter, timing, and other skills.

Miser's Dream *n.*   the classic trick of apparently plucking coins from thin air. "If we magicians could *really* work magic, the *Miser's Dream* is the effect we'd do."

move *n.*   a sleight-of-hand technique. "Did you go south with that last ace? I didn't catch the *move.*"

out *n.*   any ploy by which a magician gets out of trouble or covers up a mistake. "If I miss on the card prediction, I've got several *outs.*"

palm *v.*   to hold something concealed in the hand.

pass *n.*   a move in which the halves of the deck are secretly transposed. "If you want to judge a card man, ask to see his *pass.*" Syn. **shift.**

patter *n.*   the carefully rehearsed talk that accompanies a trick. "I've got to come up with some good *patter* for my Ambitious Card routine."

readers *n.*   marked cards.

real work *n.*   advanced technique for doing a trick, often guarded by an inner circle of magicians. "No, no—let me show you the *real work* on that deck switch."

session *n.*   a get-together in which magicians brainstorm. Also, *v.*   "Earl Nelson and I are going to *session* tomorrow night."

shade *v.*   to physically obscure a secret move. Also, *n.*   "He maneuvered a spectator into position to provide *shade* for the move."

shiner *n.*   a small mirrored reflector used to secretly glimpse something for later revelation, such as a chosen playing card. "Contrary to popular opinion, magic is not 'all done with mirrors'—but I do have one trick that uses a *shiner.*"

silk *n.*   a scarf or handkerchief.

sleight *n.* a sleight-of-hand move. "Here's a trick you can do with no *sleights* at all."

spring flowers *n.* compressible paper flowers containing wire springs that make them expand into bouquets as they are produced.

steal *v.* to secretly acquire an item or load from a concealed location. "You'll never see Lance *steal* a dove, but he produces quite a few during his act."

strippers *n.* a deck of cards cut at a taper, so that any card removed, reversed, and replaced can be stripped out simply by sliding the fingers along the length of the deck.

sucker gag *n.* an effect that makes the audience believe they've discovered the secret, but in the end fools them with a surprise ending.

switch *n.* when one item is secretly exchanged for another. "After performing a few card effects, do a deck *switch* and ring in the strippers."

table hopping *v.* performing from table to table at a restaurant. "I'm *table hopping* Saturdays at the Spaghetti Factory."

tip *v.* to reveal a trick's modus operandi either intentionally (to another magician) or inadvertently. "The fifth coin slipped from his hand onto the table, *tipping* the secret to the audience."

underground *n.* a loose cadre of magicians privy to the latest tricks, sleights, and ideas, particularly if not yet published or widely circulated. "That move was going around the New York *underground* in the '70s."

volunteer *n.* a layman brought up from the audience to assist with a trick.

work *n.* a trick's method and technique. "Bill's going to show me the *work* on his Three Card Monte routine." Also, a gimmicked state imposed on an ordinary object; e.g., a telltale crimp in a playing card. "The Professor put the *work* into the cards while he was shuffling them."

Zig-Zag *n.* a standard stage illusion in which the magician's assistant stands in a vertical cabinet with three sections. The center part is then pulled out of line and the girl appears to be separated into thirds.

JUGGLERS

Albert *n.*   throwing a club between your legs, from front to back. Named for juggler Albert Lucas. Rel. **Treblas:** a reverse Albert.

bounce juggling *n.*   when the balls move downward and bounce off the ground; a sort of reverse juggling. "I've got to buy some sillies so I can learn *bounce juggling.*" Rel. active bouncing, passive bouncing. In active bouncing, the balls are hurled at the floor, while in passive bouncing they are simply allowed to fall.

breakdown *n.*   a continuous reduction of juggled objects, which are parked between the legs, under the arms, around the neck, etc. Ant. **buildup:** when objects are returned to the juggle again, often following a breakdown.

build up a trick *v.*   to take a twenty-second stunt and turn it into a five-minute bit, with verbal banter.

California dirtbag *n.*   a throw to a juggler who is doing a trick with his right hand and may not be expecting to catch with the same hand. He must pause in his pattern to deal with the incoming "dirtbag." Invented by California jugglers. "Hey, nice *California dirtbag,* but you botched my set-up."

cascade, shower, fountain *n.*   the most common juggling patterns. The water imagery implies a fluid motion, which jugglers strive to attain.

clawing *n.*   catching a ball with a downward grabbing motion rather than the usual palm-up method.

columns *n.*   when the juggler throws balls in upright formations.

combat juggling *n.*   a free-for-all sport played by disrupting the other jugglers' patterns and making them drop things. The winner is the last person left juggling. "My favorite strategy in *combat juggling* is to claw the other guy's ball while it's in the air, leaving him a ball short." Syn. **gladiators.**

contact juggling *n.*   an elegant style in which the moving ball stays in contact with the juggler's body; there is no throwing. Identified with Michael Moschen, who performs with crystal balls.

drop line *n.*   stock patter used to cover a mistake, such as a dropped prop. Examples: "Whoops, a sudden gust of gravity!" or "I'll just set that one on the floor for a few seconds."

everies *n.*   when every throw from your right hand is a pass to another juggler. Syns. **two-count, shower.** Rel. **one-count:** pattern in which each throw from both hands is a pass. Syns. **onesies, thundershower.** Rel. **three-count:** when every third throw is a pass. Syn. **waltzing.**

exchange *v.*   to throw a prop in order to empty your hand and immediately catch another prop. The core move of juggling. Also, *n.*

feed *n.*   the passing of objects from one juggler, the feeder, to others, the feedees.

Fergies *n.*   colored beanbags for juggling, manufactured by Michael Ferguson.

flash *v.*   to execute one cycle of a particular pattern. Also, to get a large number of objects in the air and catch them again. Useful for publicity photos or as a way of learning a trick. "I think I'll practice *flashing* my five-ball cascade." Also, to throw objects higher than usual, buying time to do such stunts as clapping hands, pirouetting, or doing a flip.

flats *n.*   club throws that don't spin.

floaty *adj.*   describes club tosses that go higher and spin slower than they normally would. "This ceiling's not high enough for my *floaty* double flips."

flourish *v.*   to twirl a club like a baton while juggling. Also *n.*

free-standing ladder *n.*   a single ladder used without a supporting wall. The juggler ascends, walks around by moving the ladder's legs, and juggles while at the top.

head rolls *n.*   the rolling of a ball around a juggler's head; it is sometimes balanced on the ears, eyes, or the bridge of the nose. "When it comes to *head rolls,* Sarah is lucky to have those dimples."

helicopter *n.*   when a club is flipped horizontally, like the rotor of a helicopter.

joggling *n.* juggling while jogging. "Does Ashrita Furman still hold the Guinness world record for *joggling?*"

kick-up *n.* when a juggler uses his foot to propel a dropped prop back into a juggling pattern. Also *v.*

loopy *n.* a club pass that goes behind the back and then up over the shoulder of the throwing arm.

milking the cow *v.* performing a basic three-ball column pattern, two up the outside and one in the middle.

multiplexing *n.* when two or more balls are in one hand during the pattern.

numbers juggling *n.* juggling a large number of objects. To be considered a numbers juggler, you must generally work with five clubs or six balls.

pancakes *n.* when the juggler flips rings like coins; considered very difficult.

passing pattern *n.* a pattern in which two or more jugglers throw props to each other. Some patterns are: The Box, Bruno's Nightmare, Odd-God, Oogle Boogle, Random Feed, Rotating Feed, Shooting Star, Tick Tock, The Torture Chamber.

pulldown *n.* when the juggler lodges all the rings around his neck, often to finish a routine. "I'm not fast enough to do an eight-ring *pulldown.*"

qualify *v.* to make twice as many catches as the number of objects being juggled. "I thought I could *qualify* eight rings, but I only got 15 catches."

scissors catch *n.* when a club is trapped between two clubs held in one hand. A crowd-pleaser often used to end a juggle.

Scud *n.* when passed clubs collide in mid-air (like Scud missiles) and crash to the ground.

shower curtains *n.* when each hand throws one ball in a column and the third ball travels back and forth between the hands underneath.

sillies *n.* silicone balls used for bounce juggling.

site-swap *n.* the numerical description of a juggling pattern. Examples: a 552, a 7131.

solid *adj.* when a juggler has learned a trick so well he can do it every time. "Jason has that new trick *solid*."

solo pattern *n.* a pattern performed by one juggler. Some patterns are: Boppo's Wimpy Pattern, Burke's Barrage, Half-Reverse Cascade, The Machine, Mills Mess, Rubenstein's Revenge, The Statue of Liberty.

stage balls *n.* hollow plastic balls large enough for easy visibility on stage; often brightly colored or glow-in-the-dark.

Stumpy *n.* a joke name for someone who juggles chainsaws.

take-aways *n.* when one juggler takes all the props from another juggler while keeping the pattern going. Syn. **steals.**

tennis *n.* a cascade-like pattern in which one ball sails back and forth over the top, like a tennis ball over a net.

whirlwind *n.* when three clubs are thrown high and the juggler pirouettes once before catching each successive club.

CRIME AND PUNISHMENT

MOBSTERS

associate *n.*   a person who works with wiseguys and is almost (but not yet) accepted as a Mafia member.

babbo *n.*   an idiot; a useless underling.

boss *n.*   the head of a crime family.

broken *adj.*   demoted; lowered in mob rank.

capo *n.*   a high-ranking crime family member with his own crew of soldiers. Syn. **skipper.**

chased *adj.*   cast out of the Mafia and barred from contact with members.

cleaning *v.*   taking evasive action to prevent being tailed, usually by driving around and making random stops.

clock *v.*   to monitor a person's movements and doings. "Better *clock* Nicky; I don't trust him these days."

come in *v.*   to go see the boss when summoned. "There were complaints he wasn't *coming in.* So we whacked him."

do a Houdini *v.*   to vanish; often refers to someone who has been killed. "Carlo stole from his uncle and a week later *did a Houdini.*"

empty suit *n.*   a wanna-be who tries to spend time with mobsters but has nothing to offer.

flip *n.* to turn one's loyalty and inform on family members to gain clemency from authorities. Syn. **turn.**

get a place ready *v.* to find a burial site. "Johnny flipped. You'd better *get a place ready* for him."

gift *n.* a bribe. "The jury got nice *gifts* and failed to reach a guilty verdict."

give a pass *v.* to grant a reprieve from being killed. "Stay in Staten Island, lay low, and I will *give you a pass.*"

going *adj.* about to be killed. "Right after the trial, he was *going.*"

hard-on with a suitcase *n.* a mob lawyer. Rel. **half a hard-on with a suitcase:** a female lawyer.

joint *n.* prison.

made *adj.* sworn in as a Mafia member. Syn. **straightened out.**

meat eater *n.* a corrupt police officer.

off the record *adj.* refers to something done without advance approval from the crime family. Ant. **on the record.**

omerta *n.* the vow of silence made when becoming a member of the Cosa Nostra. A pledge never to reveal secrets. Breaking the vow is punishable by death.

problem *n.* a person who is a liability and likely to be killed. "He started taking drugs and became a *problem.* So we whacked him."

rat *n.* an informer.

sit-down *n.* a meeting with upper-level Mafiosi to straighten out a dispute.

swag *n.* stolen property.

take a walk *v.* to talk while walking up and down the block in order to avoid being overheard by means of a listening device. "Sammy tells me you and him *took a walk* about a concrete plant in New Jersey." Rel. *n.* **walk and talk:** such a discussion.

trunking *v.* popping open an auto trunk to steal the contents; a criminal activity done by mob hopefuls.

whack *v.* to murder, execute; often done to a friend, relative, or business associate. Syns. **break an egg, burn, clip, do a piece of work, hit, ice, pop, off, whack in the mouth.**

wiseguy *n.* an accepted member of a mob family. Syns. **button, friend, goodfella, made member, Man of Honor, soldier.**

CON ARTISTS

addict *n.* a mark who falls for the same scam over and over again.

big con *n.* a confidence game in which the sucker is prompted to go home or to the bank to obtain money. Ant. **short con:** when a mark is conned only for the money he has with him. "The Three Card Monte is a classic *short con.*"

big store *n.* a fake business furnished to look legitimate. The close attention given to details is meant to deceive the mark into trusting the situation and the con artists.

bleat *v.* for a mark to go to the police. Syn. **beef.**

blow-off *n.* the act of ditching the mark after the con, without making him immediately suspicious.

boarding house deceiver *n.* old-fashioned term for an inexpensive, empty suitcase left in a hotel room to make it appear occupied after a con artist decamps without paying his bill.

boiler room *n.* a telephone-sales solicitation office.

the boost *n.* shills working in big cons.

bucket shop *n.* a fake investment enterprise that promises to deliver inside information to a mark for use in arbitrage. "One *bucket shop* was taking marks to the Bahamas to see satellite dishes that were supposed to deliver price information so fast that the sucker could buy in one market and almost instantly sell in a higher market somewhere else. Of course, after the mark made a big investment, then came the blow-off."

button *n.*   a blow-off in which fake policemen "arrest" the con artists, but allow the mark to talk his way free.

chill *v.*   when a mark's interest in the con game grows cold.

con(fidence) game *n.*   any swindle in which a con artist gains a mark's confidence, then fleeces him. Often the mark is allowed to make a profit (usually a dishonest one) before the final shearing.

convincer *n.*   money that a mark is allowed to keep, in order to lure him deeper into the con.

crack out of turn *v.*   for someone in a con mob to speak his lines out of sequence, missing his cue. "A big con is as carefully rehearsed as a play, so nobody better *crack out of turn.*"

cross-fire *n.*   conversation between con men intended for overhearing by a mark, so as to influence or convince him.

flue *n.*   the envelope that holds the cash in a con game.

grifter *n.*   a swindler who lives by his wits, rather than by violence.

inside man *n.*   the member of a con mob to whom the victim is brought for fleecing.

mark *n.*   victim. Syns. **John Bates, Mr. Bates.**

the office *n.*   any private signal between con men.

outside man *n.*   a member of a con mob who finds and befriends a mark, and brings him to the inside man. Syn. **roper.**

pigeon drop *n.*   currently a term for a bank swindle in which con artists pose as bank officials and approach a depositor with a suspicion that someone is cheating the bank. The depositor is asked to make a large withdrawal in order to test the bank employee's honesty; he turns over these funds to the phony bank officials for redeposit—which, of course, never happens. Formerly, the term referred to a common swindle in which a con artist approaches a mark on the street with a cash-filled wallet he has supposedly found. After suggesting they split the money, the con man sends the mark to obtain an equal amount of cash to show his "good faith." After the blow-off, the mark discovers that the wallet contains only scraps of newspaper. Syn. **the poke.**

pluck the chicken *v.*   to fleece a mark.

the send *n.*   when a mark is sent home or to the bank to get a large amount of money.

Three Card Monte *n.*   a crooked game in which three cards are tossed face down, and the mark bets that he can find the "money card," usually an ace or queen. Because the dealer employs sleight of hand and subtle dodges, the mark can't win.

PICKPOCKETS

cannon *n.*   a pickpocket; the person who actually takes the money from the victim's pocket. Syns. **instrument, tool.**

clean the cannon *v.*   when a confederate takes a stolen wallet handed off by the cannon, who never retains it longer than a few seconds.

fix *n.*   an arrangement with local police to allow a pickpocket gang to operate in return for a share of the profits. "In the old days we always worked with a *fix* in Atlantic City."

kick *n.*   pocket. "You've gotta clean the cannon right after he takes the wallet from the *kick.*"

lush worker *n.*   a pickpocket who victimizes drunks.

mark *n.*   the intended victim.

sandwich *n.*   a ploy in which a female stall stands in front of a male victim and backs into him. Her buttocks press him into the cannon standing behind, who takes the wallet during this distraction. "What's the best place for the *sandwich?* On an elevator, just before the doors open." Rel. *v.* **prat the mark:** to work the sandwich maneuver.

stall *n.* a confederate whose job is to distract a mark so that the cannon can lift his money.

whiz mob *n.* a gang of pickpockets. "In three years with that *whiz mob,* I worked every parade and ball game in the state." Syn. **cannon mob.**

GAMBLING CHEATERS

agent *n.* a blackjack cheater in cahoots with a dealer who gives him advantages. Rel. **index dealer:** one who exposes the index of his hole card to his agent as he takes it off the deck to place it under his face-up card.

basement dealer *n.* one who deals from the bottom of the deck. Syns. **cellar dealer, subway dealer.**

black-and-white *n.* a casino dealer, who typically wears black slacks and a white shirt or blouse.

bug *n.* a clip attached to the underside of a table, used to hold out playing cards for later use. "Johnny waited till he got a pair of aces, then added the third one from his *bug.*"

California 14s *n.* misspotted dice; one die has two facets showing five pips, while the other has two facets showing two pips. These give a shooter twice the chance of rolling a seven (hence "14" in the name).

cap *v.* to illegally add chips to your bet when you hold a winning hand. "He signaled Manny to spill his beer, and while the dealer was distracted he *capped* his chips."

chip dip *n.* adhesive on the palm of the hand. Used to steal a chip from the pot as the cheater places a bet or shoves the pot across the table to the winner.

cooler *n.* a prearranged deck, set up so the cheater wins. "Doc switched in the *cooler* and cleaned house."

cosmetics *n.*   markings on the back of a card (including ink, daub, and shading) that indicate its value and suit. "Hey, this queen seems to be wearing *cosmetics.*"

crossroaders *n.*   a gang of cheats. Syns. **air bandits, ball team.**

door poppers *n.*   misspotted dice of the type available in novelty stores. One die shows all sixes, the other all fives. So called because after trying to use such obviously crooked dice in a craps game, you'd have to pop open the door and run for your life.

drag *v.*   to steal back a few chips from your bet after losing.

fishing *v.*   looking for high cards during the shuffle, so as to stack the deck for blackjack.

flats *n.*   dice with one side shaved a fraction of an inch. The area of this side is therefore greater, creating a mathematically larger chance of the die landing on it than on a narrower side. Syn. **misshapes.**

hand mucker *n.*   a cheat who holds out cards manually, without any device.

holdout *n.*   a device that secretly delivers cards to the cheat's hand, either down the sleeve or from the shirt or vest. Rel. **machine player:** one who uses a holdout.

hold out *v.*   to secretly retain desirable cards for use in a future hand.

juice *n.*   a subtle marking substance for cards. Rel. **juice deck:** a pack of cards so marked.

mechanic *n.*   a card sharp. "He won every hand he dealt, so I figured he was a *mechanic.*"

needle ring *n.*   a finger ring with a projection used to mark cards with a raised dot, somewhat like Braille. The cheat can feel these marks as he deals the cards, but they won't be seen by other players.

the office *n.*   a signal exchanged between cheats. "I'll give you *the office* when I want you to ring in the cooler."

paper *n.* marked cards. Syn. **readers.**

shiner *n.* a reflective object that serves as a secret mirror. "Gentleman Jim always laid his pipe on the card table. It had a *shiner* in the bowl, and he could glimpse every card he dealt." Syns. **glim, light.**

shirt player *n.* a cheat who uses his shirt front to stash and procure cards for his hand. *"Shirt players* sometimes have a tailor sew a special pocket in each shirt front."

silent partners *n.* two poker players in cahoots. Typically, one signals that he has a likely winning hand, and the other bets heavily in order to build the pot. At the end of the night, they split the take.

slug *n.* a group of cards controlled during a shuffle.

subway tickets *n.* cards dealt from the bottom of the deck.

tops and bottoms *n.* misspotted dice, one die showing only ones, twos, and threes and the other die showing only fours, fives, and sixes.

weights *n.* loaded dice. Rel. **first flops:** loaded dice so heavily weighted that the cheat can't lose.

FAKE PSYCHICS

Psychic readings given by charlatans rely on clever psychology and human gullibility, not on supernormal powers.

boilerplate *n.* general information, accurate for almost anyone, used to buy time while the so-called psychic sizes up the client. Example: "I can see that things haven't been progressing as rapidly as you desire."

bomb *n.* a prediction almost certain to come true, prompting the gullible to remember it with awe. "I left a *bomb* in her lap: 'You will travel across a large body of water.' "

case the mark *v.* to induce a client to return with further payment in exchange for exerting psychic influence. Example: "Bring me another $500, and I can get your husband to come back to you." Only the lowest hustlers stoop to this ploy.

cold reading *n.* the art of making vague or ambiguous pronouncements that nonetheless seem to precisely describe a client and her situation. Also, the reading itself.

lay out land mines *v.* to suggest a variety of situations to see which ones make a client react. Example: "This Tarot card represents someone who is thinking about moving to a new place. . . ."

loaves and fishes *n.* clients who visit psychics to witness miracles. Derived from the biblical miracle. Syn. **psychic cruisers.** "Most of these *psychic cruisers* just want a buzz from an encounter with the unknown."

missile *n.* a guess about a client that proves to be a dead-on hit. "When I said, 'Your husband is a cross-dresser,' it was a *missile.*"

Mr. Carlisle *n.* code words cuing a confederate to be alert. Probably derived from the protagonist in the novel *Nightmare Alley.* When a fake psychic is doing a reading for an audience, the name signals a confederate to play along. "I'm getting the name 'Mr. Carlisle.' Is he here? Ah, there you are. Is it true that you just recovered from a serious illness? Yes? A heart attack? Remarkable!" Also used in storefront psychic offices, where a statement like "I told Mr. Carlisle to come back with the check" cues an assistant to follow the psychic's lead.

shut-eye *n.* a true believer in psychic marvels; a psychic reader who believes what he or she does is real. "I worked the Psychic Fair last weekend, and it was crawling with *shut-eyes.*"

spook worker *n.* a fake medium who gives readings for spiritualists, people convinced that the departed can communicate from beyond the grave.

take a Brody *v.* to go out on a limb with a guess. Derived from the name of a man who claimed to have survived a jump from the Brooklyn Bridge. "I *took a Brody* and told him he'd had three wives." The opposite of safe boilerplate.

.38 repeater *n.* a client who returns repeatedly to a psychic reader even when readings are inaccurate and predictions fail. "My *.38 repeater* comes in so often, I'm running out of stuff to tell her."

Travis Bickle *n.* a frustrated, often angry, male client who must be handled with care. From the character played by Robert De Niro in the film

Taxi Driver. "I told this *Travis Bickle,* 'Sure, life dealt you a bad hand, but everything will get better if you work at it.' I just hope he doesn't come back."

DRUG USERS

acid *n.*   LSD. Syns. **blaze, blotters, dose, fry, gel, microdots, purple haze, pyramid, tabs, trips, white lightning.**

angel dust *n.*   PCP (phencyclidine). Syns. **angel dust, dust, elephant, hog, peace pills.**

artillery *n.*   paraphernalia used to shoot drugs. Syns. **gun, rig, works.**

back up *v.*   to let blood move up into a syringe to verify that the needle is in a vein.

balloon *n.*   a small quantity of contained narcotics.

bang *v.*   to inject drugs.

bean *n.*   a capsule for drugs.

bombita *n.*   a blend of cocaine and heroin. Syn. **speedball.**

burned *v.*   to be cheated by a drug seller. "That guy *burned* me on the dust."

chasing the dragon *v.*   inhaling heroin.

coke *n.*   cocaine. Syns. **blast, blow, cola, flake, ivory flakes, nose candy, rocks, snow, star dust, toot.** Rel. **coke broke** *adj.*   bankrupt due to a cocaine habit.

crash *v.*   to sleep off the effects of drugs.

deck *n.*   a packet of drugs.

dollies *n.*   Methadone.

downers *n.*   barbituates. Syns. **barbs, goofballs, peanuts, rainbows, reds, red devils, yellow jackets.**

drop *v.*   to swallow a dose of drugs.

dust *v.*   to sprinkle a powdered narcotic on another drug (e.g., PCP on marijuana).

flea powder *n.*   drugs of poor quality. Syn. **lemonade.**

flip out *v.*   to become irrational or mentally disordered. "I hope she never drops acid again after *flipping out* that way."

freebase *v.*   to smoke cocaine.

hit *n.*   a single dose. "How much will 10 *hits* cost me?"

holding *v.*   in possession of drugs. "It makes me nervous to be *holding.*"

hot *adj.*   wanted by the police or drug agents.

hot shot *n.*   an injection of drugs that proves fatal.

huffing *v.*   inhaling solvents or glue from a bag. Rel. **huffer** *n.*   a glue sniffer.

hype *n.*   a drug addict.

key *n.*   one kilogram.

line *n.*   a dose of cocaine laid out in a line to be inhaled.

ludes *n.*   Quaaludes.

mainline *v.*   to inject drugs into a vein. Syn. **shoot up.**

Miss Emma *n.*   morphine.

poppers *n.*   amyl nitrate vials, which are popped open and inhaled. Syn. **snappers.**

skin popping *v.*   injecting drugs under the skin.

smack *n.*   heroin. Syns. **horse, H, junk, mother of pearl, scat, whack.**

speed *n.*   amphetamines. Syns. **bennies, black beauties, crank, crystal, dexies, leapers, meth, .357 magnums, uppers.**

step on *v.*   to cut or dilute drugs. "This coke has been *stepped on* at least twice."

tolley *n.*   toluene, an extremely dangerous paint solvent that is inhaled.

tracks *n.*   a line of needle marks on the skin.

POLICE OFFICERS

Adam Henry *n.*   an asshole. From letters A and H in the police's military-style code alphabet. "Normally, I'd have let the guy off with a warning, but he was such an *Adam Henry,* I gave him the ticket."

ate his gun *v.*   committed suicide with his service revolver. "I can't believe Dick *ate his gun.* He was retiring in six months."

bolo *exp.*   abbreviation for "be on the lookout" for someone or something.

bullet *n.*   a one-year sentence in prison. "That punk only got a *bullet* for robbing the convenience store."

bus *n.*   an ambulance. "Send a *bus.*"

choo-choo *n.*   a police van. "Put this guy into the *choo-choo.*"

circling the drain *adj.*   near death; usually said of a traffic victim. "Bad accident; the driver is *circling the drain.*"

code 7 *n.*   a coffee or lunch break. "Jim and Danny are at the donut shop on *code 7.*"

corset *n.*   a bulletproof vest.

dead presidents *n.*   currency, bills; often drug money. "He had a suitcase full of *dead presidents* in his hotel suite."

divorce *n.*   a shooting involving a married couple. "We'd already answered three domestic violence calls at their house, so the *divorce* was no surprise."

drive-by *n.*   a shooting from a moving car.

drop a dime *v.*   to telephone the police with a crime tip or information.

duck *n.*   a stolen car that's been abandoned. "By the time we found that *duck,* somebody had stripped the tires, engine, seats, radio—everything but the decal on the windshield." Syn. **sitting duck.**

electric lips *n.*   the officer who negotiates through a bullhorn with a suspect who's holed up in a building; a SWAT term. Syn. **mouth marine.**

ERA *n.*   Earned Ram Average. How many blows it takes a SWAT team to ram down a door.

flip *v.*   when a criminal turns against associates and provides testimony or evidence to the police.

get small *v.*   to get away, vanish. "The perp was standing on the corner, but when he saw the squad car, he *got small* real fast."

gimme *n.*   a handgun. So called because it is often held by somebody saying "gimme all your cash and jewelry."

Gray Bar Hotel *n.*   jail. "I just checked a couple of guests into the *Gray Bar Hotel.*" Syn. **bucket.**

G-ride *n.*   a stolen car. Short for "gangster ride." Syn. **hot roller.**

he-she *n.*   a transvestite; a man wearing women's clothes and makeup. "No wonder Mitch got into a fight at the bar after work. He realized he'd been hitting on a *he-she.*" Syn. **it.**

hubcaps *n.*   the vehicle-theft detail. "What a strange twist: Frank was transferred to *hubcaps,* and his new Grand Am got stolen the very next day!"

IBM *n.*   Italian Business Man. A Mafia member.

kick *v.* to release from custody. "I'm going to *kick* the suspect when I get back to the station."

Kojak light *n.* a flashing red light that can be quickly mounted on the roof of an unmarked police car. From the television show, *Kojak*. "Somebody's hitting the 7-11 on South Crenshaw! Slap on the *Kojak light*, and let's go!"

master key *n.* a large steel pipe filled with cement; used (with a search warrant) to knock down doors. "We heard every toilet in the house flushing, so we used the *master key*."

Metro tux *n.* a white T-shirt with the sleeves rolled up to accentuate the biceps, blue uniform pants, and black patent leather shoes. Worn by officers of the Los Angeles Police Department's elite Metro detail when visiting the training academy bar in their off-hours to look for female cadets. "You can't drink in uniform, rookie. Better take off your official blue shirt and get into your *Metro tux*."

on the muscle *adj.* refers to an excited horse in the LAPD Mounted Unit. By extension, also describes a suspect who seems hyperactive.

paper *n.* traffic tickets. Syns. **greenies, tags.** "How many *tags* did you get this month?"

perp *n.* perpetrator; someone who commits a crime.

pop a cap or **pop some caps** *v.* to fire a gun. "The perp reached into his glovebox for a pistol, so we had to *pop some caps*."

popcorn machine *n.* the lights mounted atop a squad car. Syn. **Christmas tree.**

rock and roll *n.* gunfire on full automatic.

roll *v.* to take fingerprints. "I *rolled* a set of prints."

rubber-gun detail *n.* a rehabilitation unit for officers with emotional or family problems.

shake, rattle, and roll *v.* to prowl the streets searching for bad guys in general.

stinker *n.* a decayed, putrid corpse. "His first day on the force, he did the investigation on a *stinker*. New officers always get that duty."

strawberry *n.* a hooker who turns tricks for drugs. "I've arrested that *strawberry* named Teri about ten times. I wish she'd move to some other part of town."

tube *n.* a police shotgun. Syn. **gauge.**

Uncle *adj.* code for "undercover." "*Uncle* Bob, this is *Uncle* Dan."

wagger *n.* a man who exposes himself, a flasher.

FBI AGENTS

bad guy *n.* a suspected criminal.

desk *n.* the person in charge of a crime investigation, usually in Washington, D.C. "Who's the *desk* on that kidnapping?"

Disneyland East *n.* The Department of Justice in Washington, D.C.

heavies *n.* serious crimes investigated by the FBI, such as kidnappings and airplane hijackings.

melt *v.* when a suspect under surveillance disappears.

SAC *n.* Special Agent in Charge. The person who runs a field office.

tail *v.* a television-detective term for keeping someone under surveillance. Syn. **shadow.** "A good tip for *tailing* someone is to blend in with the crowd. If everyone on the street is wearing coats and ties, but you're wearing a clown suit, you'll be obvious. But if you're *shadowing* a guy who works at the circus, wearing a clown suit may be a great idea."

tasked *v.*   to be given an assignment. "Regis was *tasked* to arrest the bad guy." Also used informally. "Regis was *tasked* to pick up the burgers and fries."

UFAC *n.*   Unlawful Flight to Avoid Confinement. A criminal's escape.

PRISON INMATES

all day *n.*   a life sentence in prison. "The guy that Marcellus blew away was a scumbag crack dealer, but he still got *all day.*"

armor *n.*   weapons.

boneyard visit *n.*   a conjugal visit.

bullet *n.*   one year in jail. "I did two *bullets* for popping a cap."

Chester *n.*   a convicted child molester. "That *Chester* may end up dead in the joint." Syn. **chicken hawk.**

convict *n.*   a prisoner of age and experience, whose bearing of dignity and pride earns him respect. "If you want to survive in here, make friends with a *convict.*"

dance hall *n.*   the chamber where executions take place.

deck *n.*   a pack of cigarettes used as jailhouse currency.

Dr. Seuss *n.*   scrambled eggs made from powder and having a green tinge. From Seuss's picture book, *Green Eggs and Ham.*

dump truck *n.*   a bad or less-than-diligent criminal defense lawyer. "What a *dump truck*. This guy won't even get me a hearing for an appeal."

fish *n.*   new prisoner(s). Syn. **candy.**

the green room *n.*   San Quentin's gas chamber.

house *n.* cell. "I got a new poster in the mail today, so I guess I'll redecorate my *house.*" Syns. **casa, crib.**

inside *adj.* within prison walls. Ant. **outside.** "I was a mechanic when I was *outside.*"

joint *n.* prison. Syns. **the place, slammer.**

juice *n.* pull or connections in prison. "That convict has a lot of *juice,* so if you need anything . . ."

kite *n.* a note received from another inmate, often surreptitiously.

knot *n.* a wad of currency. "I keep my *knot* in the elastic waistband of my pants."

lock down *v.* to place an inmate in a maximum security cell. "He was caught with a shank in his cell and got *locked down.*"

minute *n.* short prison time, generally under one year. "I only spent a *minute* at Tehachapi." Rel. **short** *adj.* refers to an inmate with little prison time.

Mr. Ed *n.* "mystery meat" served in the prison mess hall.

piddle *v.* to make craft items from everyday articles such as matchsticks. "During his entire ten years in the joint, he never read a book. But he got real good at *piddling.*"

pruno *n.* alcohol made by prisoners from water, fruit, and bread fermented in a plastic bag.

rack the gate *v.* to open the cell doors, using an automatic mechanism.

raise up *v.* to be released from prison. "I'm *raising up* on August 1."

regulate *v.* to beat up another inmate as punishment for some offense. "That dude usually *regulates* the snitches."

road dog *n.* close prison friend, buddy. "You're my *road dog,* man. Don't let me down."

shank *n.*   a knife or homemade blade.

snitch *n.*   an informer.

soup *n.*   money or things to barter such as packets of dried soup, cigarettes, or coffee.

toss up *n.*   a search of inmates' cells. "There's supposed to be a *toss up* tonight after dinner. You better hide that blade in the spine of a book or somewhere."

Waldorf-Astoria *n.*   solitary confinement.

wood *n.*   a Caucasian prisoner. Short for peckerwood.

SPORTS AND RECREATION

BASEBALL PLAYERS

all wood, no leather *adj.*   bats well, but can't hit. Ant. **all leather, no wood.**

ant killer *n.*   a ball batted into the dirt by home plate. Syn. **worm killer.**

bang-bang play *n.*   a close call on the bases.

Baseball Annies *n.*   player groupies.

beanball *n.*   a pitch thrown intentionally at the batter's head.

Blue *n.*   generic name for an umpire. "Aw, c'mon, *Blue,* that pitch was a foot off the plate!"

brush-back pitch *n.*   an inside pitch meant to scare the batter away from crowding the plate.

camped under it *adj.*   when a fielder is able to get into position early and wait for a fly ball.

can of corn *n.*   an easy fly ball. Said to be derived from the old practice of grocers getting a can from the top shelf by flicking it with a long stick, then catching the can in their apron. "It's a *can of corn* . . . Johnson snags it . . . and that's it for the Dodgers."

chin music *n.*   a brush-back pitch that barely misses being a beanball.

climbing the ladder *v.*   pitching fastballs a little higher each time, causing the batter to swing even though the balls are out of the strike zone.

cup of coffee *n.* a short stint in the major leagues. "Joe Smith played nine years in the minor leagues, but had only three major league at-bats in his *cup of coffee* with the Phillies."

cycle *n.* a single, double, triple, and home run made by a single player in one game.

dial 8 *v.* to hit a home run. So called because in hotels, dialing 8 connects you with long distance. "He was up against Tweksbury and *dialed 8.*"

ding-dong! *exp.* hollered by players in the dugout when a foul tip hits the opposing catcher's protective cup.

dinger *n.* home run. Syn. **'tater** (as in potato) Rel. **moonshot:** a very long home run.

dragging a piano *v.* moving slowly; said of a base runner.

drunk *adj.* loaded, referring to bases.

ducks on a pond *n.* runners in scoring position (on second and third bases) and a batter having the opportunity to hit them in. "Jones comes to bat with a couple of *ducks on the pond.*"

dust the jewel *v.* when the umpire sweeps off home plate with a whisk broom.

55-foot curve *n.* a curve ball that doesn't make it all the way to the plate. (Home plate is 60.5 feet from the pitcher's rubber.) The pitch hits the dirt and usually bounces past the catcher.

foot in the bucket *adj.* when a batter steps toward the third baseline with his front foot; usually occurs when a batter is afraid of the pitcher. "The kid lifted up his leg and put his *foot in the bucket.*"

free trip *n.* being walked to first base on balls.

gas *n.* fastball. Syns. **cheese, heat, heater, hummer, smoke.** A batter returning to the dugout after striking out: "Watch out, Clemens has his *heater* today. He's throwing nothing but *smoke.*"

go grab some bench *v.* to sit down.

greenflies *n.* people who pester batboys to obtain autographs, free tickets, etc.

gun *n.* a good arm; usually refers to an outfielder who can throw the ball accurately a long way. "He's got a *gun.*"

happy feet *n.* when a hitter moves around in the batter's box, never getting set in one spot.

heavy ball *n.* a pitch that is deceptively fast and breaks batters' bats.

hose *n.* an arm, especially a pitcher's.

keystone *n.* second base.

kissed *adj.* describes a ball hit with the optimum part of the bat, called the "sweet spot." Rel. **hammered:** hit extremely hard. "Griffey *hammered* that ball, even though he didn't hit it in the sweet spot." Syn. **tattooed.**

loves to dance *adj.* enjoys squabbling; said of managers by umpires.

painting the corners *v.* placing pitches over the edge of the plate, so that they are called strikes but are very difficult for batters to hit. "Hershiser was erratic last week against the Tigers, but tonight he's *painting the corners.*" Rel. **on the black** *adj.* when a pitch crosses the black border around the edges of the plate.

pepper *n.* a warm-up during which players stand close together and throw the ball around their backs, do feints, throw from between the legs, etc.

pick it *v.* to field a ground ball; said especially of good infielders. "He can really *pick it.*"

pull the string *v.* to throw a slower pitch after a very hard fastball; a tactic designed to make the hitter swing too early. It's as if the pitcher pulls the ball back with an invisible string, so the hitter can't connect.

rope *n.* a line drive. Syn. **frozen rope.**

rubber arm *n.* a pitcher who seemingly can pitch forever. Rel. **rag arm:** a bad or slow pitcher.

seeing-eye grounder *n.*   a grounder that is slow but nevertheless eludes all the fielders, traveling a path between them as if it could see where it was going.

shooting BBs *v.*   making a hard, accurate throw from the outfield to gun down a runner trying to advance. Also refers to a pitcher throwing very hard.

the show *n.*   the major leagues.

slap hitter *n.*   a batter who hits mostly singles.

stick a fork in him *exp.*   said of a pitcher who isn't performing well, just before the manager removes him from the game. Also said about a player at the end of his career. Derived from baking, in which you test a cake's doneness by sticking in a fork and seeing if batter clings to it. Probably coined in 1988, when writers were pestering Reggie Jackson about whether he was really going to retire. "Hey, *stick a fork in me,*" he said. "I'm done!"

Texas leaguer *n.*   a high, weak hit that drops between the infielders and outfielders. Usually considered a lucky base hit.

toast *n.*   a player whose skills are eroded and career finished. "Hall of Fame pitcher Jim Palmer tried a comeback when he was forty-five years old. He just didn't realize he was *toast.*"

Uncle Charlie *n.*   a curve ball. "Lots of minor leaguers can hit the fastball, but when they get to the show they can't handle *Uncle Charlie.*" Syns. **hook, yakker, yellow hammer.**

wearing the collar *adj.*   when a hitter has gone hitless in a game. Rel. **in the doghouse:** when a player's poor playing causes his manager to bench him in frustration.

wheels *n.*   legs; running speed.

winning ugly *v.*   doing everything wrong, but still winning somehow. "The 1983 champion White Sox were known for *winning ugly.*"

work the rocking chair *v.*   when an umpire is assigned to third base, which is a slow, often dull, duty. Rel. **work the stick:** assignment at home plate, where batters swing "the stick."

worm burner *n.*   a hot ground ball.

wounded duck *n.*   a high, weak throw from a fielder. From the image of a shotgunned duck falling from the sky. "It looked like they had a play at the plate on the slow-running Piazza, but the relay man threw a *wounded duck* and Piazza beat the throw easily." Syn. **dying quail.**

BASEBALL CARD COLLECTORS

back door *n.*   the avenue by which cards become available before the official release date. "Yeah, I know the other shops won't have them till June; these packs came in the *back door.*"

beaters *n.*   cards so badly beaten up—with lost corners, pen marks, pin holes—that they have no real value on the market. "I've got some *beaters* I use to fill in hard-to-get sets until I can find cards in better condition." Syn. **Tipton Mints.**

Beckett's *n.*   the guidebook on which market prices are based. "I really can't sell this card for less; just check *Beckett's.*" Syn. **Buckets.**

book *v.*   to be priced in a guide such as Beckett's. "That Frank Thomas *books* for five dollars."

card shark *n.*   someone who rips you off when buying, selling, or trading cards. "Don't trade with Gary, he's a *card shark.*"

Charbonneau *n.*   a rookie card that enjoys a boom market, then crashes. Named for Cleveland outfielder Joe Charbonneau, who was named 1980 Rookie of the Year and after that saw his career plummet.

cherry picking *v.*   obtaining inserts by a clever dodge. A collector will search for them by first opening a few boxes of cards to see if a pattern emerges; then he'll use his knowledge of that pattern to go to a shop and obtain all the inserts in a box, while buying only a few packs. This practice is frowned on by most collectors and dealers, but happens regularly.

clean box *n.*   a virgin box of cards, still in the manufacturer's seal; a box that hasn't been pawed through yet. "I wish I had a few *clean boxes* for you, but a guy came in and scooped up every hot rookie card I had."

common *n.*   a card of a player who is not a star and therefore commands no special premium; usually costs next to nothing.

crack some wax *v.*   to open several packs (usually a whole box) of cards in one sitting. "Let's go over to Jimmy's house and *crack some wax.*" Syn. **busting wax.** A pack of cards is called "wax" because until 1991 baseball cards were wrapped in waxed paper to keep the accompanying gum fresh. "The idea that *wax* packs can 'keep the gum fresh' ignores the fact that most of the little pink slabs could be carbon-dated to the Mesozoic Era."

Doc Jimmy *n.*   Dr. James Beckett, founder of Beckett's guide.

first day *n.*   a card from the first day of the print run. These cards have an extra stamp on them, are limited to two thousand, and are available only in the Topps Stadium Club series, although the idea has been imitated by other companies under such names as "artist's proof" and "printer's proof."

good pull *n.*   a good card. "That Michael Jordan autographed card was a *good pull.*"

hobby *adj.*   refers to packs that are sold only through hobby dealers and not available in Kmart or Wal-Mart. "This insert is *hobby* only." Rel. **retail:** available from dealers and retail outlets. "These cards come only in hobby packs, but you can get those in *retail* packs."

insert *n.*   a special card, not part of the regular set, that is included in each main set. It is numbered independently and often preceded by a letter (for example, A1).

loaded *adj.*   describes a set of cards with many nice-looking inserts. "That new Leaf '95 set is *loaded.*"

mail in *n.*   a card or set that can be obtained only by mailing in wrappers or a special redemption card.

mint *n.*   a card in perfect condition.

pack wars *n.*   a competition in which collectors buy various packs, see whose contains the most valuable card, and award that player all the packs.

pages *n.*   soft plastic pages that hold nine regular-sized cards; used for storage and protection.

penny sleeve *n.* a single-card holder made of the same material as pages. "Usually, you put a card in a *penny sleeve* before it goes in a top loader."

rookie card *n.* a player's first card to appear in a major league set.

short print *n.* a card of which the company purposely prints fewer, in order to drive up the value.

top loader *n.* a hard plastic case into which you drop a card from the top. It is used to store and protect the more valuable cards.

BASKETBALL PLAYERS

air ball *n.* a shot that doesn't even come close to the rim. "The crowd jeered, '*Air ball!*' "

aircraft carrier *n.* a big, strong player whose drives to the basket score lots of points for a team.

alley-oop *n.* a lofty pass aimed toward the rim and meant to be dunked by another player.

boarding *v.* rebounding.

brick *n.* any shot that misses badly, such as one that clanks off the front of the rim.

bucket *n.* basket.

camp *v.* when a player installs himself in a certain location.

chairman of the boards *n.* a good rebounder.

cleaning the glass *v.* rebounding well. Rel. **windex** *n.* a good rebounder.

coast to coast *adj.* when a player makes a rebound at the opponent's basket and takes the ball all the way down the court to score.

the cords *n.* the basketball net.

does windows *v.* is able to dunk the basketball.

downtown *adj.*   far from the basket, in the three-point zone. "Michael shoots from *downtown*—and unbelievable, it's in for the score!"

face *v.*   to make a jump shot when an opponent is guarding so closely that he's "in your face." The shooter may yell "Face the nation!" after he sinks the shot.

facial *n.*   when two opposing players jump simultaneously and one dunks the ball into the other's face.

fake someone into the popcorn machine *v.*   to fake a shot or a move toward the basket, making the defender jump in the air, and then going around him for a basket or pass. Coined by Chick Hearn, longtime announcer for the Los Angeles Lakers. "Pippen *faked him into the popcorn machine.*"

handle *n.*   dribbling ability. "That guard has a nice *handle.*" Also, *v.*   "He can really *handle* the pill."

hang time *n.*   the period when a leaping shooter is suspended in the air. "Jordan's *hang time* on that shot approached the supernatural."

hit me off *exp.*   pass me the ball.

hops *n.*   jumping ability.

in the paint *adj.*   in the free-throw lane, which is painted a color.

in the refrigerator *adj.*   refers to a game that's as good as won. From a saying of Chick Hearn: "This game is *in the refrigerator.* The lights are out, the eggs are cooling, the Jell-O's jiggling, and the butter's getting hard."

jam *v.*   to dunk the ball. Also, *n.*   "With four seconds left on the clock, Magic makes the *jam!*"

pill *n.*   the basketball. Syn. **rock:** "Pass me the *rock!*"

scrub *n.*   a poor player.

shake and bake *n.*   a move including fakes that advances toward the basket to score. "A nice *shake and bake!* Two points!"

take to school *v.* when a player dazzles another with moves, in order to embarrass him. "I *took that guy to school,* man. Between my legs, around my back, then through the hoop!"

triple double *n.* when a player in a single game achieves double digits in three or more categories: points, rebounds, assists, blocked shots.

waterbug *n.* a short, fast point guard who moves faster than almost anyone else on the court. "Damon Stoudamire is a real *waterbug.* Just look at him bring the ball up the court!"

white man's disease *n.* not being able to jump very high. "Larry Bird suffers from *white man's disease.*"

BOWLERS

apple *n.* a bowling ball. Also, a bowler who chokes in a tense, critical situation.

baby split *n.* when the 2-7 or 3-10 pins are left standing. So-called because it is relatively easy to score a spare. Syn. **Murphy.** Rel. **baby split with company:** when the 2-7-8 or 3-9-10 pins are left standing.

bam-bam *n.* a beginner who lofts the ball onto the lane, making a loud thud.

bench work *n.* chatter or shenanigans designed to disturb an opponent who is bowling.

birthday cake *n.* a 5-7-10 split.

block city *exp.* refers to a lane that is blocked, which means that oil was applied to form a track, to help imperfectly thrown balls hit the pocket. This practice is against the rules. "Hmm . . . my ball was at least two inches outside, but I got a strike anyway. *Block city.*" Rel. **Berlin Wall:** when the center of a lane is oily and the sides dry, creating a strong contrast.

blow out *v.* to knock down all but one of the pins.

box *n.* one frame.

Brooklyn *n.* a shot that hits the pocket on the wrong side; e.g., when a right-handed bowler hits the 1-2 pocket, to the left of the head pin. "You crossed into *Brooklyn* on that shot." Syn. **Jersey.** Rel. **Brooklyn strike:** a strike scored with a Brooklyn shot.

cherry *n.* when the front pin drops on the second bowl, but other pins are left standing.

chicken wing *n.* when a person juts his elbow out to the side during the swing; considered poor bowling form.

Christmas tree *n.* a split that leaves either the 3-7-10 or the 2-7-10 pins standing. Syn. **Faith, Hope, and Charity.**

Cincinnati *n.* an 8-10 split.

clothesline *n.* when the 1-2-4-7 or 1-3-6-10 pins are left standing.

cranker *n.* a bowler who puts a lot of revolutions on the ball, thereby creating speed and a hooking action. Rel. **crank** *v.* to bowl in this manner. "Joe really *cranks* the ball."

dime store *n.* a 5-10 split. Syn. **Woolworth.** Rel. **Kresge:** a 5-7 split.

dinner bucket *n.* four pins left in a diamond formation.

D.O.A. *n.* Dead On Arrival. A weakly bowled ball that is likely to leave a split. Syn. **dead apple.**

dodo *n.* a bowling ball that is heavier than regulation weight or out of balance.

Dutchman *n.* a 200 score achieved with alternating spares and strikes.

fat *adj.* hitting more or less in the pocket, but a bit toward the center of the lane. Syns. **heavy, high.** Ants. **thin, light, low:** hitting more or less in the pocket, but a bit toward the closest gutter.

field goal *n.*   when the ball passes between the two pins of a wide split. "When Jim made a *field goal,* the other team all raised both arms in the air like football referees."

the fire's out *exp.*   when a bowler's series of strikes ends.

frozen rope *n.*   a ball bowled too fast, but right into the pocket.

goal posts *n.*   the 7-10 pins left standing. Syns. **bed posts, mule ears, snake eyes, telephone poles.**

Golden Gate *n.*   a 4-6-7-10 split. Syns. **big ears, big four, double pinochle.**

go out the door *v.*   to finish a game with all strikes from any frame onward. Syn. **punch out.**

grandma's teeth *n.*   a random group of pins left in gapped formation. "I don't think Phil can make a spare with *grandma's teeth* out there."

Greek church *n.*   either the 4-6-7-9-10 or the 4-6-7-8-10 pins left standing; the formation resembles the steeple of a church.

in the ditch *adj.*   where a gutterball goes.

kindling wood *n.*   pins that are lighter than regulation; these tend to produce higher scores as well as shorter games (which are to the benefit of a bowling alley owner). Syn. **light wood.**

love tap *n.*   when a pin, usually bouncing off a wall, gently knocks down another pin.

moat *n.*   the gutter.

Moses ball *n.*   a shot that parts the pins like Moses parting the Red Sea, turning what should have been a split into a strike. "Whew! That *Moses ball* saved me!"

mother-in-law *n.*   the 7 pin.

off the sheet *adj.*   refers to three strikes in the tenth frame.

pie *n.*   an alley where it is easy to score. Ant. **graveyard.**

pindicator *n.*   the illuminated display board above the pins that shows which ones remain standing.

pocket *n.*   the area between the 1 and 3 pins, where a right-handed bowler aims for a strike. A lefty aims for the pocket between the 1 and 2 pins.

poison ivy *n.*   the 3-6-10 pins left standing.

poodle *v.*   to bowl a gutterball. Syns. **play the gray board:** so called because some alleys have gray gutters; **trench.** "Man, I got all upset and *trenched* that one."

powder puff *n.*   a slow ball that hits the pins softly. "I can't believe he got a strike from that *powder puff!*" Syns. **creeper, mush ball, puff ball.**

pull the rug *v.*   when the ball grazes the head pin, the pins wobble, and then they all fall down simultaneously for a strike.

scenic route *n.*   the course followed by a breaking curve ball.

Schleifer *n.*   a strike in which the pins wobble suspensefully before falling down apparently one by one.

six pack *n.*   six strikes in a row.

sleeper *n.*   a pin concealed behind another pin. If the 2-8 pins were left standing: "You have a *sleeper* behind the 2." Syns. **barmaid, bicycle, double wood, one in the dark, tandem.**

snow plow *n.*   a ball that makes a strike by clearing all the pins entirely off the alley.

solid ten *n.*   when the 6 pin flies around the 10 pin without hitting it. "Rats, another *solid ten!*" Rel. **weak ten:** when the 6 pin falls into the channel and doesn't trip the 10.

spring cleaning *v.*   widely missing a lone remaining pin, whether the ball goes into the gutter or to the opposite side of the lane.

stroker *n.* a bowler with a smooth, flowing delivery.

Swiss cheese ball *n.* the sample ball used at a bowling pro shop, drilled with many holes for customers to determine proper fit.

tap *n.* an apparently perfect throw that leaves one pin standing. Syns. **burner, touch.**

ten in the pit *n.* a strike that knocks all the pins off the upper deck area into the back (lower) pit area of the lane.

throw rocks *v.* to accumulate strikes with fast balls.

tumbler *n.* a strike in which the pins seem to fall one at a time.

turkey *n.* three strikes in a row.

washout *n.* a split with the head pin left standing; for example, a 1-2-10 split. "I slid by the head pin and left a *washout.*"

FOOTBALL PLAYERS

barn burner *n.* a wildly exciting game whose outcome is in doubt until the final gun.

blitz *n.* a play in which linebackers (or sometimes cornerbacks or safetys) join the defensive linemen in trying to tackle the quarterback before he can pass. "The down side of a *blitz* is when it turns out not to be a pass play. Your players are way out of position for defending against a run." Offensive players warn each other of an impending blitz by shouting "Red dog! Red dog!"

bomb *n.* an extremely long pass, often for a touchdown. "We'd have won the game, except for those two *bombs* Marino threw."

call an audible *v.* when a quarterback declares a new play at the line of scrimmage—either because the defensive setup may foil the planned play or because the quarterback spots a defense weakness to exploit.

chain gang *n.* the officials who move the ten-yard chain and poles along the sidelines, indicating where the team on offense will earn a first down.

chip shot *n.* a field goal attempt from a short distance. "And the Forty Niners go for the *chip shot.*"

clothesline *n.* a tackle in which the runner's neck is snagged by the defender's arm. From the image of someone colliding with a backyard clothesline.

the flats *n.* zones to the sides of the line of scrimmage, where short passes are often thrown.

flea flicker *n.* a play in which the quarterback hands off or pitches to the running back, who fakes toward the line of scrimmage but then tosses the ball back to the quarterback, who passes it downfield.

front four *n.* the defensive linemen (i.e., two tackles and two ends). Top units earn nicknames such as the Fearsome Foursome.

Hail Mary *n.* a desperation pass by the trailing team in the final play of the game. The offense and defense both send numerous players into the end zone, and the quarterback throws the ball without any real hope of hitting any particular receiver. "Sometimes when a team pulls a *Hail Mary,* God reaches down and puts the ball into the hands of the trailing team for the winning touchdown. But more often not."

hang time *n.* the length of time that a punt stays in the air. "He kicked a short punt with good *hang time* that left the opposition no chance for a runback."

hankie *n.* the yellow penalty flag thrown by officials. The term is used when officials are imposing lots of borderline or rare penalties. "The refs are getting *hankie* happy."

headhunter *n.* a defensive player with a reputation for intentionally injuring ball carriers who are unaware they are going to be hit.

juke *v.* when the ball carrier makes a deceptive move that fakes a defender into missing an easy tackle. "He *juked* him out of his jockstrap on that one."

kneel-down *n.* when the quarterback of the leading team makes no attempt to advance the ball but kneels down to end the play and let the clock wind down. *"Kneel-downs* are those boring plays at the end of a game when the trailing team has no time-outs left."

pick *n.*   an intercepted pass. "Ken Norton, Jr., had two *picks* in one game last year, and none for the rest of the season."

playbook *n.*   the list of a team's planned plays, each with a code name such as "One Red Right."

play both ways *v.*   to handle both offensive and defensive jobs.

pocket *n.*   the protected area created by the offensive line for the quarterback. "Dan Marino of Miami is known as a quarterback who has to remain in the *pocket* to be effective. He's not much of a scrambler."

red zone *n.*   the area between the twenty-yard-line and the goal line. "The Rams have been abysmal in the *red zone* this year, scoring only two out of sixteen times they've had the ball there."

reverse *n.*   a play in which the quarterback hands off to a running back, who runs parallel to the line of scrimmage for a few yards, only to hand off to another running back coming the other way, who then heads upfield.

ring his bell *v.*   to hit another player hard.

sack *v.*   to tackle the quarterback behind the line of scrimmage before he can pass or hand off the ball. Also, *n.*

scatback *n.*   a small, lightweight running back whose chief assets are speed and agility rather than steamroller size and weight.

scramble *n.*   a quarterback's evasive maneuvers after the defenders break through his protective wall of linemen. Rel. **scrambler:** "When it comes to good *scramblers,* it's hard to beat John Elway of Denver."

shotgun *n.*   a play in which the quarterback lines up three or four yards behind the center, instead of taking the ball directly. This distance gives the quarterback a few extra seconds to survey the defensive array.

spearing *n.*   attempting to impale a runner with the head-first impact of your helmet; this move is illegal.

stunt *n.* a shift of positions by defensive players at the line of scrimmage, designed to disrupt the offense's blocking efforts; often a presage to a blitz.

two-minute drill *n.* a special set of plays used late in the half, when time is at a premium. Examples: passes thrown to the sidelines so that ball carriers can step out of bounds and stop the clock; no-huddle plays set up in advance so players can race back to the line of scrimmage when the clock is still running.

x's and o's *n.* chalkboard symbols used by coaches to map out plays. "A well-coached team has more *x's and o's* to fall back on."

zebras *n.* field officials such as referees, line judges, and umpires. So called because of their striped jerseys.

GOLFERS

airmailing the green *v.* hitting the ball over the green. Syn. **flying the green.**

alice *v.* to hit a putt too softly to even reach the hole.

big dog *n.* the driver. Syn. **big stick.** Rel. *exp.* **Let the big dog eat!** use a driver off the tee.

bikini wax *n.* a very short cropping of the greens.

bite! *exp.* an encouragement to stop one's ball from rolling too far. Syns. **grow teeth! sit!**

boomerang *v.* to slice or hook in the extreme. Also, *n.*

chili dip *v.* to make an unsuccessful attempt at a short-range shot, often out of a bunker.

chunk *v.* when the club hits the ground before hitting the ball, which results in a short shot. "He *chunked* it." Rel. **fat** *adv.* describes a shot that's been chunked. "Tommy hit *fat,* and the ball went nowhere."

dawn patrol *n.* golfers who get up early in the morning to be the first onto the course. "I see the *dawn patrol* is already on the third hole. Did they camp out overnight?" Syn. **dew sweepers.**

does your husband play? *exp.* said to a male opponent who strikes his putt weakly. Syn. **hit it with your purse next time.**

down the hole like a rat *adj.* describes a putt that was always going to get to the bottom of the cup.

duck hook *n.* a shot that curves severely from right to left. Syn. **quaker.**

duffer *n.* an amateur or inept golfer. Syn. **hacker.**

duffer swing *n.* the type of swing that keeps teaching pros (and ball collectors) in business.

emergency nine *n.* nine extra holes after the regular round; often needed when a player has lost all bets on the earlier round.

fried egg *n.* a ball that lands in a sandtrap, making a round depression with the ball in the middle.

gangsome *n.* a Saturday or Sunday morning game with as many as twenty groups. "*Gangsomes* are a common occurrence at Willie Nelson's Pedernales Country Club in the hill country outside Austin, Texas."

heel ball *n.* a shot hit off the heel of the club.

inside the leather *adj.* describes a ball lying within a club's length of the hole. The putt may be granted in informal circumstances.

jar *v.* to hit a shot into the hole. "He *jarred* his chip shot." Syn. **hole.**

knee-knocker *n.* a short putt.

knock it stiff *v.* to hit an approach shot that lands within a short putt from the cup.

lip out *v.* when a putt touches the rim of the hole but doesn't go in.

make the ball dance on the green *v.* to hit an approach shot with side or back spin that causes the ball to "dance" when it lands on the green.

military golf *n.* a style of play in which a player is unable to control the direction of his shots—left, right, left, right.

mulligan *n.* a golf shot that doesn't count on the score; allowed in informal games after a poor shot, especially from the tee.

19th hole *n.* the clubhouse bar.

on a string *adj.* describes a controlled and/or straight shot. Rel. **remote control.**

on the dance floor (but not close enough to hear the music) *adj.* when a ball is on the green, but still far from the hole.

pulley *n.* a putt longer than the length of the flagpole.

rainmaker *n.* a shot popped high and not very far. Syn. **skyball.**

reel it in *v.* when an approach shot rolls back toward the player, due to spin on the ball, after landing on the green.

rub of the green *n.* golf's equivalent of the luck of the bounce. Any odd or accidental occurrence during a game.

rug *n.* a large divot. Syn. **pelt, slab.**

skull *v.* to hit the ball at or above its equator.

snowman *n.* a score of eight on any hole. Derived from the shape of the numeral 8.

Texas wedge *n.* a putter when used off the green.

toe jam *n.* a ball hit off the toe of the club. Syn. **toe ball.**

waggle *n.* a back-and-forth motion of the club, created by wrist flexing.

wheels coming off *adj.* when a player's game is going from bad to worse. "Yikes! The *wheels* are *coming off* Bill's game again."

wiff *v.* to completely miss the ball.

work the ball *v.*   to make a controlled draw or fade shot.

worm burner *n.*   a shot that never leaves the ground and rolls a long distance. Syn. **daisy killer.**

yank *n.*   a putt hit to the left of the hole (for a right-handed player). Syn. **pull.** Ant. **shove, push.**

the yips *n.*   the persistent inability to sink putts that were once easy for you.

Caddies

birdwatcher *n.*   a caddy whose mind is elsewhere. Syn. **flytrap.**

foot mashie *n.*   a caddy's subtle nudge of his player's ball to improve the lie. "Mr. Barrett tipped me fifty bucks! Maybe it was my *foot mashies.*"

goat track *n.*   a poorly maintained course.

HOCKEY PLAYERS

banana *n.*   a wicked, curved hockey stick.

bandwagon fans *n.*   those who adopt a team only when it's doing very well. "There are more *bandwagon fans* for the Rangers than for any other team, thanks to ESPN."

barn burner *n.*   an exciting game with high drama. "Oh, baby! We've witnessed a *barn burner* here all right, with three lead changes in the third period alone . . . and we're not done yet!"

blades *n.*   skates. "He's not injured, he's just having his *blades* sharpened in the dressing room."

blast *n.*   a slap shot with high velocity. "Man, did that Danny Daoust ever split open Bunny Larocque's mask with a wicked *blast!*"

boarding *v.* driving or riding an opposing player into the boards from behind; illegal. "That was a nasty bit of *boarding* by Claude Lemieux, who clobbered Draper."

butt-end *v.* to hit another player with the blunt end of the hockey stick; illegal. "Luckily for him, Alexander Semak's dangerous *butt-end* to Shanahan's neck went undetected by the referee."

cherry picker *n.* a player who spends his time behind opposition defenses waiting for breakaway passes. "Hull is the *cherry picker* on the Blues. He lays low in the weeds, waiting to use his tremendous talents on a top-speed breakaway."

crease *n.* the four by eight foot area defined as belonging to the goalie. "The fiery Ron Hextall used to clear his *crease* with surgical precision. With a stick here. And a stick there."

deke *n.* a quick fake-out move against an opponent. Also, *v.* to show puck-handling skill. "Wow, Fedorov really *deked* his way around Leetch."

drop his gloves *v.* to fight. "Players say that Ulfie is such a coward, he wouldn't *drop his gloves* to go to the lavatory." Ant. **turtle:** to not fight. "Ulfie hits from behind, then *turtles.*"

five-hole *n.* the space between a goalie's pads. "Rumor had it that Allan Bester was having such a rough time with players scoring on his *five-hole* that he threw himself in front of the team bus. But wouldn't you know it, the bus went through his legs!"

floater *n.* a player interested only in scoring; not a physical type. "A *floater* defined is Sergei Federov—the 1993 NHL Most Valuable Player."

freeze the puck *v.* to stop the progress of the puck. "With the Flyers pressing heavily, Hasek bolts out of his net to *freeze the puck* against the mesh."

garbage goal *n.* a goal scored from the crease and generally involving little skill. "With his tremendous wing-span, Dave Andreychuk has made a living from scoring goals within four feet of the net. He's a *garbage goal* type player."

Gretzky, in his office *adj.* when Wayne Gretzky has the puck behind the opponent's net. (Gretzky is known as the most dangerous player behind the net that the game has ever seen.)

Hardy Astrom special *n.* when a goaltender lets a goal slip in from far beyond the blueline. Named after a terrible Swedish goalie who routinely let in huge, deflating goals from stupendously long distances. "The goalie served up a *Hardy Astrom special.*"

hat trick *n.* three goals scored by one player in a single game. "Mario Lemieux scores his third goal to complete the *hat trick!*"

have the jets *adj.* to be a very fast skater. "Todd Marchant *has the jets* to overtake even the best skaters!"

the ice is tilted *adj.* when a superior team plays the role of aggressor in another team's defensive zone. "It's been another one of those nights for the Sharks. *The ice is tilted,* and so are the shots on goal, 50 to 24 in favor of the Penguins, who are on the happy end of this 6 to 0 blowout."

lid *n.* helmet. "Theo Fleury's lost his *lid* again, as the feisty center takes another run at Stu Grimson of the Wings." Syn. **top.**

The Mug *n.* Lord Stanley's Cup. "The question being asked in Detroit after another playoff flop, is 'Will the Red Wings ever drink from *The Mug* again?'"

one-timer *n.* a shot made immediately from a pass without stopping it. "During their days in Edmonton, Kurri and Gretzky worked many picture-perfect *one-timers.*"

pick 'em up and put 'em down *v.* to skate fast and powerfully. "Just watch him go! Big Eric Lindros can really *pick 'em up and put 'em down!*"

play in traffic *v.* to skate in a fast-moving throng of players. "Gretzky's *playing in traffic* again . . . he makes his move . . . and he makes the steal!" Also, to skate where you're not wanted, while putting up with checking, sticks, and other abuse. "Lindros will take his lumps and isn't afraid to *play in* heavy *traffic.*"

plumber *n.* a hardworking, gritty player. Syn. **grinder.**

poke check *v.* to knock the puck from an opponent's possession by jabbing at it with the blade of your stick. "The worst feeling in the world for a goalie is to miss on a *poke check* when he's one-on-one with a shooter. But a sniper like Mario Lemieux will *make* you miss."

power play *n.* a numerical advantage on the ice given to a team whose opponent has one or more players in the penalty box. "The Pens' *power play* is downright deadly."

practice player *n.* one who shows good skills in practice but looks horrible in games. "Vladimir Ruzicka was a great *practice player*. Was he ever fun to watch! But by the end of his stay in Boston that's all the coach let him do—watch."

puckhead *n.* an avid fan. "Lenny hasn't missed a game for twelve years—he's a total *puckhead*."

put the biscuit in the basket *v.* to score a goal. Syn. **dent the twine.** "That last shot really *dented the twine*."

roof it *v.* to score a goal that hits the top of the net. "Bure was in close, saw the opening, and *roofed it*."

run the goalie *v.* to bowl over the opposing goaltender for the purpose of putting him off his game; illegal. "Rob Pearson wasn't afraid to *run a goalie*. Unfortunately, his forays were often ill-timed and drew penalties."

separator *n.* a maneuver in which a player tries to distract an opponent by lifting his stick between the other player's legs; usually greeted by extreme anger.

sin bin *n.* the penalty box. "When the Montreal Forum closed, the Montreal Canadiens gave the actual penalty box to Chris Nilan, since he'd spent so much time in the *sin bin*."

slot *n.* the area directly in front of the net, outside the crease. "Hull is deadly accurate from inside the *slot*."

smother the puck *v.* to cover the puck by falling on it; illegal except when done by the goalie.

spin-o-rama *n.* a 360-degree pivot executed while in control of the puck. "Sergei Fedorov does a nice *spin-o-rama* in the Nike ad."

stand on his head *v.* when a goalie performs unbelievably well, stopping everything in sight. "Roy is simply incredible tonight! He's been *standing on his head* to make save after save."

stone *v.* when a goalie stymies shots as if he were a stone wall. "Roenick gets the puck, breaks down the right wing, and passes in front to Daze for the one-timer. Oh, my—Roy *stoned* him."

top shelf *adj.* when a shot scores in the upper part or top corner of the net. "Yzerman puts it *top shelf* . . ." Also, top shelf, where they keep the peanut butter. Syns. **high-rent district, lingerie department, penthouse, upstairs.**

twinkle toes *n.* a former figure skater who has moves but isn't a good player.

undress *v.* to fake out, outwit, or mesmerize a defensive player and beat him on the attack. Rel. **lose your jockstrap:** to be badly fooled by a fake-out move.

wraparound *n.* a goal scored when a player skates from behind the net and stuffs the puck between the goalie and the goalpost. "Holy Mackinaw, hockey fans! Doug Gilmour scores on a spectacular *wraparound* in the second overtime period, to give the Leafs a win over the St. Louis Blues."

HORSERACING PEOPLE

baby race *n.* a race for two-year-olds.

back down *v.* to have the odds on a horse lowered by heavy betting. "Charlie J. was *backed down* to 3–5."

beagle *n.* a nag; a dog of a horse.

big train *n.* an affectionate term for a great horse. "Equipose was the original *big train.*"

blanket finish *n.*   a race so close that the winners could figuratively be covered by a single blanket.

blow out *v.*   to do a final (usually short) speed workout prior to a race. "Night Bandit will *blow out* three furlongs before the big race today." Also, to gradually slow a horse's pace after a workout, letting the animal cool down. "That's enough work for Jimmy's Pride today; go ahead and *blow him out.*"

bridge jumper *n.*   a gambler who bets heavily on a favorite, usually to show. Based on the notion that if the gambler loses such a large amount of money, he'll commit suicide.

bug boy *n.*   an apprentice jockey given an allowance for inexperience. A "bug" is the asterisk noting this fact on the racing form.

buy the rack *v.*   to purchase various ticket combinations for the daily double.

chalk eater *n.*   a bettor who always plays favorites. From the old-time practice of writing odds on a chalkboard, with the favorites heavily chalked. Rel. **chalk horse:** the logical favorite.

colors *n.*   the silk shirt and cap of a jockey's uniform.

come home early *v.*   to win a race by going to the front of the pack and staying there. Often an order from the owner to the jockey: "I want you to *come home early,* understand?"

crawl down *v.*   to push a horse for a final burst of speed. "Eddie *crawled down* on Kokomo when he hit the stretch."

crossfire *v.*   when a horse clips his back hooves together while running.

distaff runner *n.*   a female horse.

dutch the board *v.*   to hedge one's bet. Example: A gambler on a daily double may add new bets on the second race after his horse has already won the first race.

educated currency *n.*   "smart money," the bets placed on a horse by the owner, trainer, stable workers, and others with supposedly authentic information.

educated horse *n.* an animal that is apparently able to read the odds board, since he never wins except at a good price.

emergency *n.* the replacement horse when a starter is scratched.

feather *n.* a very light jockey. "Night Bandit has a *feather* up."

finger horse *n.* the favorite. From racing sheets that indicate a handicapper's choice by printing a finger symbol next to the name.

freak *n.* a horse who outruns his pedigree and performs better than expected.

get him a drink of water *v.* to allow a horse to turn wide or run along the outside rail. Also, to move around the pack on the last turn instead of trying to find a hole closer in. Syn. **take the overland route.**

goat *n.* a horse completely outclassed by his competition. "The fifth at Hollywood paid a $495 Exacta—two *goats* came in."

go to bat *v.* to use a whip on a horse, especially in the stretch.

grass specialist *n.* a horse that runs best on the turf.

gumbo *n.* mud; a muddy track.

handle *n.* the total sum of money bet on the entire race card or on a single race. "Wow! The *handle* for the sixth was at least 450,000 bucks."

has the call *v.* when a jockey is given the ride on a horse. "Bill *has the call* on Royal Midnight in the Derby."

herder *n.* a jockey who crosses his horse in front of the pack, forcing them to bunch up.

Ingersoll Willie *n.* the official timer at a morning workout.

lobster *n.* a horse that doesn't generate the bets expected by the oddsmakers.

looking out the window *v.* when a gambler bets consistently on a horse without winning; then on the day the horse finally wins, he bets on another horse or doesn't bet at all. "Noble Prince caught Eddie *looking out the window.*"

maiden *n.*   a horse that has yet to win a race.

meatball *n.*   a blend of laxatives given to a horse.

monster *n.*   a horse that based on past performance should predictably win a race, even if the rest of the field had a quarter-mile head start. "In the '73 Belmont, you had to take Secretariat—he was a *monster.*"

morning glory *n.*   a horse that runs well in the morning workout but poorly in the actual race.

mudder *n.*   a horse that runs well on the mud.

Nakatani betting *v.*   choosing a horse according to which jockey in the race has the highest percentage of wins. Named for Corey Nakatani, a winning jockey on the California circuit. The term means that when horses look otherwise evenly matched, a hot jockey who's on a winning streak might be the deciding factor when choosing which horse to bet. "These four horses look evenly matched, so I'm *Nakatani betting* this one."

open the meeting *v.*   to win the first race on the program. "Our Delight *opened the meeting* at Belmont."

ouija board *n.*   the official odds board at a racetrack.

parking lot *n.*   the part of the track along the outside rail, constituting the longest distance from the start to the finish line.

peep *v.*   to finish a race in third place; to show. "Thunderbird *peeped* for me last Tuesday." Rel. **peephole** *n.*   the third place at the finish.

picture *n.*   a photo finish. "High Diver won in a *picture.*"

pinhead *n.*   a lousy jockey. "I lost $150, thanks to that *pinhead.*"

plate *n.*   a horseshoe for a racehorse. Rel. **plater:** a cheap racehorse.

railbird *n.*   an amateur observer at a morning workout who times and checks the performances of various horses. "Hah! Look at those *railbirds* with their stopwatches and clipboards. A lot of good that'll do them when the money's down."

rear-viewing *v.*   when a jockey is watching his competitors too much during a race. "If that idiot Chico hadn't spent all his time *rear-viewing,* he could have won the fourth."

red-boarding *v.*   making a case in favor of the winner after the race is over, usually when you did not pick that horse. From the old practice of posting race results on a red board.

ride with *v.*   to bet on a horse, thus riding with it in spirit.

run up an alley *v.*   to fail to win, place, or show, and be left entirely out of the money.

salty *adj.*   having poor luck. "Joe hasn't backed the right horse since 1994, that's how *salty* he is."

scrape paint *v.*   to run along the inside rail. "I knew Quibble couldn't lose; he was *scraping paint.* "

scratch *v.*   to withdraw a horse from a race. A famous blooper made by a racetrack announcer: "Harass has been withdrawn! Be sure to *scratch* Harass!"

sharpen his skates *v.*   when a horse develops speed through short, fast bursts during training sessions. "Happy Secret has been *sharpening his skates* all week."

slop-eating fool *n.*   a horse who runs well on a sloppy track.

smoke your socks *v.*   to be all wrong. "You're *smoking your socks* if you think High Pockets can even show in that race."

stanza *n.*   a single race on a program. Syn. **spasm.**

sucker horse *n.*   a horse that is always heavily bet but seldom wins; it usually has a lot of second- and third-place finishes.

tote *n.*   the Totalisator, or betting system in which the winning bettors share the total amount of money wagered, minus, of course, a percentage for the track.

up *adv.* when a jockey has contracted to ride a horse. "True Grit has Willie Shoemaker *up* in the fifth."

worry *v.* to ride a horse. "How many did you *worry* yesterday?"

VOLLEYBALL PLAYERS

barbecue *adj.* the style of volleyball often seen at picnics, in which inexperienced players slap at the ball.

bump *v.* to pass the ball by clasping your hands and letting the ball bounce off your forearms. Also, *n.* "The first play is usually a *bump* to the setter."

butter *n.* a great set. "Thanks, Jimbo—that was *butter!*" Syn. **nectar.**

campfire *n.* when the whole team stands around while an easy ball drops into their court. Syn. **gravity check.**

Charlie Tuna *n.* a novice player who constantly runs into the net. Rel. **tuna surprise** *n.* the act of hitting the net.

cheesecake *n.* a ball that is easy to dig. Syn. **cake.**

chester *n.* a spike that hits an opposing player in the chest.

chicken wing *n.* a last-ditch way to dig a ball using your elbow and a bent arm.

clamp *v.* to block a shot. Syn. **jed:** so called because the blocker tries to "clamp it," an allusion to Jed Clampett of *The Beverly Hillbillies.*

dig *n.* the bumping of a spiked ball. Syn. **up.** "Nice *up!*" Also, *v.*

dink *n.* a softly hit spike. Syn. **tip.**

dish *v.* to make an overhead pass by using all your fingers to create a deep-dish cradle around the ball. "Chuck really *dishes.*"

facial *n.* a ball that hits a defensive player in the face. "Donna received a *facial* in the game this morning." Rel. **facial disgracial:** a hard facial that causes a player to leave the game.

family picnic *n.* when someone on a team puts the ball over the net on the first or second hit, especially on an easy play. "Hey, did your Aunt Susie teach you how to play *family picnic* ball?"

floater *n.* a serve that seems to float through the air because it has no spin; like a knuckleball in baseball. Syn. **marshmallow.**

fluff *v.* to make a spike attempt that is weak and unsuccessful. "You really *fluffed* that one." Also, *n.* "That was the ugliest *fluff* I have ever seen."

Fluffallupagus *n.* someone who fluffs consistently. Named after Snuffallupagus of *Sesame Street* fame. "Whoops! Just call me *Fluffallupagus.*"

golden stack *n.* when three hitters are in the air at the same time in a combination play.

hammer *n.* a good hitter. "That John is a *hammer.*" Rel. **nail:** a good pass-off of a serve. "I passed a *nail,* and John hammered it down."

hops *n.* a player's vertical leap. "Dave really has great *hops.*"

hubby-wife *n.* when a serve drops untouched between two receivers who fail to move, each thinking the other is going to get it.

joust *v.* when two players on opposing sides try to block a ball by vying to push it onto the other side of the net.

juice me *exp.* set the ball to me.

jump out of the gym *v.* what a player with great hops can do. "Marie Laure can *jump out of the gym!*"

jungle ball *n.* barbecue-style volleyball with wild play.

Kong block *n.* a one-armed block.

lollipop *n.* an easy serve. "If you serve any more *lollipops,* our team may get licked."

meatball *n.* a set with a high, predictable arc. "Okay, Olivia, gimme a *meatball* and I'll kill it."

Midas *n.* a player who sets the ball extremely well and so is thought to have a golden touch.

moosehead *n.* when the ball is spiked so hard that it hits the gym floor and then the ceiling.

paintbrush *n.* a spike missed completely or just off the tips of the fingers. Syn. **waffle.**

pancake *n.* when a ball is played off the back of the hand near the floor, usually during a dive. Resembles a pancake being flipped off a griddle.

roof *n.* a great stuff block. Rel. **roofing company:** a group on the same team who do a great job of blocking the ball.

Roto-Rooter *n.* a killer spike.

shake-and-bake *n.* when a beach player dives for a ball and gets coated with sand.

shank *v.* to bump the ball directly sideways; an error that usually can't be recovered from. "Debbie *shanked* that hard serve into the wall." Also *n.*

shank you *exp.* used when an opposing player shanks a pass. Also, **shanks a lot, shanks for the memories.**

six-pack *n.* a spike that hits someone in the face, usually in the course of blocking a shot. "Nice *six-pack*. Would you pass me a towel to rub the logo off my forehead?" Rel. **Spalding tattoo:** getting hit with the ball on any other body part.

sizzling the pits *v.* spiking a ball so that it flies under a blocker's outstretched arms.

sky ball *n.* a very high serve, often done to confuse the opponent in bright sun or windy conditions. Syns. **moon ball, mortar.** Also *v.*

spank *n.* a great spike. Syn. **crush.** Also, a big win. "We *spanked* the other team."

stud *n.* an awesome player, either male or female.

stuff *n.* a block that sends the ball straight down to the floor with no chance of being picked up by an opposing player.

swinging from the vines *v.* attempting a spike but instead hooking the net with your wrist or elbow. Often followed by a Tarzan bellow and beating of the chest. "Hey Scott, stop *swinging from the vines!*"

tapeworm *n.* a player who regularly hits the tape that runs across the top of the net.

terminator *n.* a player who regularly ends play by hitting the ball as hard as possible, resulting in either a kill or a ball that hits the net or goes out of bounds.

tomahawk *n.* an overhead bump.

tool *n.* when a ball is intentionally spiked off a blocker's hands to make it go out of bounds, thus using the opponent as a tool. Also, *v.* "You really *tooled* that blocker." Syn. **use.**

toss a salad *v.* to make a bad set. "Boy, did you ever *toss a salad!* Do you eat with those hands, too?"

unguided missile *n.* a spike so wild that it flies far out of the court.

wipe *v.* to tool an opponent by pushing the ball off his or her hands.

WRESTLERS

angle *n.* a planned event in a wrestling story line. Often part of a feud. "Mr. Perfect getting injured by Rick Rude was just an *angle.*"

arena rat *n.* a promiscuous woman (beauty immaterial) who hangs around arenas to make liaisons with wrestlers.

blade *v.* to cut oneself with a small piece of a razorblade, so the blood will excite the crowd. Often done on the forehead. No longer acceptable for family entertainment nor allowed in World Championship Wrestling. Also, *n.* "Fabulous Fred carefully pulled a *blade* from his tights."

booker *n.* the person in a wrestling promotion who is responsible for planning story lines and angles and deciding who wins and loses matches. "Vince McMahon and Jim Ross are the *bookers* of the World Wrestling Federation." Syn. **carpenter:** "The *carpenter* worked a new angle and drew a big crowd."

boys *n.* wrestlers.

bump *n.* a body blow that may actually hurt, or a fall taken harder than intended. "The title belt hung above the ring, and the first wrestler to climb a ladder and grab it would be the champ. When Razor Ramone knocked Shawn Michaels off the ladder, Michaels took a big *bump.*"

bury *v.* to try to sully a wrestler's image among fans.

calling the spot *v.* planning the next move with an opponent while the match is in progress. Wrestler A: "Okay, what next?" Wrestler B: "Lift me up and throw me onto the ropes. After that I'll stomp you." Wrestler A: "Okay, let's do it." Syn. **lead the dance.**

card *n.* a lineup of wrestling matches.

chairshot *n.* hitting another wrestler with a chair.

crimson mask *n.* the effect produced when blading the forehead yields too much blood.

face *n.* a "good guy" wrestler; a fan favorite. Short for babyface. "A match usually features a *face* versus a heel."

feud *n.* a pretended, prolonged quarrel between wrestlers, designed to attract fans to the matches.

finishing move *n.* a wrestler's trademark move for polishing off his opponent. "When Diesel executes the power bomb, the match is usually over. It's his *finishing move.*"

gimmick *n.* the persona that a wrestler adopts in the ring; a hook designed to attract the fans' interest. "Shawn Michaels uses a pretty-boy *gimmick,* Sgt. Slaughter a military *gimmick,* and the Undertaker an undead *gimmick.*" Also, a foreign object, such as a dog's steel choke chain, that a wrestler brings into the ring and uses during a match. Also, a souvenir or novelty sold either by the promotion, or in smaller arenas, by the wrestlers themselves.

go over *v.* to win, as planned ahead of time. "Tommy Gunn is supposed to *go over* and take the title."

ham 'n' egger, jobroni, scrub. Rel. **JTTS:** Jobber To The Stars. A name wrestler who is no longer pushed and loses regularly to bigger stars. "Adam Bomb is a WWF star, but he loses most of his televised matches because he's a *JTTS.*"

heat *n.* crowd response, including boos and jeers, clapping and cheering. An important measure of a wrestler's ability to sell tickets or get the fans involved in the match. During an interview, a heel might turn to the crowd and shout, "You're all a bunch of washed-up, freeloading, moronic idiots." They respond by booing and yelling back. He has just successfully generated heat. Heat is also built up during a match, reaching a climax right after a pin. "In his heyday, no one drew *heat* like the Iron Sheik." Rel. **canned heat:** recorded cheering and booing added to a TV broadcast to create excitement.

heel *n.* a "bad guy" wrestler; the villain. A heel may win some early battles, but the face always wins the war. "In the 1950s Gorgeous George was a handsome *heel.* Men booed him, but women threw roses."

hood *n.* a mask. "Black Tiger is Eddy Guerrero under the *hood.*" Also, a masked wrestler.

hot tag *n.* when a face tags his partner after getting severe punishment from the heels. Usually happens near the end of a tag-team match, when the crowd is at fever pitch. "Scott Steiner, barely able to move from the beating he'd taken, crawled over to his brother Rick, who stretched out his hand for the *hot tag.* Rick came in and cleaned house on both heels, with the crowd going wild."

international object *n.* a foreign object or weapon not permitted in the ring. Jocular term derived from a Turner Broadcasting order not to use the word "foreign" on its television stations.

job *n.* a planned, intentional loss. Rel. **do the job** *v.* to lose cleanly to another wrestler. "Last night, Bob Holly *did the job* for Double J."

jobber *n.*   a wrestler paid to lose to "name" wrestlers, usually on TV. Like a straight man in comedy, he makes the other guy look good. "Iron Mike Sharpe is classic *jobber*. I love that cheesy armband he wears, and every time he gets trapped in a corner and yells, 'Noooo. . . . nonononono!' I fall on the floor laughing." The going fee paid to a jobber is $50 to $150. Syns.

juice *n.*   blood, usually the result of blading. Syn. **color.** Rel. **hardway juice:** blood flowing from a genuine injury. Also, *v.*   "Van Hammer *juiced* after getting hit with a chair." Also refers to taking steroids. "Dangerous Dan is *juiced* to the gills."

kayfabe *n.*   professional wrestling's code of secrecy and silence, similar to that of magicians. "Keeping it *kayfabe*" means never revealing to fans or media that pro wrestling is scripted and fixed. For example, two wrestlers in real life may be friends, but because their wrestling personas are having a feud, they can never be seen socializing publicly. Also a code word. When an outsider approaches, a person in the know will say "kayfabe" and everyone will stop talking openly. Rel. **breaking kayfabe** *v.*   failing to protect industry secrets or stepping out of a scripted character.

knock *n.*   any injury, from a black eye to something more serious, such as a broken tailbone. "Man, have I had my share of *knocks* this year!"

loose *adj.*   having gained weight, especially in the stomach. "Lou Albano got *loose* once he stopped wrestling." Also describes holds applied with less force than usual.

mark *n.*   a fan who believes that wrestling is real, goes to the shows, and buys wrestling merchandise. Ant. **smart mark:** a fan who enjoys pro wrestling, but knows it is fake. Rel. **mark out** *v.*   to let yourself get very excited, as if you were a mark, to increase your enjoyment of the match.

married *adj.*   when two wrestlers are used in a feud angle for a long time, working together in many markets. "Those guys are *married* until the pay-per-view."

no show *n.*   a wrestler who without notice, fails to show up when he is booked to appear. Also, *v.*   "Sabu *no showed* the Three-Way Dance because he was in Japan."

paper *v.*   to give away free tickets in order to fill an arena, often for TV tapings.

piledriver *n.* a classic move that consists of a wrestler holding his opponent's head between his knees, lifting him vertically by the waist until he is upside-down, and then jumping up and landing in an extended sitting position, driving the opponent's head into the mat. "Paul Orndorff hits a *piledriver* on Hulk Hogan!" Other common wrestling moves are the brainbuster, DDT, 450-degree splash, ghostbuster, moonsault, schoolboy, Steiner's Frankensteiner, tombstone, and vertical suplex.

policeman *n.* a wrestler who works closely with the promoter to keep uncooperative wrestlers in line by giving them legitimate beatings during a match.

pop *n.* a loud cheer or round of applause. Note that a "pop" is a short-lived response, while "heat" refers to a sustained reaction. Thus, a crowd will pop for a good move, while an entire match will be described as having good heat. "Shawn Michaels got the biggest *pop* of the night." Also, *v.* "All Tornado has to do is walk down the aisle and the crowd *pops.*"

post *v.* to slam an opposing wrestler's head into one of the metal poles in the corners of the ring.

potato *v.* to throw a punch or kick that accidentally connects harder than it is supposed to. "Stan Hansen often *potatoes* his opponents because he's blind as a bat without his glasses." Also, *n.* an errant punch that hurts like a real one. Syns. **potato shot, 'tater.** "Pillman took a *potato shot* when Sid Vicious power-bombed him in the War Games. Then he caught a *'tater* in the stomach and threw up."

push *v.* to promote a wrestler by having him win, interviewing him, and otherwise raising his standing among fans.

put over *n.* to lose to another wrestler to make him look good. "Horowitz *puts* another superstar *over!*"

rest hold *n.* a non-decisive hold, such as a headlock or scissors, used to buy rest time during a match. "Frequently, it's the older or out-of-shape wrestlers who engage in *rest holds.*"

run in *n.* when a wrestler races in from the locker room and attacks another wrestler or a manager.

screw job *n.* a controversial loss or less-than-conclusive win. "The Sandman was pinned, although it was clear that the other guy's foot was on the ropes. What a *screw job.*"

sell *v.* to pretend to be injured, anguished, or groggy, thus making your opponent's moves look real and painful. An important element in pro wrestling. "The Masked Marvel really *sold* the Crusher's moves."

shoot *n.* when two wrestlers throw away the script and stop cooperating, turning the match into a legitimate fight; this can change the planned outcome. Also, *v.* "When the Cowboy started punching Fatboy full-force in the face, the ref stopped the match. The Cowboy got fined for *shooting.*"

show *n.* a wrestling match. Rel. **house show:** a match in a local arena or gym that is not taped for TV or pay-per-view. Offers a chance for fans to see the wrestlers live. "The Boston Garden's last *house show* is on May 13th." Rel. **dark match:** a match that does not air (although it may have been videotaped) on a televised wrestling program.

showing light *v.* unintentionally making it obvious that a punch or other maneuver did not connect.

spot *n.* a move or series of moves. "Superfly Jimmy Snuka's splash of the top rope is one of the most famous *spots* in wrestling." Rel. **high spot:** a move (often aerial) that rivets the crowd's attention. "Boy, did that brainbuster *high spot* get the crowd to pop."

squash *n.* a match won quickly by the star, with little defense from the jobber. "There were two *squashes* on tonight's card."

strap *n.* a championship belt.

stretched *adj.* injured.

telegraph *v.* to signal your next move to an opponent unintentionally, allowing him to prevent or reverse the maneuver. Often done intentionally by jobbers to make their opponents look smarter. "Barry Horowitz *telegraphed* that maneuver, and Hulk Hogan now has the upper hand."

tope *n.* pronounced "toe-pay." A maneuver in which a wrestler flies over the top rope and lands outside the ring.

turn face/turn heel *v.* when a wrestler changes his role from a bad guy to a good guy, or vice-versa. "Boss Man hasn't been cheered since he *turned heel* on Sting." Rel. **face turn/heel turn:** the shift of roles. "Diesel was a heel until Shawn Michaels superkicked him in the face for the third time. Then he did a *face turn.*"

work *n.* an event with a predetermined outcome. "The marks never realized that the match with the 1-2-3 Kid was a *work.*" Also, *v.* to make a match look misleadingly real. "Those two guys are good. They *work* a match just like movie stuntmen fake a barroom brawl." Also, to participate in a wrestling-related event. "I've got to *work* an interview after the match."

work rate *n.* the pace and ratio of action to non-action (particularly rest holds) during a match. "Younger, more athletic wrestlers generally have the best *work rates.*"

zombie sit-up *n.* a move performed by the Undertaker, who sits up slowly after a knockdown like a zombie rising from the dead.

BOATERS

asshole *n.* a kink in a line traveling through a block, or pulley, preventing it from passing through. "What's holding up the starboard side jib sheet?" "There's an *asshole* in the line!" "Well, free it up quick, before we go overb—(blub, blub, blub)."

ballast *n.* a guest or crew member who is thoroughly useless on a boat. "We need a new foredeck man. Mike is just *ballast.*"

boom babe *n.* a pretty female, usually in a bikini, who helpfully sits on the boom to hold it out when a sailboat is racing downwind. Syn. **bow decoration.**

check the tension on the backstay *v.* to pee off the back of the boat. (The backstay cable from the top of the mast is convenient for hanging onto.) "When Mike said, 'Take the wheel, I need to *check the tension on the backstay,*' everyone else politely turned their heads and examined various other interesting bits of rigging."

chute *n.* a large spinnaker that balloons ahead of the boat like a parachute.

Clorox bottle *n.* a cheap fiberglass boat with a thin hull that flexes excessively.

death roll *n.* an out-of-control rocking from side to side when a sailboat tries to carry a spinnaker (a large triangular racing sail) in too much wind. "Hey, check out the *death roll* over there! Ha ha."

Dutch pennants *n.* the free ends of knots or splices left long enough to reveal poor seamanship. "Look at the *Dutch pennants* on that barge!" Syn. **Irish pennants.**

floating clothesline *n.* a sailboat, to a powerboat operator; derogatory. Syns. **blowboat, ragboat.**

furniture store *n.* a yacht with elaborate cabin appointments. "Have a look below. His boat's a regular *furniture store.*"

gunboat *n.* a souped-up, Miami Vice-type powerboat; usually derisive. Derived from the ethnically offensive "guinea gunboat," referring to the supposed popularity of this kind of boat with Italian-Americans.

gunkholing *v.* hauling a trailerable sailboat to a lake or stretch of river that is otherwise inaccessible to boats, and cruising around.

hard water *n.* a rock. "We ran into some *hard water* out beyond the cove." Also, ice, in northern waters.

Harvey Wallbangers *n.* rental boats. So called because their inexperienced captains usually don't negotiate docks or lock walls skillfully.

head dweller *n.* a seasick person.

hobbyhorse *v.* when a sailboat pitches lengthwise, like a rocking horse.

hole *n.* an area with no wind. Ant. **puff.**

hydraulic sandwich *n.* a beer or other liquid refreshment served on board.

iron jenny *n.* the engine. (A jenny is a large genoa, or jib sail.) "All right, the race is over. Someone want to raise the *iron jenny?*"

Iron Mike *n.* an autopilot steering system. "When they collided, both vessels were being operated by their *Iron Mikes* and no one was on watch."

lift *n.* the raising of a drawbridge. "Tug *Barbara Ann* to the Route 88 bridge. I'm southbound and requesting a *lift.*"

mooring anchor *n.* a heavy and frustrating piece of equipment. "This *&@% engine just won't start. It would make a better *mooring anchor.*"

pointy end *n.* the bow. Used to spoof the jargon that sailors seem to have for every piece of equipment and part of the boat. Others include basement or downstairs (cabin), big rag (mainsail), big stick (mast), parking hook (anchor), puller uppers (halyards), strings (lines).

rag top *n.* a cloth sunshade.

rail meat *n.* someone whose most useful function on a boat is using his or her weight to balance it.

slimy side down! *exp.* encouragement shouted to a dinghy before a race.

squids *n.* the dock and cleaning staff at a marina.

squirt boat *n.* a jet-driven boat, to a powerboater; derogatory. Rel. **squirt jerk:** jet boat operator.

stinkpot *n.* a powerboat, to a sailboat operator; derogatory. "That *stinkpot* threw up a wake that stopped us dead in the water."

T-bone *v.* to have a collision in which the bow of one sailboat hits the middle of another boat at a ninety-degree angle. "*Impressions* was T-boned by *Chasing Rainbows* right at the finish of the race."

tea-bag *v.* when a sailing dinghy heels to windward, dunking the crew on the trapeze into the water. "Joe got *tea-bagged.*"

FISHERMEN

barndoor *n.* a California halibut.

birds nest *n.* a backlash on the reel when casting.

black belly *n.* a large gray grouper, usually over thirty pounds.

blowing black smoke *v.* when a fishing boat is backing up to gain line when a big fish is on.

bucketmouth *n.* a largemouth bass.

Cadillac *n.* a red snapper between ten and twenty pounds.

cherry-picked *adj.* when a fish has taken the bait from a hook without the fisherman knowing it.

chickens *n.* red snappers up to ten pounds, which tend to peck at the bait. In the Northeast, a type of short-tailed seabird that often hovers over baitfish.

chopper *n.* bluefish. Rel. **gorilla bluefish:** over twelve pounds.

cross their eyes *v.* to set the hook hard. "When you feel the bite, you need to *cross their eyes.*"

dink *n.* little fish. "Hey, did you catch any big fish today?" "No, just *dinks.*"

doormat *n.* a large fluke or summer flounder of ten pounds or over.

drifting snakes *v.* using eels as bait for striped bass. Rel. **slinging snakes:** fishing in the surf with eels.

drop a fish at the boat *v.* to lose a fish near the boat. Rel. **Palm Beach release** *n.* when a large saltwater game fish is dropped at the boat.

DuPont spinner *n.* a stick of dynamite. When exploded, the fish are stunned and float to the surface for easy netting. An unethical, nonecological, and usually illegal method of fishing.

farm *v.* to let a fish get away. "Dude, you *farmed* that bass."

fishing the suds *v.* surf fishing. Syn. **rock hopping.**

'gator trout *n.* a large sea trout.

get eaten *v.*   to have a bunch of large fish—tuna, marlin, etc.—hit your lines while trolling. "The port rigger bait had just passed the weedline when we got *eaten.*"

grand slam *n.*   catching a sailfish, white marlin, and blue marlin on the same day.

Hawaiian Eye *n.*   a large trolling lure with movable eyes like those of some dolls.

hawg *n.*   a largemouth bass weighing more than ten pounds.

head boat *n.*   a vessel that takes paying customers fishing, at so much a head. Syn. **party boat.**

hit a home run *v.*   to catch a mangrove snapper, red snapper, and grouper in one day.

hole in the water the size of a garbage can cover *v.*   when a big fish rises to a surface plug, misses it, and creates a hole in the water.

honey hole *n.*   a favorite hole where you can consistently catch fish. "I've been going to that *honey hole* since I was a kid."

lockjaw *n.*   what the fish have when they're not biting. "Everyone has a line in the water, but no one is getting bit. The fish have *lockjaw.*" Also, what a fishing boat captain is said to have if his crew is catching fish and he doesn't notify nearby boats.

Mexican salmon *n.*   a Pacific mackeral.

mosquito fleet *n.*   idiots on jet skis. Also, a bunch of small boats that follow a commercial fishing boat.

motorhead *n.*   someone in a big speedboat who races by the fishing boats.

nester molester *n.*   a fisherman who exploits the period in spring when bass spawn, by fishing for them on their nests.

on the chew *adj.*   when the fish are biting. Syn. **snapping.**

outboard *n.*   a small private boat, to a commercial fishing boat captain. Syn. **skiff.**

overboard *adj.*   when your boat is located out past the drop-off of the continental shelf, in thousands of feet of water.

parking lot *n.*   the ocean during extremely flat conditions.

puppy drum *n.*   a smallish redfish of two to five pounds. Syn. **rat red.**

put it on a Ritz *exp.*   used when someone lands a very small fish.

rats *n.*   small striped bass in the surf.

run and gun *v.*   to dash from one fishing spot to another, as in a tournament.

slicker flicker *n.*   someone who uses trout, which are slick to the touch, as bait for big bass; this practice is disliked by trout fishermen.

soaking bait *v.*   engaged in non-productive fishing. "I spent the morning *soaking bait.* Not even a bite!"

spooled *v.*   when a fish runs all the line off the reel. "I got spooled by the tuna." Rel. *n.*   **screamer:** any fish that tears the line off the reel. Syn. **smoker.**

squidhead *n.*   striped bass. Syns. **greenhead, linesider, pajamas.**

sweeten *v.*   to put a small piece of shrimp on a jig.

talking to Ralph *v.*   getting seasick. Syns. **chumming, feeding the fish.** Rel. *n.*   **chumchucker:** a person who is seasick.

telephoning *v.*   using electric currents to stun fish; illegal. So called because old telephone wires were once used.

tennis shoe *n.*   a remora. So called for the appearance of its sucker.

toad *n.*   a very big fish.

trash fish *n.*   a fish of no value for food or sport. "On the West Coast, *trash fish* include lizard fish, tom cod, and, with apologies to our British brethren, carp." Also, any type of fish you catch that you weren't fishing for.

unbuttoned *adj.*   when a fish gets off the line. "That bass came *unbuttoned.*"

way back *adj.*   when the bait is put 150 yards behind the boat. Rel. **way, way back:** 250 yards behind the boat; **way, way, way back:** 350 yards behind.

William Club *n.*   a billy club for delivering the coup de grâce to a large saltwater fish; usually aluminum, it resembles a small baseball bat. Fisherman to his buddy: "I've almost got the fish in the boat. Where's *William Club?*"

winnie lure *n.*   a very large #6 hook baited with a foot-long hotdog.

Fly Fishermen

Ay, caramba *n.*   an exclamation when you lose a fish. "I caught two rainbows and had two *Ay, carambas.*"

boiling water *n.*   a prime condition for dry fly fishing, when many trout are rising to feed on a hatch of insects and disturbing the water's surface. Rel. **boil:** "Up here on the Oriskany, the brookies come to a *boil* every night around seven-thirty."

flogging the water *v.*   futilely casting without a single strike. "I spent three hours *flogging the water* and finally had the good sense to call it quits—until tomorrow." Also, having both front and back casts hit the water sloppily.

footballs *n.*   big, fat trout. Syn. **pigs.** "Holy guacamole, Bill, your fish is a real *pig.*"

garden hackle *n.*   worms. A hackle is a tuft of feathers on a dry fly.

hardware specialist *n.*   a spin caster or bass fisherman who uses plugs and lures made of cork, balsa, or metal. "I was flogging water under the bridge last week, when this *hardware specialist* shows up and pulls out the biggest brookie I've ever seen!"

in 'em thick *adj.* when one is catching many fish. Related sayings include "I think I've hooked the Thick Ness monster," and "Oh, you thick bathtard you."

Jimi *n.* a Hendrickson fly.

liar *n.* a fisherman.

little red Corvette *n.* a prince nymph fly.

long-distance release *n.* when a fish gets off the hook with lots of line out. Syn. **LDR.**

long wand *n.* fly rod.

Mr. O *n.* a man wearing high fishing fashions. Derived from Orvis, a company that makes fine fly fishing gear. *"Mr. O* over there is right out of the catalog."

noodle rod *n.* a long, lightweight rod that absorbs most of the shock of a big fish's fight and so allows the use of light line.

on the rise *adj.* when trout are feeding on the surface.

pork chops *n.* nightcrawlers. "They won't take nuthin', so I guess I'll serve 'em up some *pork chops."*

priest *n.* a small club for knocking a trout on the head, in order to kill it as quickly and humanely as possible.

rippin' lips *n.* what you sometimes find on your barb when you've tried to set the hook on a fish too hard and lose the fish.

slumby *n.* an uneducated fisherman with no motor skills or common sense. Fishing guide: "My *slumby* hooked his ear four times today."

smokin' *adj.* yielding lots of fish. "Hat Creek was really *smokin'* this morning. I got four rainbows."

snit *n.* short for "standard nine-inch trout." A term used on Atlanta's Chattahoochee River, which is so heavily fished that the stocking truck barely stays ahead of the fishermen, and most fish caught are fresh from the hatchery. "No big ones today, but at least I got a couple of *snits.*"

speak Latin *v.* to use the "elitist" Latin names for insect species rather than the common names; e.g., *Baetidae* instead of blue-winged olive. "This yuppie on the river last Sunday *spoke* more *Latin* than the Pope."

VFT *n.* Valuable Fishing Time. A rallying cry for a group that is fishing or about to fish. Also, a curse to shout when stuck in traffic or otherwise delayed on the way to fishing.

SURFERS

backside *adj.* when a surfer rides with his back to the wave. "Jimmie went *backside* on that ride."

bail *v.* to jump off the board to end a ride. "I fully *bailed.*"

barney *n.* idiot; someone who doesn't surf well. Slightly dorkier than a kook. Derived from Barney Rubble, a character in *The Flintstones* cartoon series. Also, *v.* to act like a barney. "Check out that grommet *barneying* all over the wave." Rel. **wilma:** a female barney.

barrel *n.* a wide-open tube.

beached *adj.* full of food. "We ate donuts till I was so *beached* I couldn't stand up."

betty *n.* a pretty girl; cool girl; girlfriend. Derived from Betty Rubble in *The Flintstone* cartoon. "State Beach was full of *bettys* today." Syn. **chick.**

big mama *n.* the ocean.

bitchin' *adj.* great; killer.

black ball flag *n.* a yellow flag with a black circle, raised by Southern California lifeguards to indicate "no surfing." Syn. **meatball flag.**

blown out *adj.* when wind blowing onshore ruins the shape and rideability of the waves.

body wompin' *v.*   body surfing.

bogus *adj.*   not right, phony, rude, lame, weird, bullshit. "The black ball flag at the Wedge is completely *bogus.*" Rel. **bogosity:** "The utter *bogosity* of the guy, cutting me off on that wave!"

bro' *n.*   friend, buddy. Short for brother. Also, a substitute for "dude." "What's up, *bro'*?"

butt floss *n.*   a G-string bikini. Syn. **butt thong.**

cake *n.*   money. "I need some *cake* to buy some beer."

capitalize *v.*   to ride aggressively. "You entirely *capitalized* on that wave."

choiceamundo *adj.*   great. "How were the waves this morning?" "*Choiceamundo!*"

clamshelled *adj.*   said of a surfer when a wave closes over him.

close out *n.*   a wave breaking along most or all of its length at the same time, so it offers very short rides only. Also, *v.*   "That barrel had a real chance of *closing out.*" Syn. **wall out.**

corduroy to the horizon *adj.*   waves lined up in straight lines, like the parallel ribs of corduroy fabric.

curl *n.*   the hollow area under the lip of a breaking wave.

dawn patrol *v.*   to hit the waves at sunrise.

dial in on *v.*   to talk with. "Let's *dial in on* those chicks."

diape *adj.*   awful. Derived from the image of a dirty diaper. "The waves were blown out and completely *diape.*"

ding *n.*   a dent or puncture in a surfboard.

dingo *n.*   an Australian surfer; derogatory. "There were a bunch of *dingos* in the water." Syn. **beer-drinking marsupials.**

drop in *v.*   to take off on a wave that another surfer already has. Also, *n.*

dude *n.*   guy, friend. Also a substitute for "man," added to the end of almost any statement. "Let's get some food, *dude.*" Sometimes tongue in cheek; "du-u-u-u-ude" is a self-mocking parody of Valleyspeak in 1980s Southern California. Rel. **dudette:** girl.

epic *adj.*   large, magnificent. "The surf was completely *epic* when we dawn patrolled this morning."

freak show *n.*   a place that's too busy or crowded. "The parking lot was a full-on *freak show.*"

fully *adj.*   completely, absolutely. Syns. **heavily, totally.** "Like, I *totally* imagine I can help you out."

get air *v.*   to leave the water with your board. Syn. **catch air.** "Hey, did you see Jason *catch air?*"

gnarly *adj.*   big, nasty, dangerous, scary, in the challenging-to-deadly range. Refers to waves and, by extension, to situations. "If you get mixed up with the Federales in Mexico for some imagined offense, it can be pretty *gnarly.*" Rel. **gnarlatious:** cool, huge, awesome; **your gnarlyness:** jocular term of respectful address for a friend. "Want a burger, *your gnarlyness?*"

goofy foot *adj.*   surfing with your right foot forward instead of the usual left foot.

green monsters *n.*   very large waves.

grommet *n.*   a young or novice surfer. Also, a surf punk or little tough guy.

grovel *v.*   to purposely bounce oneself along the wave, trying to get up speed and find a decent section to ride. "It's pretty embarrassing to *grovel,* but I didn't have much choice." Syn. **hop.**

gunga *n.*   the residue of surf wax that won't come off a board.

hair *n.*   guts, courage. "It took real *hair* to go surfing on such a big day."

hair ball *n.*   a big wave. "Check out that *hair ball!*"

huevos *n.* pronounced "WAVE-ohs." Waves. From the Spanish word for eggs. "Shoulda been at Malibu Sunday, dude. Gnarly *huevos!*"

in the green room *adj.* inside a perfect tube. Syn. **in the Pope's living room.**

jonesing *v.* feeling a strong desire. "I haven't gone surfing all week, and I'm *jonesing* for some waves."

kick out *v.* to leave a wave with a sharp turn up its face and over to the back of the wave.

killer *adj.* great; a degree below epic. "Man, the surf was *killer* this morning. Also describes girls, situations.

kook *n.* a surfer of limited ability who nonetheless overestimates his skill and knowledge of the surfing world.

mackin' *v.* when the ocean is producing large waves, reminiscent of Mack trucks.

monkey show *n.* a bad scene; a mess. "With all those kooks in the water, it's a total *monkey show.*"

mushy *adj.* shapeless, blown-out, slow, boring; refers to waves. Rel. **mushburger** *n.* a slow, shapeless wave.

nailed *adj.* hit hard by the falling lip of a wave in a wipe-out.

over the falls *adv.* caught in the water that is falling from the lip of a wave to the bottom. "Did you see Chris get sucked *over the falls?*"

pearl *v.* when the nose of a board digs into the water, throwing the rider off head-first, as if diving for pearls.

plank *n.* a big, unwieldy surfboard, especially the type of mammoth redwood board used before the 1950s.

plugged *adj.* crowded with other surfers. "Rincon was really *plugged* on Saturday."

punch through *v.* to push the board and oneself through the back of a breaking wave.

quiver *n.* one's arsenal of surfboards.

R&D *n.* research and development; i.e., searching for new surfing spots. "We're doing some *R&D* in Mexico next month."

rip *v.* to surf aggressively, a term of admiration. "Corky really *rips.*" Syn. **torque:** "He fully *torqued* out that wave."

set *n.* a sequence of bigger-than-usual waves.

snake *v.* to take a wave away from someone else by dropping in on it in front of him. "*Snaking* on this beach may lead to fights."

sponger *n.* a body boarder.

stick *n.* a surfboard. "Check out my new *stick.*"

stoked *adj.* happy, up, energized, exhilarated. Refers to surfing and by extension to all kinds of situations. "I'm *stoked* that I didn't have to sit in traffic."

stylish *adj.* very cool. "That was a way *stylish* turn." Rel. **stylin':** to be doing very well. "You were *stylin'* out there, dude."

surf god *n.* a great surfer. "Kelly Slater is a *surf god.*"

Team Satan *n.* evil corporate yuppies. "We were in town today, and it was full of *Team Satan.*"

tube *n.* a wave shaped like a tunnel, through which a crouching surfer can ride. Syn. **pipe.**

veg *v.* pronounced "vej." To chill out, do nothing.

way *adj.* very. "The waves were *way* good." Syn. **so.** "The surf was happening at the pier this morning" translates as "The surf was *so* happening. . . ."

wipe out *v.* to take a messy fall. Rel. **blasted, drilled, lunched.**

worked *adj.*   held under the waves and churned in the water. "I got nailed and then *worked.*" Syn. **prosecuted:** "Terry really got *prosecuted* out there."

zip-locked *adj.*   trapped inside a tube as it collapses.

LIFEGUARDS

banana hammock *n.*   a man's bikini-type swimsuit.

blitz *n.*   when a number of swimmers need rescuing at once. "With this riptide, we can expect a *blitz.*"

buff *adj.*   in great shape. Also, **buffed.** Rel. **buffasaurus:** a fit, muscular guy.

camels *n.*   wooden objects in the ocean, such as logs or timber.

can *n.*   the sausage-shaped, air-filled float that lifeguards use to aid people in trouble. Rel. **can flip:** the stunt of spinning the can through a couple of revolutions and catching it, mainly to impress girls.

drop zone *n.*   the perilous area where a wave breaks.

dumped *adj.*   knocked down by the surf. "Check that older woman who got *dumped.* She okay?"

fluff and buff *v.*   to shave, shower, shampoo, and otherwise groom oneself.

inside *adj.*   inside the surf line, close to shore. "Stan, make sure those little kids stay *inside.*" Ant. **outside:** past the surf line.

juice head *n.*   an obsessive body builder, probably a user of steroids (juice).

sinker *n.*   a swimmer going down. Rel. **potential:** someone to watch, a swimmer who might be in trouble. "Looks like a *potential* out by the jetty."

soup *n.*   the foamy water left after a wave breaks.

sun spot *n.* a sun glare on the water that makes it difficult to see swimmers in an area.

towelside manner *n.* a lifeguard's style and rapport with beachgoers, particularly of the opposite sex.

tumble dry *v.* to be churned by the force of a large wave after it has broken; usually embarrassing to a lifeguard. "Ha ha! Did you see Shawn get *tumble dried?*"

Victory at Sea *n.* choppy conditions, too rough for swimming.

watching the water *v.* lifeguarding.

SKATEBOARDERS

clean *adj.* stylish and confident.

deck *n.* the wooden part of a skateboard; commonly seven plies of maple, but can be plastic, aluminum, etc. Also, a skateboard.

dope *adj.* nice.

gear *n.* clothes. "Hey, man—dope *gear!*"

GQ *adj.* describes nice, pricey clothes. Rel. **Lo'ed out:** outfitted in Polo or other good clothes.

grinding *v.* jumping onto a curb and sliding along it on your trucks.

grip tape *n.* an adhesive, sandpaper-like material stuck to the deck to improve footing. "I put electric yellow *grip tape* on my blue board."

grommet *n.* a little kid who isn't a good skater but is obsessed with stickers and other skateboard-related items.

krew *n.* a bunch of people a skateboarder hangs out with.

lame *adj.* terrible, wimpy.

meeting Mr. Wilson *v.*   falling because of being stiff legged. Now an old-fashioned term. "I shoulda been looser when I tried that McTwist, but I ended up *meeting Mr. Wilson.*"

ollie *n.*   a jump in which the deck remains against the skateboarder's feet without his holding it. The most basic trick in skateboarding. Accomplished by kicking the tail down and popping the board into the air. Also, *v.*   "I love to *ollie* over garbage cans."

phat *adj.*   huge, insanely large.

poser *n.*   someone who doesn't skate but tries to look like he or she does, especially by wearing skate clothes, carrying a board around in the mall, and so on. Sometimes spelled "poseur."

rad *adj.*   good, cool. Not short for "radical."

shove-it *n.*   a trick in which the board flips along a vertical axis. Other tricks include the heelflip and the kickflip.

sick *adj.*   when someone does a really difficult and usually dangerous trick.

slam *n.*   a fall. "Skate videos often include a segment devoted to particularly horrifying *slams.*" Syns. **beef, biff** (both now slightly archaic).

straight edge *adj.*   refers to people who don't do drugs.

trucks *n.*   metal mounts for the wheels, under the deck.

SNOWBOARDERS

air it out *v.*   to make a jump as fast and high as possible.

barney *v.*   to approach a jump too slowly and stop at the top, flattening it and creating a traffic jam while you slowly ride down the other side. "Snowboarders hate it when the skiers *barney* all the jumps."

betty *n.*   a desirable female. Also, a snowboard groupie.

bomb *v.* to speed without stopping.

bonk *v.* to strike something with the nose or tail of your board as you jump over it. "The management at Aspen discourages boarders from *bonking* trash cans and picnic tables." Syns. **poke, shaboink.**

bulletproof *adj.* impenetrably icy. "That run is *bulletproof* today."

butt plant *n.* to fall hard in the snow and land on your rear end. Ant. *face plant.*

Canadian bacon *n.* grabbing the board between your legs during a jump.

carving *v.* making good, smooth turns.

chowder *n.* deep, newly fallen snow with a thick consistency.

cut *adj.* out of style, passé. "That trick is really *cut.*"

egg beater *n.* a dramatic crash in which plenty of snow is churned up.

fakie *adj.* riding backward, with the tail of the board forward. "Jimmy hit a bump, got good air, and landed *fakie.*"

freshies *n.* the first tracks in new powder.

gaper *n.* a person lacking skill or coordination, especially a skier. "I was just landing when this *gaper* dive-bombed me from the trees and hit me in the head with his ski pole."

get air *v.* to leave the ground.

get schooled *v.* to wipe out.

grommet *n.* a young rookie boarder.

half-pipe *n.* a U-shaped launching pad carved out of the snow by a machine called a Pipe Dragon.

hit *n.* a hollow in the snow that makes a good launching ramp. Rel. **taking a hit** *v.* taking a jump.

hospital air *n.* lots of air time on a risky jump. Syn. **sick air.**

jib *v.* to ride over something other than snow, such as stumps or trash cans.

Kodak courage *n.* when the sudden appearance of a camera or a cute member of the opposite sex prompts an act of risky bravery, such as jumping off a cliff.

launch *v.* to jump. Syn. **spank.** "Erin *spanked* off the groove around the lift line and got a little air."

pat the dog *v.* to stoop down and touch the snow with your hand.

phat *adj.* baggy or loose, referring to clothes. Also, cool, good, hip.

posers *n.* boarders who have the latest clothes, haircut, equipment, and attitude, but much less riding ability than style quotient. Syn. **pimps.**

posse *n.* a group of boarders who ride together. Syn. **pack.**

pow *n.* snow.

ride *v.* to ride a snowboard. "Snowboard" is never used as a verb.

riding trees *v.* boarding through dense trees, usually off-trail; best in deep powder. Rel. **wompin':** riding trees at high speed.

rolling down the window *v.* when someone goes for air or rides off a cliff, then starts losing balance so that his arms rotate in large backward circles.

ruler *n.* a boarder with great riding skills, usually the best on the hill.

session *n.* a period of time spent snowboarding.

shiftie *n.* a maneuver with the board twisted ninety degrees one way and the body twisted ninety degrees the opposite way.

shredder *n.* a now outmoded term for a snowboarder; still used by the media but not in the snowboard culture.

sitting on the toilet *adj.*   describes a rider who thinks he is carving well, but is actually hanging his rear end out.

slam *v.*   to fall or crash. Syn. **pack.** Rel. **mackeral slap:** to crash very hard.

slurpee *n.*   slushy conditions. Syn. **oatmeal.**

snake the line *v.*   to cut in front of someone in the lift line or on the approach to a hit.

starfish *v.*   to take a high-speed fall, cartwheeling down a hill with all limbs extended.

stick *n.*   a snowboard. Syns. **deck, plank, ride, snow toy.**

stick it *v.*   to pull off a trick.

switchstance *adj.*   trailing the foot you normally lead with. "This season I learned *switchstance* frontside 360's." Syn. **switch.**

wanker two-planker *n.*   a skier as seen by a boarder, if they aren't the best of friends. Syns. **dual planker, two-plank wank.**

yard sale *n.*   a big crash with a skier, whose clothes and skis end up strewn on the hill as if laid out for a garage sale.

INLINE SKATERS

bacon-in-the-pan *n.*   when a skater wipes out badly on a ramp and slides back down to the bottom.

bashing *v.*   skating down a flight of stairs. This can be done forward, backward, even sideways. Syn. **bumping.**

black snake *n.*   a tar line on the street. Rel. **black ice:** a street that was recently paved and is smooth.

chunk *v.*   to damage your wheels so they have pits or missing pieces. "I *chunked* my tires."

fakie *adj.*   on launch ramps, refers to tricks that start backward. In a half-pipe, refers to tricks in which the rider comes back down backward, or in which he goes up backward and comes down facing forward. One such example is the fakie 360.

grinding *v.*   jumping onto a curb and sliding along it on your skates.

home run *n.*   a fall while grinding, when both feet slip out from under the skater, as if he were sliding into home plate.

inline skating *v.*   the preferred term for Rollerblading.

layed out *adj.*   a prefix for tricks executed with the body fully extended. "A *layed out* backflip is not recommended!"

McTwist *n.*   a ramp trick in which a skater turns upside-down, does a 540, and lands back on the ramp.

180 *n.*   half a revolution during a jump; i.e., 180 degrees. Rel. **360, 540, 720, 900.**

rail slide *n.*   sliding on your skates down a handrail.

rewind *n.*   a 180 performed off a handrail while sliding and rolling backward.

road rash *n.*   any wound due to unintentional momentum reduction through contact with pavement.

rocket air *n.*   a ramp jump made while holding on to your skates. Rel. **Japan air, method air, mute air.**

skitch *v.*   to hold on to a moving automobile and get a free ride; may be up a hill or across part of town. Short for skate-hitch. "I *skitched* a ride on a Mercedes this morning."

stall *n.*   when a skater jumps onto an object, holds the position for a few seconds, then jumps off.

Superman slide *n.*   a forward-facing slide, done on protected hands and toe wheels.

tires *n.*   skate wheels.

tweak *v.*   to fully extend or compress the body during a trick; to do a trick to the maximum. "Davey really *tweaked* that back flip."

ICE SKATERS

be chacked *v.*   to have an outstanding performance be inexplicably excluded from a TV broadcast. Named for Michael Chack, to whom this has happened repeatedly. "Kurt Browning appeared in the benefit show, but not on TV—a classic *chacking*. Some observers noted that the event was sponsored by Pepsi, and Kurt was endorsing Coke."

biff *v.*   to crash in a self-induced wipeout.

blade *v.*   to be cut with a skate blade; to cut oneself or another skater. "Michael was *bladed* during the practice drills and couldn't make the competition." Rel. **spike:** to be injured with the toepick of a skate blade.

butt-magnet *n.*   a skater whose rear end hits the ice repeatedly, as if by magnetic attraction.

doughnut-on-a-stick *n.*   a spin in which a skater bends her free leg so that it forms a horizontal circle.

flutz *n.*   a screwed-up lutz jump; it becomes a flip jump at the last moment.

flying Tweety *n.*   a flamboyantly biffed jump.

kiss 'n' cry *n.*   the area just off the ice surface where skaters go to wait for their competition marks.

Midori Ito *n.*   a jump that lands too close to the boards, resulting in a crash into the boards or camera pit. Olympic medalist and world figure skating champion Ito made such a crash during the 1991 world championships. In a playful, apologetic manner she patted the TV camera and returned to the ice to finish her routine.

Nasty Tangle *n.* the Canasta Tango, a dance performed on skates. Rel. **Clutch Waltz:** Dutch Waltz; **Hickory Showdown** or **Slippery Slowdown:** Hickory Hoedown; **Siesta Tango** or **Fiasco Tango:** Fiesta Tango.

nosebleed seats *n.* spectator seats located very high up in an arena.

Oksana *n.* someone who comes out of nowhere to win a major event on her or his first try.

playing Zamboni *v.* when a skater is falling down so much, he appears to be wiping up the ice with his body. Syns. **doing a Zamboni impersonation, doing a human Zamboni.**

pop *n.* when a skater intends to spin a certain number of times during a jump, but isn't able to do all of the rotations. "One of Nancy Kerrigan's programs had more *pops* than Orville Redenbacher." Also, *v.* "Damn, she *popped* the lutz!" Double and triple axels usually pop to singles.

pretzel people *n.* skaters with unusual flexibility, such as Natalia Mishke-tuneok.

Thomas *n.* a spinning butt-fall. Coined by humorist Dave Barry. Comes in both single and double varieties.

tollering around *v.* flouncing around on the ice with greatly exaggerated dramatics such as waving one's arms, running across the ice, flinging one-self down, making overwrought facial expressions. Named for its primary exponent, Toller Cranston.

waxel *n.* an axel that takes off from the back or side of the blade instead of the toe pick; it almost always results in a major crash landing.

woetzel *n.* an unintentional face-dive onto the ice. Also, a chin scar resulting from such a fall. Named after Mandy Woetzel, a German pairs skater, who tripped during the long program at the Lillehammer Olympics, and injured her chin. Also, *v.* to take such a fall.

wylie *n.* coming through with the performance of a lifetime at the best possible moment. From the silver-medal winning performance of Paul Wylie at the Albertville Olympics. Also, *v.* Rel. **manley:** a wylie when accomplished by a female; refers to Elizabeth Manley's performance at the Calgary Olympics.

SKIERS

aggro *n.* the aggressive attitude needed for skiing difficult terrain. "If you're going up on Baldy, you'd better get *aggro.*"

air mailed *adj.* refers to an unintended jump. "I got in the backseat and got *air mailed* off a mogul."

back seat *adj.* when a skier is off balance to the rear.

biff *n.* a self-induced wipeout. Also, *v.* "Talk about embarrassing! I *biffed* right in front of everybody on the deck at the restaurant."

boards *n.* skis. Syns. **slats, sticks.**

boilerplate *n.* a hard patch of ice or snow.

bulletproof *adj.* very hard, referring to snow or ice.

bump lunch *n.* a fall among moguls.

champagne *n.* extra fluffy, powdery snow. Syn. **cold smoke.**

coner *n.* a skier who has all the most expensive clothes and equipment, but skis horribly. "Did you see that *coner* do a face plant?"

corduroy *n.* groomed snow. From the ribbed pattern produced by the grooming machine.

corn *n.* snow that has thawed and refrozen for several cycles, forming kernel-sized granules that create a smooth, firm ski surface.

crash and burn *n.* a major crash. Rel. **crash and burn with no survivors:** an even worse crash.

crud *n.* hard crust over softer snow, caused when the top layer of slush refreezes. Also, heavy mush and consolidated snow, with a very irregular surface.

Daffy *n.* an aerial maneuver with one ski in front of the skier and one behind, so it looks as if he is walking in mid-air, like a cartoon character.

death cookies *n.* fast-moving clumps of snow or ice broken loose by other skiers. Also, pucks of hard snow spit out by grooming machines. Syn. **gamooties.**

digger *n.* a fall.

dust on crust *n.* light snow on top of frozen snow.

face plant *n.* a face-first crash into the snow. Syn. **eggplant.** "Man, did I take an *eggplant.*"

face shot *n.* fresh powder spraying up in a skier's face, said to produce a euphoric feeling. "That *face shot* was such a rush! The powder was flying everywhere."

fat air *n.* a big jump. Syn. **big air.**

French fries *n.* parallel skiing, as explained in children's ski school classes.

gaper *n.* a novice skier who watches a fast skier fly by. Also, a racer's term for a non-racer. May derive from "gp," short for general public, a term used by mountain management to describe the average skier. "A true *gaper* is easily recognized because he or she is wearing blue jeans, using rental skis, and probably smoking a cigarette in the lift line."

gorby *n.* short for "goof on rental boards."

iron cross *n.* an aerial maneuver made with ski tips up and crossed.

Lange bang *n.* a sore shin caused by skiing in overlap boots. Named for the Lange company, which made this kind of boot.

mashed potatoes *n.* heavy, wet snow.

Maytag *v.* to fall head over heels. Named after the tumble clothes dryer. Syn. **endo:** contraction of "end over end."

moonie *n.* an intentional leap into deep powder with one's skis up in the air and rear end down.

nose pickers *n.* inward curving tips for slalom racing skis, designed to help avoid snagging a gate. "I hooked a gate between my legs once, so I put on *nose pickers.*"

pinhead *n.* a cross-country skier. From the three-pin bindings on cross-country skis.

pizza pie *n.* the wedge or snowplow style, as explained in children's ski school classes.

poaching *v.* skiing a closed run or an out-of-bounds area.

sardine can *n.* a tram car.

Scud *n.* a fast-moving skier who has lost control. "That *Scud* went off the ridge and started washing the windows."

shredders *n.* snowboarders. Syns. **knuckle-draggers, knuckle-draggers on lunch trays, riders.**

Sierra cement *n.* heavy, deep, wet snow in California's Sierra Nevada; with the consistency of wet concrete, it can cause painful falls. Other regional terms include Aspen asphalt, Cascade concrete, and Portland pavement.

touron *n.* definitely not a local. Compounded from "tourist" and "moron."

Volkswagens *n.* moguls, or bumps in the snow. Gradually built up by many skiers turning in the same place, they resemble VW Bugs in size and shape. Syn. **bumps.**

walking out *v.* what one does when a ski binding releases unexpectedly during hard skiing.

washing the windows *v.* rotating one's arms in circles as a result of being off balance in midair.

windshield wiper turns *n.*   turns in which the tails of the skis remain in the same position while the fronts sweep across the snow like wipers. "If ultra-steep conditions require *windshield wiper turns,* you might pause for further consideration and for your life to pass before your eyes."

yard sale *n.*   a major crash in which poles, skis, and goggles end up scattered across the slopes, as if for sale. "As we rode the lift and spotted a *yard sale,* it was only polite to shout offers: 'I'll give you five dollars for the hat!' "

Zorros *n.*   the pattern that learners leave in untracked powder, in contrast to the pretty S-turns made by experienced powder skiers.

Ski Instructors

base area stone grinder *n.*   a student who can't stop and, therefore, skis right into the parking lot.

brain buckets *n.*   protective helmets for children in ski classes.

flounder *n.*   a student so uncoordinated that merely getting on the chairlift poses a serious challenge.

gumby *n.*   a beginning skier who totally lacks muscle tone.

hangers *n.*   people on the ski lift who accidentally drop their skis.

Oral Roberts *n.*   a class member who wails noisily about being hurt, but seems fine a moment later.

poodle *n.*   a ski instructor dressed in a fancy outfit.

SPORE *n.*   Spastic/Stupid Person On Rental Equipment.

MOUNTAIN CLIMBERS

beta *n.*   insider or advance information about a climb; it usually has to do with sequences or proper gear, but can be applied to almost anything. "What's the *beta* on that new Denny's in town? Is it all-you-can-eat?"

betty *n.* a cute female climber. Ant. **bertha:** a less than attractive girl.

bombproof *adj.* when a protective anchor is solid and reliable.

bongle *n.* a traditional climber who avoids gear that damages rock. Derived from the sound his gear makes when he walks.

brain bucket *n.* a protective helmet.

bucket *n.* a large handhold. Syn. **jug.** Rel. **jugfest:** a climb full of large handholds.

buildering *v.* climbing up buildings. Derived from bouldering, or climbing boulders without using ropes.

bumblie *n.* a beginning climber. Syn. **whirlie.**

catch a ride *v.* to meet climbers who have a safety rope set up on top of the climb, and use their rope. "Say, can I *catch a ride?*"

chickenhead *n.* a protrusion of rock that juts out like the head of a chicken. With a narrow neck and wide knob, it makes a good handhold or place to set a rope.

choss *n.* bad rock.

crater *v.* to fall and hit the ground, whether or not the climber makes a hole on impact. "Bill really *cratered* on that one. See, that's his leg over in the bushes." Syns. **become talus food, deck.**

crimper *n.* a small handhold with just enough room for one's fingertips.

crux *n.* the most difficult part of a climb.

Darwin in action *exp.* used when an accident was caused by gross stupidity. "Well, he's dead, but it was *Darwin in action.*"

discos *n.* men who follow the Lycra fad in sports climbing.

dogging *v.* hanging on the rope while trying to figure out the next sequence of moves, resting one's arms, or gathering oneself after a fall. Syn. **hang dogging.**

dyno *n.* a dynamic lunge for the next, often distant, hold.

Elvis *v.* to have a leg begin shaking and jerking in the manner of Elvis Presley on stage; usually a sign of fatigued muscles under tension. Syn. **sewing machine leg.**

epic *n.* any unforeseen event that is outrageously dangerous or annoying during a climb. "On El Capitan, Jack's knot came untied and he watched his rope fall a thousand feet to the meadow below. At this point, his *epic* began, a struggle that lasted for hours."

flamed *adj.* refers to forearms getting so tired they burn; caused by gripping the rock.

flapper *n.* a cut on the hand with a flat piece of skin left hanging.

flash *v.* to climb a route for the first time, without falling but with beta.

gardening *n.* the removal of loose plants and rocks to clear a path. "I've done all kinds of *gardening,* from pulling out tufts of grass to bringing in a chainsaw."

goby *n.* a skin abrasion on the back of the hand, caused by using cracks to climb. Also, any wound to the hand. "After a day of pulling myself up Double X, I've got serious *gobies.*"

gripped *adj.* extremely scared on a climb.

grovel *n.* a climb that is dirty, awkward, or unpleasant. "There I was, hanging on with one hand and trying to garden with the other. What a *grovel.*" Also *v.*

gumby *n.* a stupid climber.

lock *n.* a very secure hold, usually a crack in which a hand, foot, or leg can be slotted.

lockoff *v.* to use one's bent arm to hold on to the rock, while the other hand seeks the next hold. Also, *n.* "With that many *lockoffs* on tiny ledges, I got really pumped."

logging *v.* defecating. Syn. **launching a bag.**

manky *adj.* only marginally safe; bad. "I'm not climbing unless we can do better than this *manky* protection."

munge *v.* to damage in an ugly manner. "Pulling your fist out of a crack tends to *munge* your hand badly."

nut *n.* a metal wedge placed in a crack as protection.

onsight *n.* a flash with no beta.

party ledge *n.* a big ledge where climbers can rest together during a long, difficult climb.

peel *v.* to lose contact with the rock and fall off. "I'm really hung over this morning and feel like I could *peel.*"

pro *n.* short for technical protection gear, such as pitons, placed into the rock. "Hell! I can't get in any *pro* up here!"

pumped *adj.* when a climber's fingers are so overworked that his forearms swell up, like an inflating balloon. This reduces muscular strength. "Man, I was so *pumped* after the climb, I couldn't even hold a beer can."

pumpfest *n.* the climbing of several very strenuous routes.

pumping plastic *v.* climbing an indoor practice wall at a gym. Rel. **plastic master** *n.* someone who climbs on gym walls, not mountains.

rack *n.* the array of gear carried on a climb.

redpoint *v.* to lead a climb on an established route, with no falls or dogging.

rock rash *n.* general abrasion wounds.

run out *adj.* when a climber is a long way from his protection, perhaps risking a fall.

screamer *n.* a very long fall. Syn. **air time.** "Quentin scored some serious *air time* at Yosemite."

shaky legs *n.* a physical reaction due to fear. "I had such a case of the *shaky legs,* it took me fifteen minutes to get going again."

slime *v.* to have a hand or foot slip from a hold, usually causing a fall. "After I *slimed* off the crimper, I ended up with a flapper on my index finger."

smear *n.* a small friction hold; usually a foothold.

sphincter factor *n.* a subjective fear index used to rate climbing routes, based on the tightening of this muscle. One climber explains: "In some situations the sphincter actually shrinks so much as to become a black hole, and a dense gravity field begins pulling in nearby articles of clothing. You may also encounter the related 'supernova,' a sudden explosion of gaseous and sometimes solid matter."

strobe *v.* to climb rapidly, so that one's movements appear to be images caught in a flashing strobe light. "Jimmy *strobed* the summit this morning."

trundle *v.* to purposely roll a dangerous rock off a cliff. "That last rock on Meat Sandwich was just supported by dirt. We knew it would come loose if you climbed on it, so we *trundled* it."

UXB *n.* UneXploded Bomb. A large, loose rock that could easily be dislodged and fall.

way honed *adj.* describes a climber in perfect physical shape.

whipper *n.* a long fall on a rope. "I took a gnarly *whipper* on that last section."

wired *adj.* when a climber knows by heart the moves for climbing a route.

yo-yo *v.* to climb, then lower, then climb again, until a higher position is successfully reached.

zipper *v.* to sequentially rip out many pieces of protection during a fall.

MOUNTAIN BIKE RIDERS

air *n.* the open space between the ground and a bike's tires. "I got big *air* on that last jump."

auger *v.* to take samples of the local geology involuntarily, usually with one's face.

bacon *n.* a scab.

bail *v.* to jump off one's bike in order to avoid an imminent crash.

barney *n.* a novice rider. Syn. **squid.** "Stay away from those guys—they're *squids.*"

betty *n.* a female rider.

biff *n.* a crash. Syns. **involuntary dismount, stack, wipeout.** Also, *v.* "I *biffed* it into a tree." Rel. **spew:** to do a long, drawn-out biff. "I lost my traction on the gravel and *spewed* for twenty feet."

boing-boing *n.* a bike with full front and rear suspension.

bolt-on *n.* a woman with breast implants. From the term for aftermarket bike parts that are bolted on.

bonk *v.* to run out of energy on a ride, as though hitting a wall. "I *bonked* so early it was embarrassing."

bring home a Christmas tree *v.* to ride or crash through dense bushes, so leaves and branches hang from the rider's bike and helmet. Syn. **prune.**

bunny hop *n.* a jump in which both wheels leave the ground. "A *bunny hop* is useful for clearing obstructions like gullies, logs, hikers. . . ."

can-can *n.* a jump during which a rider throws one leg forward over the top tube to the other side of the bike, and then returns it to the pedal before landing. It resembles a can-can dance step.

carve *v.* to speed around turns. "Man, I really *carved* on that fire road."

cashed *adj.* to be too tired to ride any farther.

chain ring tattoo *n.* a scar that resembles a dotted line, caused by gouging one's shin on the chain ring.

chainsuck *n.*   when the bike chain jams between the frame and the chain rings.

clean *v.*   to negotiate a trail successfully without crashing. "I *cleaned* that last section."

corndog *v.*   to become covered in silt, usually after a fall.

crotch-testing *n.*   a sudden impact between a male rider's private parts and something hard and pointy, such as a handlebar stem or seat.

curb grind *n.*   the expensive erasure of low-hanging parts of a bike on a curb or rock.

dab *v.*   to put a foot down in order to catch one's balance on a difficult section of trail. "I made it without crashing, but I had to *dab* twice."

death cookies *n.*   fist-sized rocks that knock the bike in every direction.

death march *n.*   a ride that becomes a test of your endurance. "The bridge was out, so I had to go all the way back. My easy ride turned into a Bataan *death march.*"

dialed in *adj.*   when a bike is set up perfectly and everything works just right.

drillium *n.*   any part with holes drilled in it to make it lighter.

endo *adj.*   when a rider goes flying unexpectedly over the handlebars. Short for "end over end." "I hit that rock and went *endo* like nobody's business." Syn. **superman.** Also, intentionally applying the front brake and allowing the back wheel to come off the ground in a front wheelie; this is the basis for many tricks.

face plant *n.*   hitting the ground face first. "Joe hit a tree root and did a spectacular *face plant.*" Syns. **digger, soil sample, spring planting.**

first blood *n.*   credit given to the first rider in a group who crashes and starts bleeding as a result.

foot fault *n.*   when a rider can't disengage his cleats from the pedals and falls over. "A *foot fault* is worst when performed in front of members of the opposite sex, especially after doing something cool first." Rel. **horizontal track stand:** a foot fault at a stop sign.

fred *n.*   someone who spends lots of money on his bike and clothes, but can't ride. "What a *fred*—too much Lycra and titanium and not enough skill." Syn. **poser.**

giblets *n.*   all the colorful parts and pieces that can be added or changed out on a bike.

gonzo *adj.*   treacherous, extreme. "That vertical drop was sheer *gonzo.*"

granny gear *n.*   a bike's lowest gear, which only a grandmother would need to use. Designed for steep climbing, it is extremely easy to use on flat ground.

gravity check *n.*   a fall.

grunt *n.*   a very hard climb, requiring use of the granny gear.

gutter bunny *n.*   a bicycle commuter.

hammer *v.*   to ride fast and hard. "I *hammered* that ride up Ajax Mountain." Rel. **hammered** *adj.*   tired, exhausted. "I would have gone faster, but I'm too *hammered.*"

HOHA *n.*   Hateful Old Hikers Association. "*HOHA* members hate mountain bikers with a fervor exceeding that of rabid wolverines."

kack *n.*   an injury to the shin.

male blindness *n.*   results from watching a female ride over rough terrain and staring at her jiggling anatomy until the male viewer becomes too dizzy to see straight on his turn to ride.

mantrap *n.*   a hole covered with leaves, resembling solid earth. "That *mantrap* was very effective at eating my front wheel."

mo *n.*   momentum. "If you don't get in gear at the bottom of that hill, you'll lose your *mo.*"

mojo *n.*   a charm or icon worn by a biker or attached to the bike.

mud diving *n.*   what happens when a bike slows abruptly in mud, and the rider is thrown into wet goop.

nard gard *n.*   an attachment to the stem that helps prevent injury to male riders.

newbie *n.*   a person new to mountain biking. "He's a great racer but a technical *newbie.*"

over-the-bar blood donor *n.*   a rider injured while doing an endo.

pogo *v.*   to bounce on a full-suspension bike like a pogo stick. Also, when a full-suspension bike bounces annoyingly and uncontrollably.

rag dolly *v.*   to be tossed like a cartwheeling Raggedy Ann doll after a crash. "Did you see me *rag dolly* back there? I'm lucky to be walking."

retro-grouch *n.*   a rider who disdains new, high-tech equipment.

'rhoid buffing *n.*   touching the rear wheel with one's rear end while going down a steep hill.

roadie *n.*   a pejorative term for a rider who sticks to paved surfaces. "A *roadie* is a lower life form."

road rash *n.*   large abrasions from a crash, particularly on cement.

rocket fuel *n.*   the mandatory pre-ride coffee.

rookie mark *n.*   chain grease on a rider's pant leg. "Give that newbie extra points for his *rookie mark.*"

roost *v.*   to come to a sudden, complete stop. "Whoa! Did you see Mike *roost* on that log?"

singletrack *n.*   a trail wide enough for one bike. Rel. **doubletrack:** a rutted road made by vehicles, creating two parallel singletracks.

skid lid *n.*   a helmet.

sky *v.*   to jump extremely high.

snake bite *n.*   inner tube damage caused when a wheel hits something so hard that the rim slices two holes in the rubber.

snowmine *n.*   an object hidden under snow on the trail. "Watch out for *snowmines*—rocks, logs, hibernating bears."

steed *n.*   one's bike.

strokin' *v.*   to be making an all-out climb, during which blood pressure and heart rate rise to critical levels. "Man, I was *strokin'* on that last hill!"

taco *v.*   to bend a wheel into the shape of a taco shell during a crash. "When I smashed into the picnic table, I *taco'd* my wheel."

tea party *n.*   when a group of riders stops and chats, and nobody seems to care about riding on.

technical *adj.*   describes a trail section difficult to negotiate because of rocks, tree roots, steep drops, and turns.

techno-weenie *n.*   a rider obsessed with components. Rel. **weight weenie:** one obsessed with reducing the bike's weight. "Alan's such a *weight weenie,* he cares more about how many milligrams he can lose than about being a better rider."

three-hour tour *n.*   a ride that looks like a piece of cake at the outset but turns out to be a death march. From the theme song to *Gilligan's Island.*

trail swag *n.*   equipment or accessories dropped by other bikers and found on the trail.

tricked out *adj.*   when a bike has the latest and hottest components.

tweaked *adj.*   when a trick is done to an extreme degree. "The more you twist the handlebars on that jump, the more *tweaked* it is." Also, *v.*   to injure oneself or the bike slightly in a crash. "I *tweaked* my wrist when I fell."

unobtanium *n.*   a mythical metal used in expensive, high-tech bike parts. A play on "unobtainable" and "titanium."

vegetable tunnel *n.*   a heavily overgrown singletrack trail.

wang chung *n.* what can happen to a male rider whose bike stem doesn't have a nard gard.

washboard *n.* small undulations of the soil that create a rough ride.

wild pigs *n.* poorly adjusted brake pads that squeal.

wonky *adj.* not functioning properly. "I bailed, and now my wheel is all *wonky.*"

yard sale *n.* a horrendous crash that leaves a biker's gear—water bottle, pump, tool bag—scattered as if on display for sale.

the zone *n.* a mystical state of mind wherein a rider doesn't need to think, but simply does everything perfectly.

CAVERS

air rappel *n.* an accidental fall down a pit.

bang *n.* explosives. Syns. **chemical persuasion, Instant Cave, rock solvent.**

birth canal *n.* a cave passage reminiscent of this area of the female anatomy.

BNC *n.* Big-Name Caver. Usually complimentary, but sometimes connotes self-styled.

booty *n.* a virgin cave passage.

bottomed *adj.* having reached the lowest point of a vertical cave.

brain bucket *n.* helmet.

carbide *n.* a carbon compound that, when mixed with water, generates acetylene; used for cavers' lamps. Syn. **stink.** Rel. **stinkies:** carbide lamps.

carbide assist *n.* when you move too close to a slow caver ahead of you in a crawlway, and end up burning his rear end with the flaming carbide lamp on your helmet.

carbide pig *n.* a length of automobile inner tube, knotted and used for carrying carbide in caves.

cardboard caver *n.* a caver who turns back at the first sign of water; a joking reference, since cardboard falls apart when wet.

ceiling burner *n.* a belt-generator carbide lamp with a vertical flame.

chest compressor *n.* a crawl that cannot be negotiated by someone without exhaling.

crap out *v.* when a passage ends.

cave burritos *n.* containers of fecal waste, normally tripled-bagged in Ziplocs and carried out in one's pack.

dangle *n.* a strap used to hang packs below cavers' feet and out of the way while they rappel.

eardip *n.* a water passage that becomes so low-ceilinged a caver must drag one ear on the ceiling, while the other dips below the water.

e-caver *n.* one who spends more time caving electronically (via e-mail and the Internet caving newsgroup) than actually going underground. Syn. **keyboard caver.**

enduro caver *n.* one who often goes on challenging and gruelling cave trips.

entrance fever *n.* when a caver is very anxious to get out of a cave. "After the last squeeze, I could see *entrance fever* in Mark's eyes."

flail *v.* to show poor climbing technique. "I saw this guy try to get over a rock lip, and he was *flailing* all over the place!"

GNURDS *n.* Goodies Nibbled Under Really Desperate Situations. Example: chocolate chips that must be separated from pocket lint.

gorp *n.* good ol' raisins and peanuts. A popular energy food.

grimbly *adj.* greasy.

grunt *n.* a challenging and rugged caving trip requiring extra effort.

hog *n.* a long coil of rope carried through a cave.

knobbly dog *n.* a half-ladder consisting of a single length of wire threaded with rungs.

lipping *v.* puckering one's lips to breathe in an extremely shallow air space between water and the rock ceiling. Syn. **MASUing,** from the acronym for Minimal Air Space Utilization.

little black rocks to make fire *n.* calcium carbide.

mundane *n.* a non-caver.

nerd gate *n.* a natural but surmountable barrier in a cave passage, which prevents wimps from going any farther.

route *v.* to head toward the way out. "We were exhausted, so we *routed* for the entrance."

scoop *v.* to discover a virgin cave or passage.

sherp *v.* to carry, as if one were a Sherpa. "We *sherped* eighty pounds of rope up to the pit."

squeeze *n.* a tight spot or constriction. Also, a speleobabe.

speleobabe *n.* a pretty female caver.

speleobopper *n.* a teenybopper in a cave. Also, a person who participates only in sport caving.

speleorectal ambiguity *adj.* doesn't know his ass from a hole in the ground.

sporting *adj.* a term to lend a positive image to a challenging, wet, muddy, difficult cave. "It's a *sporting* cave!"

virtual caver *n.* one who talks about caving more than he goes underground. Syn. **armchair caver.**

winker *n.* a fray in a caving rope that exposes the core.

winse *n.*   a vertical shaft inside a mine. It is located between levels and does not connect directly with the surface.

wuffo *n.*   a non-caver, who asks, *"Wuffo* you go in them caves?"* Borrowed from skydiving terminology.

SKYDIVERS

air bath *n.*   a bad skydive. Also, a skydive done simply to wake up and get one's knees in the breeze. Rel. **hangover cure:** an early morning skydive after a night of partying.

bag lock *n.*   a malfunction in which the parachute is never extracted from the deployment bag.

BASE jumps *n.*   acronym for jumps from Buildings, Antennas, Spans (bridges), or Earth (cliffs).

beer line *n.*   the line on the ground beyond which a jumper is forbidden to land. Violators are fined a case of beer.

biff *v.*   to land hard, trip, or otherwise make a clumsy arrival on terra firma. Syn. **cream in.**

blot *n.*   a large formation of skydivers; there are usually specific slot assignments for jumpers but no definite pattern. Syns. **big way, mega-way.**

bomb *v.*   to jump out of the airplane without stopping at the door to assume a stable body position.

boogie *n.*   a gathering of skydivers, usually for a weekend of skydiving, parties, competitions, and so forth.

bounce *v.*   to hit the ground at high speed due to lack of a deceleration device such as a parachute. Almost always lethal. A person hitting the ground at 120 miles per hour bounces some ten feet in the air. Syns. **auger in, burn in, frappe, go in, smoke in.** Also, *n.*   "Hey, did you hear they had a *bounce* in Florida? The funeral is tomorrow."

brainlock *n.* a skydiver's paralyzed failure to react, usually owing to a high-stress situation such as a malfunction. Also, going blank during a skydive; usually caused by not paying attention during the dirt dive.

breach *n.* a student who goes up in the plane, but won't jump out.

burble *n.* a low-pressure area of dead air that forms just above a jumper in freefall.

chop *v.* to cut away one's main parachute. "I had to *chop* it because it was malfunctioning." Also, what you do to get rid of an unwanted, typically non-jumping, girlfriend or boyfriend. Syn. **cutaway** *n.*   "The last thing she heard during the *cutaway* was the sound of Velcro tearing."

chunks *n.* groups of jumpers who leave a plane while holding on to one another.

clear and pull *n.* a standard novice's task in which one first clears the airplane, then pulls the rip cord. Ant. **pull and clear:** when one overanxiously pulls the ripcord while exiting the plane.

dead spider *n.* a skydiver who ends up too far below a formation. Named for the body position he must assume—a negative arch, with extended arms and legs cupping the air—in order to slow his fall and move back up to the formation.

diaper *n.* a deployment device for round reserve chutes.

dildo *n.* a hot-dog-shaped handle for deploying the main parachute. "The other night at the restaurant Jenny forgot to lower her voice when she was talking about her *dildo*." Rel. **floating dildo:** a handle that has come loose from its attachment, making it difficult to extract and use.

dirt alert *n.* an audible altimeter worn during freefall, especially by experienced skydivers concerned about becoming so involved in the jump that they might forget about altitude. Syn. **beeper.**

dirt dive *n.* an on-the-ground rehearsal of maneuvers planned for freefall. "A *dirt dive* looks like a square dance with everyone bent over at the waist."

do cross country *v.* to maneuver far away from the drop zone and still get back before landing.

donut *n.* a type of four-way formation.

dope rope *n.* a static line used by students. It is attached to the plane and automatically initiates the deployment sequence. Rel. **dope-on-a-rope:** a static-line jumper.

dump *v.* to deploy one's main parachute.

elevator *n.* a very fast airplane that takes skydivers aloft.

Farmer McNasty *n.* the generic rural neighbor of a drop zone who harasses jumpers that accidentally land in his field.

floater *n.* a person who hangs on the outside of a moving airplane while the rest of the group lines up inside. Also, a lightweight jumper who falls slowly; often kidded because skydivers prefer rapid fall rates.

four-way *n.* four people maneuvering together in freefall. Other combinations: eight-way, twenty-way, etc. The current world record is a 222-way.

frappe hat *n.* a leather helmet. "A *frappe hat* offers little real protection."

fruit loop *n.* a stunt in which one skydiver performs a backward loop while holding on to another jumper, who is thereby flipped through the sky.

funnel *n.* a formation that collapses when jumpers fall into the burble above another skydiver and are rapidly accelerated downward, toward the lower jumper. "Sometimes a chain reaction occurs, in which a skydiver moving below a large formation can flush several dozen other jumpers down the *funnel.*"

grab the grass *v.* what a skydiver does if the parachute fails. According to a somewhat grim joke, grabbing the grass prevents you from "bouncing."

homesick bowling ball *n.* a skydiver who falls rapidly.

hop 'n' pop *n.* a jump in which a skydiver hops out of the plane and quickly pops open his or her parachute.

horny gorilla *n.* a skydive in which three or more people hold hands, swing their legs into the middle of the circle and lock them, and complete the dive on their backs, perhaps while beating their chests. "A *horny gorilla* can move at two hundred miles an hour." Rel. **cup and saucer:** a horny gorilla with eight people.

humming it *v.* approaching very low to the ground in freefall before opening the parachute.

industrial haze *n.* bears a strong resemblance to clouds. "Skydivers never fall through clouds, since this is illegal, but do occasionally pass through pockets of *industrial haze.*"

kiss pass *n.* a smooch during freefall.

logbook *n.* the record book of one's skydives.

lurking *v.* trying to get a place on a good skydive by hanging around and hoping the organizer will find a slot for you. Also, hanging around a member of the opposite sex with hopes of success. "Pete was *lurking* that new blonde."

Mae West *n.* a malfunction of a round parachute that results from a line going over the top of the canopy, creating two round segments that resemble a giant brassiere. Named for busty movie star Mae West.

Mr. Bill *n.* a two-person skydive in which one (Sluggo) hangs on to the other (Mr. Bill) as the latter deploys his chute. The two jumpers fly together under one canopy for a while, before Sluggo lets go and falls away. ("Oh no! Mr. Billllll. . . .")

Never-Never Land *n.* a designated part of a drop zone that a jumper never, never wants to land in.

peas *n.* small rocks or pea gravel, spread thickly over a landing target to help absorb the impact of landing.

people processor *n.* an airplane propeller.

POPS *n.* Parachutists over Phorty.

pud *n.* the deployment handle of a pilot chute, similar to a ripcord. Syn. **hacky,** as in the Hacky Sack toy.

rag *n.* a weathered and much used parachute; generally an affectionate term. "She's an old *rag,* but I love her anyway."

rodeo *n.* when one freefalling skydiver flies into another's burble, causing the two to collide and fall low in the formation; this looks like a cowboy jumping on a calf. "A *rodeo* formation really smokes, since the two jumpers have double the weight with no increase in air resistance. Cool!"

roman candle *n.* a malfunction in which a parachute is deployed and trails in the air, but doesn't open.

skygod *n.* a complimentary term for a very experienced skydiver who knows it all. "He doesn't act like a *skygod;* he jumps with beginners, too." Also, a skydiver who thinks he knows it all or acts conceited; meant pejoratively. "That *skygod's* logbook is thick, all right—thicker than any book he's ever read."

sky slug *n.* a big, slow, low-performance canopy. Syn. **truck.** Ant. **pocket rocket:** a fast canopy.

sniveler *n.* a parachute that takes a long time to open.

snoot *n.* any female skydiver.

snot whip *n.* what builds up on the goggles of a person who jumps with a head cold.

speed of snot *n.* the speed beyond which mucus will exit the nose; a matter of particular concern in tandem jumps.

spinning end *n.* the end of the airplane a skydiver must stay away from.

swoop *v.* to start from far above the formation and fly down into position. "Steve did a great job of *swooping* his slot in that formation." By extension, to move in fast on the ground; i.e., hitting on a member of the opposite sex. "Steve *swooped* your girlfriend."

swoop the hoop *n.* when two skydivers hold a hula hoop vertically and other skydivers swoop through it.

toad *n.* a beginning skydiver who isn't very good yet. "Yup, that Pete is a real *toad.*"

total *n.* a malfunction in which nothing deploys at all. "Johnny had a *total.*"

trash pack *n.*   a quick, sloppy job of packing a parachute. This can make for interesting openings or malfunctions.

tube *n.*   when at least three people arrange their bodies in a circle and roll out the airplane door like a wheel.

turf surf *v.*   to flare a chute just before landing, so as to skim low to the ground for a long distance. This makes an appealing picture; however, performed too late it may lead to orthopedic surgery or death.

unpack *v.*   to deploy the canopy, thus ending a freefall session.

waive *v.*   to have jumpers sign a standard liability waiver. "Hey Billy, have those students been *waived* yet?"

whuffo *n.*   a non-skydiver. Derives from the layman's common question, *"Whuffo* you jump out of a perfectly good airplane?"

wrap *n.*   when the parachutes of two jumpers attempting to join together in flight accidentally get tangled. "They'd better untangle that *wrap* fast— before the paramedics have to!"

zoo *n.*   any messed-up skydive, particularly one doomed from the start due to lack of experience or inadequate dirt diving. Often results in jumpers being scattered across the sky.

zoomie *n.*   a negative term for a toad who goes zooming past a formation.

zoo out *v.*   to be wildly unstable in freefall. Syn. **z out.**

BULLFIGHTERS

bananas *n.*   small horns.

cathedral *n.*   a huge bull.

cavalry *n.*   the picadors.

nun *n.*   an easy bull. Rel. **sweet pear:** an easier bull.

peons *n.*   the matador's helpers, called banderilleros.

pig-tailed folk *n.*   any bullfighter, picador, banderillero, or matador.

rag *n.*   the cape, or muleta, used before the kill. Syn. **flannel.**

the steel *n.*   the sword.

sticks *n.*   the darts, or banderillas.

the stroll *n.*   the parade into the arena.

sword *n.*   the matador.

theater *n.*   a derogatory term for the style of a showy bullfighter.

tobacco *n.*   a serious horn wound.

the wise monkeys *n.*   the arena attendants.

wood *n.*   the wooden sword used to spread the muleta before the actual kill.

WEIGHT LIFTERS

big boy *n.*   a massive body-builder. Also, forty-five-pound weight plates, the biggest available for the bench press. "Let's load on a few *big boys*."

blasted *adj.*   heavily worked out, referring to a muscle group. "Boy, my quads are really *blasted* from those squats."

cobra *n.*   a person with a wide, muscular back that narrows to a thin waist.

deads *n.*   dead lifts.

dime *n.*   a ten-pound plate. "Throw a *dime* on each side, will ya?" Rel. **nickel:** five pounds; **quarter:** twenty-five pounds.

doing a cycle *v.*   taking steroid drugs for a set period, then going off them.

eat the iron *v.*   to fail on a lift. "Bobby *ate the iron* big time on that clean-and-jerk."

freaky *adj.*   when muscles have size and definition to an abnormal, unnatural, and highly desirable degree. "Forget the 'big enough for football' stuff, man. I want to be *freaky* big!"

genetics *n.*   the inborn characteristics of a body type. Some body types gain mass easily, some don't. "If you don't have the *genetics,* you're gonna have to use drugs to get big."

get big *v.*   to build up muscle mass.

guns *n.*   arms. "You've got an awesome set of *guns* there, man." Syn. **pythons.** A favorite term of professional wrestler Hulk Hogan: "I've got twenty-four-inch *pythons!*"

hardgainer *n.*   someone with a body type that doesn't gain mass easily. "Don's a *hardgainer.* He gets stronger, but he never gets any bigger."

heifers *n.*   large, freaky calf muscles.

hit *v.*   to target a muscle for workout or enlargement. "Stiff-legged deads will really *hit* your hamstrings."

it's all you *exp.*   said by a spotter to indicate, "I'm not helping you at all, even though my hands are on the bar." Sometimes it's true, sometimes not.

juice *n.*   steroids. Syns. **fuel, gummi-berri juice, power, 'roids, the sauce, vitamin S, wonder water.** Rel. **juicer:** a person who uses steroids.

max out *v.*   to do a single exercise with the greatest weight possible. "Today I'm going to try *maxing out* on the bench."

meathead *n.*   a person who thinks only about lifting and getting big.

pork chop *n.*   an overweight person.

pumped *adj.*   when muscles become engorged with blood right after exercise, so they appear large and impressive. "My arms are really *pumped* after that brutal set of curls." Also, when someone's muscles look this way all the time. "Bob looks so *pumped* nowadays."

rage *v.*   to go berserk on the weights. Rel. **'roid rage** *n.*   a temporary berserk state in a steroid user.

reps *n.*   repetitions of an exercise; usually done in sets. "I just did five sets of eight *reps* in bench press." Rel. **rep out** *v.*   to do repetitions until the muscles fail. "He can't walk since he *rep'ed out* on his legs."

ripped *adj.*   having great muscular definition, low body fat, and immense muscle mass. Syns. **buff, cut, ripped to shreds, shredded, striated.** "Wow, that guy is really *ripped to shreds.*" "You're going to have to get more *cut* for competition."

'roid monster *n.*   a very big guy who uses steroids. "Tommy's turned into a real *'roid monster.*" Syn. **blowfish.**

screamer *n.*   a lifter who grunts or yells loudly while working out. "That *screamer* over there is driving me nuts!"

smooth as a pig *adj.*   when someone's skin surface is sleek due to retained water and a lack of bulging veins.

superset *v.*   to alternate between two exercises with minimal rest between sets. "I'm *supersetting* bench presses and pull-ups."

thick *adj.*   dense and muscular. "Jim's pecs are really looking *thick.*"

FRISBEE PLAYERS

backhand *n.*   a throw made by pulling the disc across the body, as in a tennis backhand stroke; the most common delivery.

bail *v.*   to fall short, quit. "He could have done a flying gitis, but he *bailed.*"

Berkeley power grip *n.*   a hold with the thumb on top of the disc and fingers clenched against the inside of the rim; this allows for a more powerful throw.

biff *v.*   to make an error. "You *biffed* it, Bud."

boosch *adj.* worthless, without merit.

delay *v.* to sustain a spinning disc on your fingernail. This is the basic move of advanced Frisbee work. "Jimmy *delayed* the disc, brought it under his leg, and then put it behind his back."

disc *n.* the correct generic term. Frisbee is a registered trademark of Mattel. "Hey man, toss me the *disc.*" Syns. **bee, flying disc.**

fastback *n.* a lightweight, low-profile Frisbee often available as a premium. "If you want a lot of hang time, use a *fastback,* since it's so light."

flamingo close *n.* a spectacular between-the-legs catch, in which one leg is straight up and the head is down by the ankle.

forehand *n.* a throw made by slinging the disc off the fingertips of the palm-up hand, with the thumb on top of the rim.

get ho *v.* to get horizontal, dive.

gitis *n.* pronounced "guy-tus." A reverse between-the-legs catch.

hang time *n.* the period when a disc is hovering in the air.

hein *adj.* pronounced "hayn." Very good, the best. "When it comes to throwing for accuracy, Stork is the *hein.*"

huck it *v.* to throw a disc a great distance; often done in desperation. "It was late in the game, so he just *hucked it* and went for the goal."

hyzer *n.* angling the disc with the edge opposite the hand tilted toward the ground. "To throw into the wind, use a lot of *hyzer,* or else the disc will blow back over your head."

jambuster *n.* a new player who breaks the flow or ends the game.

mac *n.* short for mid-air correction.

MTA *n.* Maximum Time Aloft, measured from the moment the disc leaves the hand until it is caught. (The all-time record is 16.72 seconds.)

phlaud *n.* a special catch behind the legs.

roll curve *n.*   a type of curving flight. If the disc hit the ground, it would roll rather than skip. Example: a right-handed backhand throw, curving to the right.

shelf *v.*   when a disc sails aloft and floats flatly in the air. "Once the disc *shelves,* you'll get lots of hang time."

skip curve *n.*   a type of curving flight. If the disc hit the ground, it would skip rather than roll. Example: a right-handed backhand throw, curving to the left.

snap *n.*   a quick wrist movement that imparts spin. "Give that disc a good *snap!* Just imagine you've got Jell-O on your fingertips and want to flick it off."

soak *n.*   a clean catch. "You should have seen the *soak* he had in the final game." Also, *v.*   "He *soaked* my hardest throw."

spaunch *v.*   to choke, fall short of expectations. "They shredded the semi's, but *spaunched* the finals."

swill *n.*   a badly executed throw in an Ultimate game.

throw, run, and catch *n.*   an event in which contestants toss the disc, run, and catch it, measuring the distance from start to finish. (The world record is 92.64 meters.)

tip *v.*   to tap an arriving disc back up into the air with one's fingertip. "Wow, I did six *tips* before the catch!"

twirl *v.*   to spin a disc around one's fingertip. Syn. **padiddle.**

Ultimate *n.*   a field game in which two seven-person teams score points by catching the disc in the end zones.

z's *n.*   spin. "That guy should have delayed that disc! A 'z' is a terrible thing to waste."

STONE SKIPPERS*

agnew *n.*   a wildly skipped stone that clonks someone in the crowd. "Did you see that *agnew?* The stone must have had grease on it."

blinchki *n.*   the Russian term for stone skipping, literally "little pancake." From the circular pattern a stone makes on the water.

chukker *n.*   an inning in which each contestant throws one stone. From polo. "Today's tournament will have the usual six *chukkers.*"

drakes and ducks *n.*   the British term for stone skipping.

Little David Trophy *n.*   a seventy-five-pound rock that is the Stanley Cup of stone skipping.

New Orleans dispensation *n.*   a rule allowing New Orleans skippers to substitute oyster shells, due to a scarcity of stones on the Mississippi River Delta.

pittypat *n.*   a short skip at the end of a run.

plink *n.*   a long skip at the beginning of a run.

plonk out *v.*   to have a stone sink without any skips at all. "I can't believe it: I make it to the finals and *plonk out!*"

run *n.*   the performance of one stone. "Arthur 'Babe' Ring set the world record with a *run* of twenty-nine skips—fourteen plinks and fifteen pittypats. His ability is the stuff of legend."

skronker *n.*   a thrown stone that never touches anything.

smut *n.*   the Danish term for a skip.

---

*The sport of stone skipping was supposedly invented by an English king who skipped gold sovereigns across the River Thames. Today, stone skippers' feats appear in the *Guinness Book of World Records.* Like many great athletes, they employ a special glossary of terms.

USS *n.* Unidentified Skipping Stone. An unauthorized stone that enters the official skipping lane. "Hey, who threw that USS? Better chase those kids away from shore!"

vet's out *n.* a rule by which the tournament veterinarian may reject rocks that are not from Mackinac Island—home of the sport's major tournament and official advisory body—if he believes they will contaminate the Straits of Mackinac. "One contestant wanted to use a lava rock from his barbecue, but the officials invoked the *vet's out.*"

TABLE TENNIS PLAYERS

fishing *v.* trying to return balls that are being slammed off the table in all directions. Distances may exceed sixty feet. Rel. **fisherman** *n.* "To be a successful *fisherman,* use high lob shots with heavy topspin to thwart the slammer."

junker *n.* a player whose paddle is faced with junk rubber (having long pips) that gives the ball a weird spin or no spin, either of which is difficult for opponents to handle. "Oh, no—I have to play a *junker* in the second round."

knuckleball *n.* a ball played off one's knuckles or fingers instead of the paddle.

Mexican jumping bean *n.* a heavily spun serve that hops around unpredictably, befuddling the opponent. It sometimes creates the equivalent of an ace in tennis.

the nedge *n.* a lucky return in which the ball strikes the top of the net, manages to go over, and then hits the table at the side or back edge. "*The nedge* is like adding insult to injury."

slime *n.* a ball hit by a paddle with long, junk pips.

spanker *n.* a fast shot that nears or hits a vital part of the body such as crotch, eyes, or bare skin.

windshield wiper *n.* a player who uses the same side of the paddle for both forehand and backhand.

POOL PLAYERS

action *n.*   gambling. "At the Ace Pool Room, there's *action* around the clock."

ball in hand *n.*   a rule that when one player commits a foul or scratch, his opponent can place the cueball anywhere on the table and start shooting from that point.

barrels *n.*   how much money per game a player is betting. "I have ten *barrels* at twenty dollars." Rel. **shooting air barrels** *v.*   gambling when one has no money. "That s.o.b. can't pay up; he was *shooting air barrels* the whole time."

clean *adj.*   when a ball has to go into the pocket without contacting any other balls. "Shots on the eight must go *clean.*"

clock *v.*   to scrutinize another player to assess his true skill level. "Minnesota Fats would sometimes miss three or four shots in a row when he thought somebody was *clocking* him."

English *n.*   spin on the cue ball, particularly side spin. "Put some *English* on it, Mick."

frozen *adj.*   when a ball is touching the rail or another ball.

go off *v.*   to start playing for small money, keep raising the stakes, and finally go broke.

handcuff artist *n.*   someone who gambles only when sure he will win. Syn. **lock artist.**

have the nuts *v.*   to be heavily favored to win. "Everyone knows that Eddie *has the nuts.*" Syns. **have the Brazilians, have the stone cold nuts.**

hook *n.*   when a player shoots and misses but by luck or design leaves his opponent no shot. "Joe is known as Captain *Hook.*"

hustle *v.*   to mislead others about your true ability and take advantage of them in gambling. Also, *n.*   "Paul has a good *hustle* going."

inning *n.*   a turn at the table.

kitchen *n.*   the zone from the end of the table to the second diamond on the side rail.

lemon *v.*   to conceal your actual ability, in order to hustle another player. "When he kept beating me by a hair, I knew he'd *lemoned.*"

like it had eyes! *exp.*   uttered when a shot is so perfect it appears to guide itself toward the pocket. Usually said by the shooter, either in self-congratulation or in declaring his opponent helpless before his powers.

liking it *v.*   when a player believes that he has real winning chances, even when he's losing. "Jimmy beat him out of three hundred dollars, and he was *liking it* so much he wanted to play Jimmy some more."

lock *n.*   a sure win. "This game is a *lock* for Joe."

money ball *n.*   the ball that, when pocketed, wins the game.

on the hill *adj.*   needing just one more game to win the set. Rel. **over the hill:** having won the set.

on the side *adj.*   describes a bet made by a bystander with one of the players in a match. "I'll bet you fifty dollars *on the side,* Bobby."

park the car *v.*   to make the cue ball stop rolling at a desired position.

poke 'n' hope *n.*   smacking the cue ball into another ball in the hope that you'll sink a ball somewhere.

put the money in the rack *v.*   when players put their money on the table when playing for a significant amount, in order to show that they have the cash, and to keep the loser from running out the door without paying. Syn. **freeze up the money.**

rat in *v.*   to sink a ball by luck, especially when you miss the intended shot but the ball falls in another pocket. "Joe seems to *rat in* the ball a lot."

road player *n.* a pool player who travels around and makes his living gambling at the game. "Buddy Hall is the best *road player* ever." Syn. **road warrior.**

rolling the cheese *v.* caroming or hitting another ball into the nine ball, in the hope that it will find a pocket. Syn. **riding the nine.**

run out *v.* to break and sink all the balls, without giving an opponent a chance to shoot.

score *v.* to win a large amount of money. Syn. **make a score.**

scratch *n.* to sink the cue ball in a pocket or knock it off the table.

session *n.* one or more sets. Typically, a session is over when one player is broke or both players decide they need some sleep. "That *session* lasted for a couple of days non-stop."

set *n.* a predetermined number of games. "They're playing a *set* for three hundred dollars."

shark *v.* to distract someone who is in the act of shooting. "He *sharked* me!"

slop counts *n.* a game in which any ball counts if it goes in any pocket, and there's no need to call shots.

speed *n.* skill level. "Fats is clocking your *speed.*" Rel. **top speed:** the best that a person can play.

stall *n.* the subterfuge of playing below one's ability level, hiding one's true skill in order to obtain a more favorable match at a later time. "Joe, get off the *stall.* I know you're a better player than this."

sweat the action *v.* when people other than the players bet on the game. "People were *sweating the action* all over the room."

tip-tapper *n.* a shot with a chance to miscue; usually a long draw shot.

tit *n.* the extended corner of the side pocket. "The ball ran straight into the *tit,* which made Neal miss the shot."

tournament tough *n.*   a player who, in the course of a tournament, never loses focus and typically reaches the finals.

turn on the torch *v.*   when a player begins to beat his opponent very badly.

weight *n.*   a mutually agreed upon modification of the game, made so players of disparate skill levels can compete against each other in a meaningful way. Example: When playing someone much worse at nineball, it can be agreed that if he makes the eight ball, he wins. "You're a champion. To play you, I need some *weight.*"

woof *v.*   to prod another player into a game. "It took me half the night to *woof* that guy. Then I took twenty bucks off him."

DARTS PLAYERS

bolo *n.*   when all three darts miss the space a player needs for his score.

clack! *exp.*   a snide comment when someone misses the dart board entirely. From the noise a dart makes when it hits a wall.

cork *v.*   to decide which player starts the game, by seeing whose dart lands closest to the bullseye. "Gents, shall we *cork?*"

good arrows! *exp.*   nice throws!

gutterball *n.*   a round of three darts that all miss the board entirely. "John's new girlfriend threw a *gutterball.*"

mug *n.*   a loser who is allowed to start the next game without corking.

Murphy *n.*   a total of twenty-six made with a five, twenty, and one. Some teams penalize their players each time they hit this combination. Syn. **bed & breakfast:** so called because the traditional cost of a B&B in Ireland was two shillings and sixpence.

nooner *adj.*   when a shot misses the board or the point that was aimed at, yielding a zero score. "I just threw a *nooner* round."

on the wire *adj.*   when a dart misses the number aimed at, but lands just on the other side of the wire from that number. (All scoring spaces are separated by wires.) "Sure, I missed—but it was right *on the wire.*"

outshot *n.*   the game-winning shot.

plug *n.*   a three-holed plastic holder for darts, to prevent their getting lost or jabbing holes in one's shirt (or oneself). Syn. **chuck, garage.**

race track *n.*   the catch ring around the board, which doesn't count in scoring and exists only to catch stray darts. "Say, Phil, why do you keep throwing at the *race track?*" Syns. **rhubarb, tar road.**

Robin Hood *n.*   a dart that sticks in the feather end of another dart. Named for Robin Hood's famous archery feat. "I should get a free drink for that *Robin Hood!*"

slop *n.*   random, unintended numbers hit by one's darts.

three in a bed *n.*   three darts in one wedge-shaped space of the dart board.

Woodstock *n.*   a poorly thrown dart that flutters toward the board. Named for the erratic flight pattern of the bird character in the "Peanuts" comic strip.

AMUSEMENTS AND LIFESTYLES

AUDIOPHILES

arc welder *n.*   a high-powered transistor amplifier. "Did you get a load of the *arc welder* that Fred bought?"

boofer *n.*   an audio store shopper who comes to listen to equipment and asks endless questions, but doesn't intend to buy.

boom-sizzle *n.*   sound quality that satisfies undiscriminating fans of cheap rock 'n' roll speakers. "The *boom-sizzle* crowd just loves those one-note-bass speakers. They don't seem to need any intelligible midrange." Syn. **thud-tink.**

cans *n.*   headphones.

Chinese bottle rockets *n.*   low-quality vacuum tubes from China.

die a hero *v.*   when equipment is destroyed under extreme conditions. "I huffed my woofer playing Pink Floyd at 110 decibels. It *died a hero.*"

golden ears *n.*   non-technical subjectivists; listeners who feel they're gifted enough to hear minute differences in sound quality. More technically oriented audiophiles would dismiss these sonic differences until proven.

letting the smoke out *v.*   opening up an old tube amp after it has died in spectacular fashion.

licorice pizza *n.*   a long-playing record, made of black vinyl.

make your ears bleed *v.*   what a harsh-sounding recording will do.

Mpingo Discs *n.*   brand name of expensive ebony-wood discs. Placed on stereo components, these four-inch discs are claimed to improve the sound of the system. Made of African mpingo ebony, a wood used on the finger-boards of musical instruments and said to absorb resonances. Many people, especially scientists and engineers, doubt the merits of Mpingo Discs, but some golden ears claim to hear the effects.

one-note bass *n.*   the boom-boom-boom of cheap rock 'n' roll speakers.

silver doughnut *n.*   a compact disc (CD).

tube-o-holics *n.*   vacuum-tube fans.

tubey *adj.*   having the warm sound associated with vintage tube components.

tweaks *n.*   people who fuss endlessly with their stereo systems, making subtle adjustments. They often care less about music than about equipment. Syn. **tweakophiles.** Also, the modifications themselves. "Do you know of any *tweaks* for a Rega 3 turntable?"

WAF *n.*   Wife Acceptance Factor. Example of a low WAF: "John, your new five-foot-tall stereo speakers don't exactly complement our early American decor. Maybe you could paint them."

BIRD WATCHERS

Big Day *n.*   an endeavor to see the maximum number of species in a midnight-to-midnight period of nonstop birding. Rel. **Big Year.** These terms can be limited to certain bird groups or geographic areas. Examples: a Big Year for shorebirds of the world; a Big Day for Washington's woodpeckers.

butterbutt *n.*   a yellow-rumped warbler *(Dendroica coronata)*. A common winter resident in most parts of the country. "Did Susan spot any good warblers?" "Nah, just a few palms and the rest *butterbutts.*"

BVD *n.*   Better View Desired. "Did you see the eagle?" "Barely; it was a *BVD.*"

dickie birds *n.*   umbrella term for all small songbirds.

dip *v.*   to miss a species one has purposely sought out. "I went all the way to New York last week, but I *dipped* on the lapwing."

dude *n.*   a laid-back bird watcher. "A *dude* is pretty much the opposite of a twitcher."

gashawk *n.*   an airplane.

GBB *adj.*   Gone Before Binoculars. Indicates that in the short time during which the bird watcher brought the binoculars up to her eyes, the bird vanished from sight. "Did you see the marsh wren?" "No, it was *GBB*."

goldielocks *n.*   an American gold finch

good *adj.*   any bird that is rare or unusual for a given time or place. "You saw a Ross' gull in Texas? That's a *good* bird!"

granny birder *n.*   one familiar only with very common birds, usually those appearing at her or his feeder. Derived from the senior women who compose much of this group, but may apply to anyone. "Adam is nothing but a *granny birder*. He's happy just watching the sparrows in his backyard."

hawkoreagle *n.*   any unidentified bird of prey. "Look Jim, there's another *hawkoreagle!*"

Holstein crow *n.*   a black-billed magpie, especially in the prairie states.

jizz *n.*   the distinctive manner in which a bird sits or flies that reveals its identity, even in a glimpse or a silhouette. "I didn't get a good look at that bird, but the *jizz* says brown creeper to me. It was zipping up that tree trunk like a windup toy!"

LBJ *n.*   Little Brown Job. A small drab bird that has escaped a bird watcher's identification; e.g., a sparrow. "Did you see that *LBJ* go behind the bush?" Syn. **LBB:** Little Brown Bird.

lifer *n.*   a bird that one has never seen in the wild before. "A Least Bittern was a *lifer* for me back in '87. I flushed it from behind the Wal-Mart on Rt. 3A."

list *n.*   a birder's list of sightings in a defined geographical area (state, county, city, backyard) or time period (month, year). Rel. **life list:** a list of birds a person has seen throughout his or her life; **whoopee list:** birds seen mating.

lister *n.*   a person who enjoys keeping lists and is often interested in seeing as many bird species as possible. Occasionally used pejoratively to imply that someone's interest in the natural world is superficial.

NFF *adj.*   No Fucking Feathers. Applies to anything that is not a bird.

owl prowl *n.*   a trip taken to see owls, usually at night.

peebeegeebee *n.*   a pied-billed grebe, which is a ducklike waterfowl.

peep *n.*   any of the small, cryptically colored sandpipers of the genus *calidris.* "I was out for three hours and only saw whimbrels and about a million *peeps* I couldn't identify."

pish *v.*   to utter the whisper-like sound "pish, pish, pish," in order to arouse the curiosity of nearby birds and bring them into better view. "Well, there's not much activity along the trail this morning. I think I'll try to *pish* something out into the open." Rel. **pisher** *n.*   a bird watcher who pishes too much. "Daniel is such a *pisher,* the birds are fleeing in terror."

prairie vultures *n.*   gulls that follow tractors that are plowing fields.

punk *n.*   a young bird. "What in the world was that?" "I think it was a *punk* red-tail."

ring and fling *v.*   taking scientific measurements of a bird that carries an ID band on its leg, then releasing it. "We had a big push in the migration yesterday. We were so busy, all we could do was *ring and fling.*"

sky rat *n.*   a feral pigeon. Rel. **sea rat:** a feral gull.

splat *v.*   when a raptor kills a bird. "My pigeon got *splatted.*"

tick *n.*   a bird that gets checked off on a birder's list. "That redshank was my first *tick* of the month." Also, *v.*   to add a new species to one's list. Rel. **megatick:** a tick that adds a new species to multiple lists, or one that was highly sought after and is rather rare.

trash bird *n.*   any bird that is very common or easy to spot at a given time or place. "Why were you so excited about seeing a starling? That's just a *trash bird.*"

TV dinner *n.*   road kill. ("TV" is short for turkey vulture)

twitcher *n.*   a person who chases after reported birds, sometimes spending excessive time and energy. "That guy's a real *twitcher.* He got up at two in the morning and drove three hundred miles to see that Ross' gull." Also, *twitch v.*   to chase obsessively after new or rare species.

WNK *n.*   We'll Never Know. Refers to an interesting bird that is spied but not identified. "I'm not sure if it was a great-tailed grackle, so I'll have to call it a *WNK.*"

zip *n.*   a sharpie or kestrel. "Whatcha been seein'?" "Oh, just a bunch of *zips.*" Also used when trying to identify a bird that is small, far-off, and usually moving rapidly. "I've got a *zip* out there over Topa Topa Mountain. Can you follow it for a minute while I scan to the east?"

COMIC BOOK COLLECTORS

ashcan *n.*   a promotional comic issued in half size (4″ × 5″), usually in black and white. Appearing in the 1940s, the publications were designed to secure copyright protection for characters or titles.

breaking the fourth wall *v.*   characters showing awareness that they exist in a comic book, a device sometimes used for humor. Derived from the theater, where the fourth wall is the imaginary barrier between actors and audience, usually associated with Brecht and Pirandello.

CBG *n.*   the "Comic Buyers' Guide." A weekly newspaper and market listing with reviews.

Claremontisms *n.*   phrases used by writer Chris Claremont, who helped the Marvel title *X-Men* rise from failure into one of the most popular books in comic history. His characters used certain phrases regularly, for example, "I'm the best at what I do . . . and what I do ain't very nice."

comix *n.* comic books that are independently produced and out of the mainstream. The term has roots in the 1960s Underground movement. "I love *Yummy Fur*—what great *comix!*"

comic-con *n.* a comic convention at which sellers, fans, and creators gather. "Are you going to the San Diego *ComiCon* this year?" Rel. **mega-con:** a large convention; **mini-con:** a small local convention.

comic condom *n.* a plastic or mylar bag used to protect comics from possible damage. "Danny keeps his entire collection of *Uncle Scrooge* in *comic condoms,* so they're mint."

dino *n.* a person who prefers the good old days; especially someone who was a fan of the *X-Men* before they became widely popular.

double bagger *n.* an extremely good comic that will probably appreciate greatly in value; thus, putting two bags on it would be prudent.

drooling *v.* what fanboys do.

eye tracks *n.* a jocular reference to "damage" caused by reading a comic, particularly a rare old issue that should be handled gently. "Hey, you're leaving *eye tracks* all over my mint *Silver Surfer* #1."

fanboy *n.* a usually adolescent male comics fan who likes stories with flashy artwork, big guns, big breasts, and lots of action as opposed to good characterization and plot development. "Only a *fanboy* could love a character with so little personality." Also, a fan who habitually buys certain comics without regard to the content of any particular issue. Rel. **Image fanboy:** one who buys Image comics, mainly because they contain a higher than average share of fanboy material.

furry *n.* an anthropomorphized animal in a comic book. "Donald Duck is still my favorite *furry.*" Also, a fan of anthropomorphic animals.

gimmicked *adj.* said of a comic with garish cover enhancements.

GnG *adj.* Grim 'n' Gritty. Describes a comic updated to be realistic or mature. *The Dark Knight Returns* was one of the first GnG comics and set a trend. Also, *v.* "Oh, no! *Suicide Squid* is being *GnG'd.* He's going to start leaving small squids stuffed in the ears of evildoers."

keeper of the flame *n.*   a fan who carries the torch for a comic character or series that is currently neglected or in oblivion, hoping that it will get more play or be revived. "I'm the *keeper of the Suicide Squid flame.*"

Kirbyesque *adj.*   imitative of the late Jack Kirby, a founder of modern comics who was influential in the 1960s and 1970s. He helped create *Spider-Man, Captain America, The Incredible Hulk,* and *The Fantastic Four.* Rel. **Kirbytech** *n.*   fancy looking, pseudo-scientific weapons and devices of the type that Jack Kirby liked to create.

Marvel zombie *n.*   a fan who buys every comic put out by Marvel, without regard to quality, and who appears to have no free will in regard to comic buying. "Brian has become a total *Marvel zombie.* He should learn to discriminate."

mutant zombie *n.*   an avid follower of Marvel's line of *X-Men* books, which feature mutants, supposedly the next step in evolution beyond *Homo sapiens.* "There's something you should know about me, Harold. I'm a *mutant zombie.*"

phone book *n.*   a large, bound collection of *Cerebus* comics. So called because of its hefty size and low-quality paper.

ploybag *n.*   an intentional corruption of polybag, the sealed plastic bag in which some comics are packaged. The "ploy" is a marketing strategy based on the fact that a comic's value plummets after the polybag is opened. Thus, if a collector wants to keep a mint version and still read the comic, he must buy two copies.

pod *n.*   a comic character whose behavior changes inexplicably when a new writer or editor takes over—a change apparently not noticed by other characters. Derived from the film *Invasion of the Body Snatchers,* in which alien invaders generated counterfeit human duplicates. Syn. **pod person.**

retcon *n.*   retroactive continuity. A process by which a writer goes back to revise an earlier characterization, story line, or character history, in order to maintain consistency with what is presently being written.

splash page *n.*   a single piece of artwork that spans one or two pages of a comic, usually at the beginning of a superhero story. The focus is on splashy art that features sex or violence designed to grab the reader.

squid *n.* an irritating fanboy. "I went to the comic-con but got stuck in a room full of *squids,* who did nothing but debate the fine points of *Sandman.*"

stoner *n.* a fan of 1960s comics whose themes revolve around drugs. "That *stoner* never gets his head out of R. Crumb comix and the *Fabulous Furry Freak Brothers.*"

Supes *n.* Superman. "I dropped all my *Supes* books last year." Rel. **Bats:** Batman. "I hate the way Jones draws *Bats.*"

COMPUTER USERS

barf *v.* when a machine or operation fails due to poor input. "The division operation *barfs* if you ask it to divide by zero."

bells and whistles *n.* computer features that are unnecessary but appealing to buyers. "That machine is yet another IBM clone, but they did add some nice *bells and whistles.*"

bomb *v.* to cease functioning; said of a software program. "Help! Microsoft Word *bombs* every time I try to print a document."

bondage-and-discipline language *n.* a computer language that ties its users to the author's ideas of proper programming. An example is Pascal.

bot *n.* a practical joke planted on a computer, online service, or site on the World Wide Web; it operates automatically, like a robot.

bounce *v.* when E-mail is returned to the sender. "Maybe I've got the wrong address for her. My message *bounced.*"

bozo filter *n.* a program that sifts through E-mail and rejects unwanted messages.

bulletproof *adj.* describes software unlikely to be botched by a novice user or wrecked by a hacker. "This new paint program is basically *bulletproof.* I even let my 7-year-old use it."

chat *n.* informal conversation between two online users in real time.

cracker *n.* someone who penetrates a computer system's security and illegally gains access to information or causes electronic mischief. Syn. **darkside hacker.** Rel. **crack** *v.*

crash *v.* to break down or freeze; said of a computer system. "My system *crashed,* and I lost the whole afternoon's work."

cruft *n.* redundant, superfluous code in a computer program; has been compared to the unappealing dust that gathers under a bed.

cybercrud *n.* technical gobbledygook about the information superhighway. "The guy who came to our office to explain the new system was a master of *cybercrud.* We'll have to figure it out ourselves."

cyberpunk *n.* a hacker, perhaps one with an outlaw streak, who operates on the Internet.

cyberspace *n.* the virtual community in which computers talk to each other. It is felt to have an almost physical sense of place and dimension. Coined in *Neuromancer,* a novel by William Gibson.

cypherpunk *n.* a hacker in cyberspace who tries to create codes the government can't crack.

denizen *n.* a low-level citizen on the Internet.

dot *n.* the cool way to refer to the period in an E-mail or Internet address. "My address is jdunn at west *dot* net (jdunn@west.net)."

drool-proof paper *n.* software or hardware documentation written at a level of simplicity suitable for an idiot. "They used *drool-proof paper* for the manual that came with my spreadsheet program."

earl *n.* the URL, or Universal Resource Locator, which is the electronic address of a World Wide Web site.

Easter egg *n.* a goody hidden in a computer program to amuse or amaze the user. "There's an incredible *Easter egg* in my datebook program. Press command-escape-3, and Mickey Mouse appears."

electronics hobbyist *n.* a tongue-in-cheek, self-descriptive name for a hacker who commits electronic pranks or damages other computer systems.

E-mail *n.* electronic mail, sent between computers.

flame *v.* to scorch someone with an insulting E-mail or newsgroup message.

flame war *n.* a fierce dispute waged in cyberspace. "You wouldn't believe the *flame wars* on CompuServe this week."

forum *n.* a formal electronic roundtable for discussing a topic online. "I'll be avoiding the music *forum*. When I said I liked the Carpenters, I got royally flamed."

hack *n.* a very good piece of programming that does the job perfectly.

hacker *n.* an ultra-proficient computer user. Also, an inspired and accomplished programmer.

handshake *n.* the transaction between two modems before they connect.

holy war *n.* an epic dispute based on opposing doctrines and beliefs. Example: "A Macintosh will always be better than a PC."

hot chat *n.* a private conversation, often sex oriented. "At night cyberspace is a whorehouse. You shouldn't have much trouble finding a *hot chat* online."

letterbomb *n.* an E-mail message freighted with data to harm the recipient's machine.

log on *v.* to sign on to an online service.

lurk *v.* to read messages in a newsgroup or online forum, but never reveal your presence.

magic *n.* technical matter that is impossible to explain simply. "How can a program search the whole Internet in just a few seconds? *Magic.*"

mouse droppings *n.* single pixels on a computer screen left when the mouse pointer moves, resembling rodent droppings. Caused by a program problem.

munge *v.* pronounced "mung." To foul up something badly. Short for "mash until no good." "Oh, my god, I really *munged* that one."

Net *n.* the Internet, the international network of computer networks that includes millions of users and computers, with facilities for E-mail, news reading, file transfers, and other services.

Net god *n.* a longtime Net user with deep knowledge.

Netiquette *n.* etiquette guiding people's behavior on the Internet.

Net personality *n.* someone who posts messages on newsgroups so often that he or she becomes known to many other users. The messages may be useful or, just as often, worthless and flaky.

Net spider *n.* a person who scrambles around the Internet or online services. Syn. **modem rat.**

newbie *n.* a newcomer to the Net; may be clueless. Used disparagingly by arrogant Net veterans.

online *adj.* when your computer is actively connected to a computer service, network, or electronic bulletin board via a telephone line.

phreaking *n.* the art of illegally appropriating telephone communication services.

return from the dead *v.* to end a period of absence from the Net.

sagan *n.* a very large quantity. Derived from the "billions and billions" phrase made famous by Carl Sagan on television's *Cosmos.* "Microsoft has invested *sagans* trying to develop an Internet browser that will take over the world."

salami attack *n.* an outlaw program that commits a computer crime in small slices that are difficult for authorities to notice. "His *salami attack* on the bank was brilliant. Once a week the program moved a nickel out of every checking account into his own account."

samurai *n.* a hacker hired to do legal cracking for legitimate reasons. "A firm of lawyers working on privacy-rights cases needs a *samurai*. Interested in the job?"

sandbox *n.* the research-and-development department at a software or computer company.

signal-to-noise ratio *n.* an estimation of the proportion of useful to irrelevant and meaningless information posted in a newsgroup. "You'd think the alt.journalism newsgroup would have intelligent discussions, but people just rant and rave. The *signal-to-noise ratio* is really low."

snail mail *n.* mail delivered by the U.S. Postal Service.

social engineering *n.* when a hacker schmoozes with or cons someone on the telephone to pry out a password or other information for breaking into a computer system.

sunspots *n.* an explanation of strange errors or occurrences on a computer. "I don't know why all the text on my screen suddenly turned green—*sunspots,* perhaps."

spam *v.* to send identical messages to many newsgroups or E-mail recipients, often with blatantly commercial intent. "Those lawyers pitching their services for personal-injury clients was the most brazen *spamming* of the Net!"

surf *v.* to look for information on the Net in an unplanned way by following links from one site to the next; a nonlinear approach to navigating the Net.

topic drift *n.* when the discussion in a newsgroup or online forum strays from the original subject, often onto a track that's not very useful. *"Topic drift!* How did we get from Israeli politics to the Beatles anyway?"

thread *n.* a series of messages about a specific topic. "There's a magicians' *thread* on alt.theater, but nobody gives away any secrets."

time bomb *n.* instructions hidden within an outlaw program that will destroy information at a specified time in the future. Also, instructions built into Beta (test version) software to make it stop functioning at a specific time.

trap door *n.* a hole in a program through which a hacker can enter.

Trojan horse *n.* outlaw instructions hidden in an apparently benign program, designed to destroy information.

vaporware *n.*   software hyped before it actually exists. Software makers use this ploy in order to claim a spot in the marketplace and hold it until the product can be developed.

vulture capitalist *n.*   a hacker term for a corporation whose contracts give the company rather than the inventor control over innovations and the profits they bring.

wave a dead chicken *v.*   to perform what you know is a useless repair ritual over crashed hardware or software to show others that you have tried to fix it.

wirehead *n.*   a person completely obsessed with computers.

wizard *n.*   someone with a gift for computing.

SMILEYS OR EMOTICONS

In electronic messages, typographical symbols are used to convey nonverbal subtleties such as irony, anger, gratitude, and sarcasm. To read an emoticon, turn your head sideways.

:-)   a smile.

:-D   a big smile.

8-)   a smile from person who wears glasses.

;-)   a wink.

;->   a wink with lewd intent.

:-O   an expression of surprise. Also, "eeeek!"

>:-)   so surprised my hair is standing on end.

<:-| dunce.

:-/   indicates perplexity or irony.

:-J   tongue in cheek.

%-)   crossed eyes. "I've spent eight hours trying to figure out why PageMaker is bombing. **%-)**"

:-&   tongue tied.

I-O   a yawn. "Went to see Barry Manilow in concert. Huge **I-O**"

:-(a frown.

:'-   tears.

:-P   raspberry; usually offensive.

@:-}   just back from hairdresser.

0:-)   angel.

}:->   devil.

:-x   a kiss.

*   a kiss.

{ }   a hug.

–/—@   a long-stemmed rose.

ABBREVIATIONS FOR STANDARD PHRASES

Users online employ a shorthand that saves time and keystrokes when sending messages or talking in a forum.

afk   away from keys.

bak   back at keys.

bbl   be back later.

brb   be right back. "I have to go to the john. *brb.*"

btw   by the way.

cul8r   see you later.

esad   eat shit and die. "Flame ME, will you? *esad.*"

faq   frequently asked questions.

ftr   for the record.

f2f   face to face.

fwiw   for what it's worth.

gmta   great minds think alike.

hhok   ha, ha, only kidding.

imo   in my opinion.

imho   in my humble opinion. "Apple should lower their PowerBook prices to compete with other laptops, *imho.*"

imnsho   in my not so humble opinion.

irl   in real life.

18r   later.

lol   laughing out loud. "Madonna = *lol.*"

m or f?   are you male or female?

otoh   on the other hand.

rofl   rolling on the floor laughing.

rtfm   read the fucking manual.

sol   shit out of luck.

ttfn   ta-ta for now.

ttyl   talk to you later.

wag   wild-assed guess.

wb   welcome back.

wylasomwtc?   would you like a saucer of milk with that comment? Usually a response to a catty remark.

ymmv   your mileage may vary.

CROSSWORD PUZZLE FANS
AND CONSTRUCTORS

abber *n.*   an abbreviation. "This puzzle has twenty *abbers* in it—and that's about nineteen too many for me."

cheater *n.*   an extra black square beyond those necessary to separate the words in the grid. Shows inferior talent in the constructor, who is supposed to weave words; black squares reduce the skill needed. *"The New York Times* didn't buy my crossword because the first square was a *cheater.*"

commuter *n.*   a small crossword puzzle (no larger than a 15 × 15 grid) of low- to middle-range difficulty. A commuter can usually complete one on the train ride to work.

cross-stitch *n.* a cross-reference to another clue, such as "opposite of 29 down."

crosswordese *n.* a peculiar language of obscure words that appear in crossword puzzles because they have convenient letter patterns, but never come up in daily conversation—such as names of some African tribes and Guatemalan lizards. "A seasoned solver is equipped with a wearisome recall for *crosswordese,* such as nene, a four-letter word for Hawaiian goose."

cruciverbalist *n.* a crossword puzzle constructor or enthusiast. "Henry and I are both ardent *cruciverbalists.*"

dirty double-crosser *n.* the intersection of two tough words.

15 *n.* a 15 × 15 grid puzzle (also called a daily). Rel. **21:** a 21 × 21 grid puzzle (a Sunday). "I have a deadline to construct five *15s* by the end of the month. Whew!"

flash *n.* an easy answer. "There were so many *flashes,* I finished the puzzle in about ten minutes."

ladder *n.* a series of words, sometimes located in the center of a large puzzle, that are all the same length and run from upper right to lower left.

New Wave *adj.* a style of puzzle full of brand names and pop culture.

six down *adj.* a term of endearment used for great crossword constructors who have passed away. "Eugene Maleska, fifteen-year crossword editor for *The New York Times,* became *six down* on August 3, 1993."

unch *n.* a letter that is part of an across entry or a down entry but not both. Short for unchecked. Because the solver can't double-check the letter's correctness, this is considered a serious flaw in puzzles. "I'm trying to solve for a 'city in Asia.' The crossing letters give me K-R-C-I, and all the unknown letters are *unches.*"

GAMBLERS

Casino Gamblers and Employees

action *n.*   a bet; the aggregate of bets being made. "We've got plenty of *action* tonight!"

betting spread *n.*   the range of a player's bets, from lowest to highest. Betting from twenty-five to one hundred dollars per blackjack hand would be a one-to-four spread. An extreme betting spread may alert the casino that the blackjack player is counting cards—i.e., he bets the minimum until his count indicates a statistical advantage over the house, then he bets the maximum.

Big Dick *n.*   a ten rolled in craps.

boat people *n.*   the throngs of gamblers who arrive in Las Vegas by bus. "Dive for cover! The *boat people* are pulling into the parking lot."

boxman *n.*   a craps dealer who handles bets and payoffs; he is seated by the drop box.

buy-in *n.*   the amount of money a player exchanges for chips at a gambling table. "Wow! Big Ed's *buy-in* was a hundred thousand dollars."

cage *n.*   the cashier's area.

carpet joint *n.*   a luxury casino. Ant. **sawdust joint.**

check *n.*   a gambling chip. "Every time the Spaniard won a hand, he rattled his *checks* like castanets."

comp *n.*   a complimentary room or meal. Also, *v.*   "The Mirage *comped* me for two nights." Rel. **RFB:** complimentary room, food, and beverage.

coupon *n.*   a certificate good for freebies and discounts. "I got a *coupon* book from Harrah's for the buffet and some free pulls on the slot machines."

crossroader *n.*   a cheater.

cut card *n.*   a colored plastic card used to cut the playing cards after a blackjack or poker dealer shuffles them.

drop box *n.*   a cash box fed through a slot in the gaming table; it holds paper money the players have exchanged for chips. Rel. **drop:** the total amount of money in the drop box.

eye in the sky *n.*   a surveillance system above the tables. A ceiling of one-way mirrors conceals employees on catwalks, who watch for cheating by dealers or players. Cameras may also be used. Syn. **Big Brother.**

fat deck *n.*   a deck with a greater than usual proportion of high cards left, which is more likely to produce a winning hand. A term used by blackjack card counters.

first base *adj.*   the position at a blackjack table that receives cards first during the deal. Pit boss to dealer: "Watch that guy on *first base*. He's trying to peek your hole card." Rel. **third base:** location of the last player to receive cards.

gaming *n.*   a genteel term for gambling; promoted by the casino industry to sound more like recreation and less like risking money. Syn. **casino entertainment.**

George *n.*   a player who tokes generously. Rel. **Super George** or **King Kong:** great toker; **Georgette:** a female version.

getting rated *n.*   the process of having a casino calculate your status, by observing your buy-in and your action. If these are high enough, you may receive comps.

handle *n.*   the total amount of money moving through a casino. "Saturday's *handle* was way up. This one Asian guy dropped $900,000 playing baccarat."

heat *n.*   casino attention on a blackjack player who may be counting cards. Counting may give a player an advantage, so is frowned on by casinos, which resort to countermeasures such as shuffling early, limiting the bet size, and intimidating or actually barring players. "Joe was only betting a one-to-four spread, but he still got a lot of *heat.*"

high roller *n.*   a gambler known to bet large sums.

hopper fill *n.*   a new supply of coins to replenish a slot machine.

hopping *v.*   betting that a certain combination of dice will be thrown on the very next roll—for example, a six and three for a nine, or four and two for a six. These bets normally pay odds of fifteen to one.

juice *n.*   influence, prestige; having friends or relatives in the right places at a casino. "He got his job at the MGM Grand because he has *juice.*"

in red *adj.*   the way a comped customer's name is noted on a maitre d's reservation list.

insurance *n.*   a side bet in blackjack, wagering that the dealer's hole card is a ten, when his up card is an ace.

ivories *n.*   dice. Syn. **Africans, Mississippi marbles.**

Little Joe *n.*   a roll of three and one in craps.

marker *n.*   the IOU of a gambler allowed to play on credit. "Harrah's is holding his *marker.*"

nickel *n.*   five dollars. Rel. **quarter:** twenty-five dollars. The standard chip colors are also used as synonyms: white = one dollar, red = five dollars, green = twenty-five dollars, black = one hundred dollars. "You won't get any heat at Caesar's unless you suddenly bet a stack of *blacks.*"

on the rim *adv.*   on credit. "Philly Joe took five hundred dollars *on the rim.*"

on the wood *adv.*   when a marker is taken to the cashier's counter in order to revise a player's tab. "The Iceman's ten-thousand-dollar marker is *on the wood.*"

paint *n.*   a ten or court card in blackjack.

pit boss *n.*   an employee who oversees a group of gaming tables, supervises dealers, and watches for cheating. The pit is the enclosed area where he and the dealers work.

pit critter *n.*   any of the pit employees, including dealers, floormen, and pit bosses.

railbirds *n.* people who hang around watching poker games from behind the rail that separates the playing area from the public area. They may be busted-out poker players, but more commonly are just curious people or tired players taking a break. "He never plays; he's just a *railbird.*"

shoe *n.* a dealing box that holds multiple decks for blackjack.

shooter *n.* the player rolling the dice at a craps table.

spoon *n.* a device used to cheat a slot machine.

spotter *n.* a skilled employee who watches the games and detects cheats.

stickman *n.* craps dealer who moves the dice around the table with an L-shaped stick.

stiff *n.* a gambler who never tokes or places side bets for the dealer. Also, a blackjack hand with a poor chance of winning no matter how it is played, typically twelve to sixteen. Rel. **superstiff:** a cheapskate gambler who tips no one. "That *superstiff* didn't even toke the cocktail girl for his free drinks."

take a shot *v.* to make a wager.

toke *v.* to tip. "Whenever Frank Sinatra won big at my table, he *toked* me one hundred dollars." Also, *n.* "We dealers have a saying on bad nights: 'All jokes, no *tokes.*'"

to the farm *exp.* used when a blackjack dealer's hand goes over twenty-one and busts. "Fourteen . . . and a deuce . . . and a jack! *To the farm!*"

wonging *v.* checking various blackjack games in order to find one where the odds have become temporarily favorable to players (as determined by card counting), then jumping in and playing until the advantage shifts back to the house.

working *adj.* refers to bets that may win or lose on the next roll. Syn. **live.** Ant. **off.** "My bets are *off* next roll!"

Poker Players

advertise *v.* to be intentionally caught bluffing on a poor hand in order to set up a win on a good hand later. The idea is to appear to play badly or too loosely. "He didn't even have a pair, but he bet like it was a royal flush. I guess he was *advertising*."

assault rifle *n.* hole cards consisting of ace, king, four, and seven of any suit in the game of Omaha.

at the river *adv.* when the seventh and last card has been dealt in a stud poker game. "We were *at the river* and I had zip, so I folded."

babies *n.* two small pairs.

big bobtail *n.* a four-card straight flush that is open on both ends.

boat *n.* a full house. Syns. **barn, full boat.**

Broderick Crawford *n.* ten and four as hole cards in the game of Hold 'Em. From the star of the 1950s television series *Highway Patrol,* whose scripts often used the police radio code "10-4."

bug *n.* a joker.

bullets *n.* aces. "Jimmy's three *bullets* shot down my pair of jacks." Syn. **oil wells.**

bump *v.* to raise. "I'll see your thousand and *bump* you three more."

calling station *n.* a player who often calls better hands when he should have folded, thus adding to the other players' profits. Derived from "call," to match a bet. Syn. **pay station.**

coffee house *n.* deceptive chatter or false assertions. A player may say, "What you got, Charlie? Two deuces?" and then watch his opponent's eyes for a revealing reaction. If Charlie is cool headed, he'll come right back with something like, "Yep! Why, do I need more?"

cowboys *n.* kings.

Dead Man's Hand *n.*   two pairs, aces and eights. From the hand held by Wild Bill Hickok when he was shot in the back during a poker game in Deadwood, South Dakota. (The cards he held were the black aces, the black eights and the nine of diamonds.)

door *n.*   the first card dealt face-up in a stud poker game.

fish *n.*   a very bad player who loses lots of money. "You know the old saying: If you can't find the *fish* at your table, you're it." Syn. **live player.**

fishhooks *n.*   jacks.

four flush *n.*   four cards of a single suit (five of a single suit are needed for a flush). Rel. **four-flusher:** "My uncle was a *four-flusher* who always bluffed when he didn't have that fifth card."

friend *n.*   a card that improves a hand. "Brandy drew a king, which turned out to be a *friend.*"

gut shot *n.*   a draw to an inside straight (i.e., four cards of a straight that can be filled only by drawing a card to the middle of the series). For example, drawing a nine to a hand consisting of seven, eight, ten, and jack.

in the pocket *adj.*   refers to face-down cards in a stud poker hand. "I knew I'd beat him. I had two cowboys *in the pocket.*"

Jackson Five *n.*   jacks and fives; named for the pop group.

Judge Bean *n.*   three tens. Perhaps from the Wild West judicial phrase "thirty days in the county jail."

mortal nuts *n.*   a hand that can't be beaten. "Raising the bet to Amarillo Slim was a mistake. He had *mortal nuts.*" Syns. **Brazilians, a lock.**

muck *v.*   to toss cards onto the face-down pile of discards by the dealer, taking them out of play. Also *n.*   the pile of discards.

outrun *v.*   to win a hand by drawing the cards one needs.

pee-wees *n.*   low cards. "Don't go dealing me a bunch of *pee-wees* unless they're four of a kind." Syn. **mice and lice.**

pocket rockets *n.* a pair of aces in the hole. Syn. **American Airlines.**

quads *n.* four of a kind.

rake *n.* a cut of the pot taken by a poker parlor as a fee for use of the room. "The *rake* is lower at the Palace Club; maybe we should play there tonight."

rat-hole *v.* to pocket some of one's stake or winnings during a game. "Jimmy looked like a loser; then we realized he'd been *rat-holing* chips all night."

rock garden *n.* a game full of very tight, patient players, known as "rocks." "I stopped playing in Gardena. It's turned into a real *rock garden*."

sandbag *v.* to play a strong hand as if it were much weaker, in order to trap other players into calling or raising bets. This strategy increases the size of the pot one stands to win.

Siegfried and Roy *n.* a pair of queens.

street *n.* a round in stud poker. "We're on Fifth *Street*, gentlemen," means the fifth card is being dealt.

stuck *adj.* when one has lost a significant amount of money. "Ray is *stuck* $650."

tell *n.* any distinctive behavioral trait that inadvertently reveals the strength of your hand. "His *tells* are so obvious you'd have to be an idiot not to notice them. The guy puffs his cigarette like a chimney when he's got a good hand and sets it down in the ashtray when he hasn't. Just watch him."

trips *n.* three of a kind. Also, **triplets.**

wheel *n.* ace, two, three, four, and five, the best hand in lowball poker. Rel. **steel wheel:** a wheel of the same suit, forming a straight flush—a very good hand in games where the high and low hands split the pot.

wired *adj.* a pair with one card face down and the other face up. "Doc started off with aces *wired,* and by the time he was on Sixth Street he had a full boat."

GAYS AND LESBIANS*

bog queen *n.* a gay man who frequents public toilets for sex.

breeders *n.* a derogatory term for heterosexuals, especially those who glorify childbearing.

circle jerk *n.* a male group-masturbation session.

cottage *n.* a public toilet. Not current usage except among older men.

drag *n.* mode of dressing usually identified with the opposite sex. Rel. **drag queen:** a man who dresses like a woman.

dyke *n.* a lesbian. Derived from nineteenth-century slang term "dike," which referred to male clothing. When first used to refer to women, it carried a derogatory connotation of masculine appearance or behavior.

faggot *n.* a male homosexual. Like dyke, the term was originally derogatory but has been adopted by many of the people to whom it refers. Syns. **fag, mariposa** (from the Spanish word for butterfly).

fag hag *n.* a heterosexual woman who socializes extensively with gay men.

fairy *n.* a male homosexual, especially one who acts or dresses in an effeminate manner. This common derogatory term has been adopted by gays.

family *n.* the lesbian and gay community. "He's a member of the *family*. He's gay."

feigele *adj.* a Yiddish term for gay, derived from the word for bird.

fist *v.* to insert part or all of one's hand into the anus or vagina of a sex partner.

French Embassy *n.* any location, especially a gym or Y, where gay sex is readily available.

---

* These terms were provided by Gay-Mart (http:www.gaymart.com), incorporating terms from the *Alyson Almanac*.

friend of Dorothy's *adj.* gay. Derived from the lead character in the movie *The Wizard of Oz,* which starred Judy Garland, whose singing and tragic life story are popular with gay audiences.

frig *v.* when two women have sex, often involving one rubbing the genitals of the other with her fingers.

gaydar *n.* the uncanny sense with which lesbians and gays detect other gay people in their midst. Coined from "gay" and "radar."

glory hole *n.* a hole carved in the partition between stalls in a men's room and used for sexual liaisons.

Government Inspected Meat *n.* a gay man in the armed forces.

Greek *adj.* having a preference for anal intercourse.

guppies *n.* gay urban professionals, or gay yuppies. Rel. **luppies:** lesbian yuppies.

helmet *n.* a circumcised penis. Ant. **turtleneck.**

honeypot *n.* a woman's genitals.

hung *adj.* having a large penis; well endowed.

in the closet *adj.* not revealing one's homosexual orientation to the general public. Ant. **out of the closet.**

in the life *adj.* gay; more common in the black community.

Kinsey six *n.* a person who is completely homosexual, as opposed to one with some bisexual inclinations. Derived from classifications by sex researcher Dr. Alfred C. Kinsey.

kosher *adj.* circumcised.

lavender law *n.* legal issues and practice pertaining to the gay and lesbian community.

library *n.* an adult bookstore.

lilies of the valley *n.*   hemorrhoids.

lollipop stop *n.*   a highway rest stop where gay men cruise for sex partners.

make a milk run *v.*   to cruise a men's room.

meat rack *n.*   a gay male cruising area.

muff diving *n.*   cunnilingus.

nancy *n.*   an effeminate man. Syns. **nancy boy, pansy, poof, poofter, queen.**

napkin ring *n.*   a ring placed around the penis. Syn. **cock ring.**

number *n.*   a casual sex partner. Syn. **trick.**

one-eyed Cyclops *n.*   the head of the penis.

Princeton rub *n.*   intercourse between two men in which one's penis rubs between the other's thigh, or between the two men's abdomens.

rim *v.*   to lick or suck the anus of a sex partner.

S & M *n.*   sadism and masochism. S & M enthusiasts derive part of their pleasure from inflicting pain or humiliation (sadism) or having pain inflicted upon them (masochism), but always within defined and mutually agreed-upon limits.

size queen *n.*   a gay man who is especially interested in partners with large penises.

tearoom *n.*   a public lavatory that is often cruised by gay men.

vanilla sex *n.*   relatively conventional forms of sexual activity, usually in contrast to S & M sex.

HARLEY-DAVIDSON MOTORCYCLE RIDERS

ape hangers *n.*   high handlebars.

bitch bars *n.*   a backrest for a passenger.

bitch pegs *n.*   foot pegs for a passenger, mounted about level with the driver's hips. "With her legs up on those new *bitch pegs,* that babe provides a picturesque curve of thigh."

brother or **sister** *n.*   another loyal Harley rider. "Ridin' a bike is like being part of a family. If you own a Hog you can always find a *brother* or *sister* to help you out."

cage *n.*   a car. "My bike isn't working, so I had to come in my *cage.*"

cattle-pusher *n.*   the engine guard. Syn. **crash bar.**

crotch rocket *n.*   a fast Japanese motorcycle. "He's got one of those whiny-chainsaw-lean-over-and-go-like-hell-until-you-hit-a-wall-and-splat-like-a-bug *crotch rockets.*" Rel. **crotch rocketeer** the pilot of a crotch rocket. "Like the typical *crotch rocketeer,* he comes equipped with a complete set of leathers and a full-face helmet in the same color scheme as the motorcycle."

dressed *adj.*   fully accessorized, referring to a Hog.

flathead, knucklehead, panhead, shovelhead, blockhead *n.*   five types of Harley engines, in chronological order.

garbage wagon *n.*   a full-dress stock Harley.

Half-a-Harley *n.*   a Harley Sportster; pejorative. "A *Half-a-Harley* is the smallest model made, but it's ridden by many large, macho men."

Hog *n.*   a Harley-Davidson motorcycle; no longer pejorative.

HOG *n.*   Harley Owners Group.

ink *n.*   a tattoo.

in the wind *adj.* on the road, riding a motorcycle.

iron *n.* a motorcycle. "Hey, Jack, nice *iron!*"

Old Lady *n.* one's wife or significant other. Syn. **bitch.** Rel. **Old Man:** one's husband or significant other.

peg scraper *n.* a tight turn made while leaning at an extreme angle.

pig on rollerskates *n.* the way a Hog handles on rain-slicked roads.

poser *n.* a yuppie biker who puts on bad-boy clothes and temporary tattoos in order to look like a real biker.

pud *n.* a rider on a Japanese motorcycle who wears fancy racing leathers and believes that since he owns a fast bike, he can ride well.

pussy pad *n.* a second seat for a passenger. Syn. **crack rack, p-pad.**

rice-burner *n.* a Japanese-made motorcycle, especially a crotch rocket.

road rash *n.* any wound caused by skidding along the pavement on one's unprotected epidermis.

RUB *n.* Rich Urban Biker. A yuppie who buys a Harley.

scoot *n.* a motorcycle, especially a Harley. Syns. **putt-putt, sled.**

scooter trash *n.* a term of endearment for a woman on a bike.

sissy bar *n.* a back rest.

skid lid *n.* a helmet. "I hate wearing a *skid lid.* The helmet law sucks! Those who ride should decide!"

speculator *n.* a person who buys a Harley motorcycle and then tries to sell it for a quick profit.

squid *n.* an unskilled motorcycle rider. So called because his arms and legs flop around in an effort to maintain balance. Also, a rider who lacks judgment, even if experienced. "If you're running up to the Rock Store this weekend, beware of the *squids.*"

toy ride *n.*   a group ride held for a toy drive during the Christmas season.

UJM *n.*   Universal Japanese Motorcycle. Coined in the mid-1970s to refer to four-cylinder, inline, mid-displacement, standard model bikes, such as the Honda cb750. Every Japanese manufacturer cloned one.

yuppie scum *n.*   yuppies. "I like to go into coffee bars with all my tattoos on display and scare the *yuppie scum.*"

KARAOKE SINGERS

barber *n.*   someone who joins in on every tune. Often inebriated. From "The Barber of Seville."

croaky *n.*   karaoke, according to bar patrons who don't care for karaoke.

flipper *n.*   a karaoke performer who tosses his or her hair around constantly.

karaoke kamikaze *n.*   a person who will get up and sing any song, anytime, often for a free drink. "If you want to hear an unbelievable version of 'Feelings,' ask that *karaoke kamikaze* at the front table."

kariography *n.*   the choreography used in a karaoke performance. "He had all the moves of the Four Tops—great *kariography*—but the voice of Kermit the Frog."

ringer *n.*   a professional singer who may get free admission and drinks in exchange for coming in regularly and keeping things rolling along in a larger karaoke bar. "That gal sure sounds and moves like a *ringer!*"

shadow *n.*   someone who stands behind a singer, but can't get up the courage to join in.

shred *v.*   to mutilate a tune.

sig *n.*   a signature song identified with a regular patron. "That virgin came up and sang Tina's *sig.* I bet she's not too thrilled about that!"

software *n.*   a singer whose performance is so faint that no one can hear it. "All I hear is the sound track. I wish the *software* would stand a little closer to the microphone."

virgin *n.*   a greenhorn who has never done karaoke before.

POT SMOKERS

baked *adj.*   very stoned, often to the point of inactivity.

beaner *n.*   a marijuana seed. "This bag has a lot of *beaners* in it."

binger *n.*   a hit from a bong.

blunt *n.*   a cigar with tobacco removed and pot inserted; a large joint rolled in cigar paper. Rel. **blunted** *adj.*   high from smoking a blunt.

Bob *n.*   marijuana; getting high. "Let's go see *Bob*." "I'm with *Bob* right now."

bogart *v.*   to hold on to a joint or pipe for too long before passing it. "Don't *bogart* that joint, my friend; pass it over to me."

bong *n.*   a pipe with a water chamber, through which the smoke is bubbled to clean and cool it. "I have *bongs* that are a few inches tall and one that's several feet." Syn. **chalice.**

bowl *n.*   the part of the pipe that holds the marijuana. Also denotes a certain measurement. "Let's smoke a *bowl*."

buddage *n.*   whole marijuana buds, or large chunks.

cashed *adj.*   empty, referring to a pipe bowl. "This pipe is *cashed*." Also, *v.*   "Here ya go, but I think I *cashed* it."

doobage *n.*   pot. "Doobie" for a joint is now nearly archaic.

double percolator *n.*   a bong with two chambers. Syn. **double perk.**

4:20 *n.*   a time of day when one "should" get high. Also, a term for pot smoking in general.

green *adj.* describes someone who smokes a lot of pot.

green day *n.* when one stays high all day.

harshing a buzz *v.* bringing someone down; annoying a stoned person. "Stop *harshing my buzz,* man." Syn. **killing a buzz.**

head *n.* someone who smokes a lot of pot.

herbalize *v.* to smoke pot; get high.

hitter *n.* a small metal pipe used for smoking the equivalent of one hit of a joint. Syns. **bat, one-hitter.**

implement of destruction *n.* a bong or marijuana pipe. From an Arlo Guthrie song.

J *n.* joint. Rel. **pinner:** small joint; **fatty:** really big joint; **torch a fatty** *v.* to smoke a big joint.

jonesing *v.* wishing you had marijuana to smoke. "I've been *jonesing* all day." By extension, aching for anything. "I'm *jonesing* for some good blues music."

(the) kind *adj.* refers to the very best buds, which are fresh, potent, and smooth-smoking. By extension, may refer to anything nice, as in, "This is *the kind* raspberry iced tea!"

kind bud *n.* a particularly bright green and powerful type of pot. Syn. **KB.**

lumber *n.* an excess of large, woody stems in a bag of marijuana buds. "These bags are pretty good, once you clear out the *lumber.*"

O *n.* an ounce of pot.

piece *n.* a pipe. "Check out this new *piece* I made."

pull tubes *v.* to smoke bongs, especially long ones. "Hey, let's *pull* some *tubes.*"

roach *n.* the burned-down end of a joint.

schwag *n.*   dry, harsh-smoking marijuana that may give the smoker a buzz, but not a good high. By extension, may refer to anything mediocre or lousy. "This restaurant has pretty *schwaggy* food."

shake *n.*   loose bits of marijuana and powder, in contrast to whole buds.

snarf *v.*   when someone takes a big hit and coughs hard, blowing the marijuana out of the bowl.

spliff *n.*   a large, fat joint. Sometimes pronounced "spleef."

stoned *adj.*   experiencing a heavy, intoxicated high, in contrast to a breezy, clear-minded high.

twenty sack *n.*   a bag of pot sold for twenty dollars. Related quantities: dime (ten dollars), nickel (five dollars).

wake 'n' bake *v.*   to smoke pot right after waking up in the morning.

walk the dog *n.*   to smoke pot. "Let's go *walk the dog.*"

weed *n.*   marijuana. "Hey, Jill, got any *weed?*" Syns. **the bomb, bud, cheeba, chronic, dope, green, green things, happy weed, hemp, herb, indo, ism, leaf, Mary Jane, MJ, pot, shit, skunk, smoke, wacky 'baccy.**

ROLLER COASTER
ENTHUSIASTS

ACEer *n.*   a member of the American Coaster Enthusiasts club.

airtime *n.*   a period of near-zero gravity when a rider feels as if he's coming out of his seat. "The Magnum has great *airtime* on the second hill." Rel. **float hill:** extended airtime, up to three or four seconds.

camel back *n.*   a series of hills, each slightly smaller than the preceding one.

chain dogs *n.*   catches beneath coaster cars that grab a moving chain and pull the train uphill.

classic coaster *n.* an older ride without lap bars, headrests, and other modern restraints or safety devices. Rel. **golden age coaster:** one built prior to World War II.

coffin cars *n.* trains with excessive safety restraints. "I hope they take the *coffin cars* off the Ripsaw."

Dinn shuffle *n.* when trains bounce from side to side, losing speed. Caused by track warped due to building methods used by the Dinn corporation. "That woodie had a severe case of *Dinn shuffle.*"

double dip *n.* a hill that has been divided into two separate drops.

ERT *n.* Exclusive Ride Time. Set aside for hard-core coaster enthusiasts only.

finé de capo *n.* the sensation that a rider is about to have his head knocked off, usually by a beam or tunnel. Syn. **head chopper.**

frequent flyer *n.* individual who has ridden one hundred or more roller coasters.

gp *n.* the general public, who prefer roller coasters tamer than enthusiasts do.

green alert *n.* a warning that someone is getting sick on a ride. "Whoa! *Green alert* on the Vortex." Syns. **Code V, 10-38.**

grubbies *n.* park employees who sweep up trash.

hang time *n.* the feeling of suspended gravity when a train reaches the top of a loop.

head banger *n.* a coaster that slams a rider's head into the restraints.

laterals *n.* being slammed to the outside of the car as the train goes around a curve. "You want *laterals?* Ride Mister Twister."

mega coaster *n.* a huge ride with tall hills and high speed.

out and back *n.*   a coaster that has an oval layout in which the train travels to a turnaround and then returns to the station. Generally faster than designs with tight turns. "My favorite *out and back* is the Blue Streak."

POP *n.*   Pay One Price. An admission policy that includes all rides and shows.

season passers *n.*   kids whose parents buy them season passes to a park and let them run free.

slammer *n.*   when a drop bottoms out suddenly, crushing a rider into the bottom of the seat.

slammer Gs *n.*   negative gravity so violent that bruises from hitting the lap bar are fairly common. "La Montana Rusa has some nice *slammer Gs.*"

speed dip *n.*   a small hill crested at high speed, usually lifting riders up off their seats.

squealer *n.*   a ride that's not properly greased. "The Cyclone was a real *squealer* tonight. Call the maintenance crew."

stand-up *n.*   a steel roller coaster designed to be ridden standing up; often features one or more inversions.

theme park mentality *n.*   a derogatory term implying a set of overly strict, safety-conscious rules and operation procedures, designed to please the general public and the park's insurance company, but not hard-core enthusiasts.

twister *n.*   a ride that has limited straight track and usually winds through itself.

washboard *n.*   a series of quick bumps that make one feel as if the coaster is rolling over a washboard.

whirl-and-hurl *n.*   a spinning ride that induces nausea; often found in older parks and carnivals. "I'll never forget the old *whirl-and-hurl* at Pacific Ocean Park—and neither will the guy next to me." Syn. **spin-and-barf.**

whoop-de-doo *n.*   the most intense and exciting part of a ride, such as a corkscrew loop.

Wild Mouse *n.* a small steel coaster with sharp turns and quick, steep drops.

woodies *n.* coasters with tracks made of laminated wood. Rel. **steelies:** coasters with steel tracks.

SCIENCE FICTION FANS

BEM *n.* Bug-Eyed Monster. A humorous reference to any sci-fi (as opposed to SF) monster. Especially pertains to the ones luridly depicted on the covers of early pulp magazines, usually shown holding a scantily clad female of a different species (ours). Rel. **LGM:** Little Green Men. (*See* **SF.**)

bheer *n.* beer. (Fans like to insert an h in various words.)

blog *n.* punch for a fannish party. Usually a combination of alcohol, carbonated beverages, and fruit punches. Also, *bhlog.*

BNF *n.* Big Name Fan. A well-known SF fan.

con *n.* a convention, which may feature book dealers, vendors, panels, guests of honor, movies, parties, costume masquerades, banquets, dances, concerts. Cons vary from fewer than a hundred attendees to nearly ten thousand. An example of this is Worldcon, or World Science Fiction Convention.

cyberpunk *n.* a school of science-fiction writing focused on a bleak and fearful future world where computers, cybernetics, and drugs have taken over.

cyborg *n.* a human being having some electronic body parts. A portmanteau word derived from CYBernetic ORGanism.

D&D *n.* Dungeons and Dragons. A game in which players act out roles in a fantasy universe. It is played with pencil, paper, and dice. Rel. **D.M.:** Dungeon Master. Someone who designs D&D stories in which players can immerse themselves and who may also referee interaction with the fantasy world.

dirty old pro *n.* a writer who has received high pay for a story.

door dragon *n.* someone who watches the door during a room party at a con, to check that arrivals have invitations or know someone in the room. "I don't want all those teenagers drinking up our scotch, so will you be the *door dragon?*" Also, *v.* "I put on room parties regularly, but I never *door dragon* them."

dragon *n.* someone who smokes tobacco.

droid *n.* a machine or robot. From the film *Star Wars*. "I have my *droid* answering the phone."

drobes *n.* derogatory term for people who wear costumes to a science fiction convention, but are not participants in the official masquerade. Probably derived from "wardrobe" and "drone."

DUFF *n.* Down Under Fan Fund. Used for sending fans between the U.S. and Australia. Rel. **TAFF:** Trans-Atlantic Fan Fund. Funds for sending fans between the U.S. and Britain; **MAFF:** Mid-Atlantic Fan Fund. Funds for sending fans into the middle of the Atlantic Ocean; this term comes into play when fans are unhappy with someone.

egoboo *n.* an ego boost, achieved through having an article or letter printed, being discussed in print (even if unfavorably), being on a con panel, and so on. Represents recognition in the SF community. *"Egoboo* is the major fannish currency, the medium of exchange."

fan *n.* a member of fandom; an enthusiast of the science fiction subculture. Plural: **fans, fen** (often joking). Rel. **faan:** someone more interested in fandom than in science fiction; **femmefan:** nearly obsolete term for female fan, from a time when there were few women in fandom.

fanac *n.* fan activity.

fandom *n.* the subculture of science fiction fans.

fannish *adj.* involved with the social side of fandom, including cons and fanzines.

fanzine *n.* a fan magazine that is an amateur publication. Often shortened to "zine."

faunch *v.* to yearn for, desire (sometimes sexually); to search for. Also, *n.* "She's on the *faunch* for a cheeseburger."

FIAWOL *exp.* Fandom Is A Way Of Life. Rel. **FIJAGH:** Fandom Is Just A God-damned Hobby.

filk *n.* folk songs about science fiction themes or fandom, often fitting new words to familiar tunes. Usually parodies or just plain humorous. Derived from a typographical error for "folk" music. "Songs about miners are folk; songs about space miners are *filk.*" Also, a place or party where filking takes place. Also, *v.* to sing these songs.

Four Basic Food Groups *n.* chocolate, Coke, pizza, beer (sometimes listed as chocolate, caffeine, alcohol, and grease). "An alternate in the *Four Basic Food Groups* is the white stuff in Oreo cookies, which is either a food or an alien life form—the jury is still out on which."

fugghead *n.* someone who is considered annoying, cloddish, or idiotic. "Listen, *fugghead,* I simply don't agree with you about that Heinlein story."

furry fandom *n.* fandom focused on anthropomorphized animals.

gafiate *v.* to drop out of science fiction and re-enter the real world. Derived from GAFIA ("Getting Away From It All"), a term for ceasing to participate in fan activity. "He *gafiated* and got a job at a photocopy shop." Rel. **FAFIA:** Forced Away From It All.

Golden Age *n.* the period of science fiction writing from the 1930s to post-World War II. Rel. **Silver Age:** the 1950s.

GURPS *n.* Generic Universal Role Playing System. A popular game system, based on the GURPS Basic Set book and designed to work in any genre: fantasy, science fiction, horror, etc. "Worldbooks" contain information on specific worlds to play in. "The *GURPS* Cyberpunk worldbook is famous for being mistakenly seized by the U.S. Secret Service, which believed it was a manual for computer crime."

hucksters *n.* vendors in the dealers' room at a con, selling books, jewelry, comics, costuming materials, and whatever else a fan might buy.

lecture *n.* the expository lump in a story where the author stops to explain something, usually science—for example, how the stardrive works. Rel. **idiot lecture:** in which the author tries to make this more interesting by having a bimbo ask the professor how the stardrive works.

meat puppet *n.* a cyberpunk character whose nervous system has been altered so he or she is not aware of what the body is doing; often this character is a prostitute, who can be miles away mentally during sex.

mundane *n.* a non-fan. The fans' equivalent of "geek"; someone not of your crowd. Rel. **Mundania:** the world outside fandom.

pro *n.* a professional writer, artist, editor, or publisher of science fiction. "Anyone who ever sold a story can call himself a *pro.*"

readers *n.* people who are avid fans of SF without participating in fandom.

S&S *n.* Swords and Sorcery. A school of fantasy writing that features barbarians, curvaceous girls, and grotesque creatures. "My favorite *S&S* stuff is books about Conan the Barbarian."

sercon *adj.* short for "serious and constructive." The attitude of early fandom, whose members regularly wrote letters to SF magazines reviewing the stories. The antithesis of "fannish."

SF *n.* science fiction. Preferred over "sci-fi," which is a term that SF fans use condescendingly for bad science fiction, usually of the Hollywood *Buck Rogers* sort. Sci-fi is sometimes pronounced "skiffy," in which case it is definitely derogatory.

SMOF *n.* Secret Master of Fandom. A person who wields authority in the organizing and running of cons and in the direction of fandom. Often used tongue in cheek. Also, *v.* to wield power (or try to) at a con, or to discuss con politics and gossip.

trufan *n.* a fan's fan. Someone who takes part in a wide variety of fannish activities and does them well. "You're a real *trufan.*"

waitron *n.* someone who serves coffee and food to guests at SF cons. May appear tired and dronelike, due to the odd hours that fans keep, and may be stupefied by fans' mind-numbing personal habits. "You should have seen the look the *waitron* gave you after you casually mentioned murdering Joey. She doesn't realize we're talking about Virtual Reality.''

Star Trek Fans

clamhead *adj.*   describes the Klingon hairstyle affected by certain Trekkers.

DSPSG *n.*   Disgusting, Slobbering, Patrick Stewart Groupie. ''That *DSPSG* even sends him birthday cards!''

IDIC *n.*   Infinite Diversity in Infinite Combination. A theory in *Star Trek* cosmology.

K&S *n.*   Kirk & Spock. Refers to homoerotic fan fiction, published in zines, that concerns a possible sexual relationship between the two.

Mary Sue *n.*   the stereotyped, overweight female Trekkie.

ST *n.*   *Star Trek.*

ST:Classic *n.*   the original series.

ST:TNG *n.*   *Star Trek: The Next Generation;* sometimes called *Star Trek: The New Guys.* Rel. **ST:DS9:** *Star Trek: Deep Space 9;* **ST:VGER:** *Star Trek: Voyager.*

Trekker *n.*   avid *Star Trek* enthusiast. Rel. **Trekkie:** now often used to mean an annoying *Star Trek* fan or groupie.

THE SOCIETY FOR CREATIVE ANACHRONISM*

aha! *exp.*   an intuitive insight that comes after it was needed. *"Aha!* This is how I could have killed him!''

* With more than forty thousand members, the Society for Creative Anachronism, or SCA, explores and re-creates the Middle Ages (except the Plague and religious injustices, which they only study). Activities include heraldry, dancing, games, armor reconstruction, and gatherings.

attack bard *n.*   someone who comes to your campsite and performs for you, especially when you don't want entertainment.

Autocrat *n.*   the person in charge of an event. "The *Autocrat* had an excellent support team, so she had a great time herself." Rel. **Democrat:** the person in charge of a demonstration. "Lady Catherine is the *Democrat* for the activities at the Fringe Festival."

autotroll *n.*   a telephone answering machine. "For further information, call (555) 555-5555; autotroll on duty." Syn. **gollum.**

bard in a box *n.*   a tape player. Rel. **artist in a box:** a camera.

brass hat *n.*   royalty. The titled nobility within the group wear circlets.

bunny fur *n.*   a barbarian. Someone whose persona falls into the "Conan" or early Middle Ages vein. May wear only patches of bunny fur as garb. "The woman with the bad sunburn? She's a *bunny fur.*"

corkscrewing *v.*   circling a tournament opponent who has had a leg "taken" as a handicap, and is therefore fighting on his knees.

dragon *n.*   a car. "The *dragon* parked illegally with the license plate of ABC-123 will be towed if not moved immediately." Also, an airplane; a mean lady.

droob *n.*   a wooden tournament sword. "Sir Extleb had no money to pay the site fee at the troll booth, so he had to leave his *droob* as collateral."

DSF *adj.*   Derrier Side Forward. A full retreat. "Let's pull a *DSF* and get out of here."

Eric the Red rope *n.*   the tourney field. Named after a red rope used to mark the first fields at SCA events. Syn. **eric.** "Sir BangedHelm! Arm and take the field in the central *eric.*"

farb *adj.*   being out of the proper period, anachronistic. Example: wearing a digital watch with your medieval garb.

farspeaker *n.*   a telephone. "Sir Grantle can be reached at his *farspeaker,* (222) 222-2222.

the Force *n.*   duct tape. "The *Force* has a dark side and a light side, it's found everywhere, and it holds the universe together."

freak the mundanes *v.*   to startle ordinary folk. Frowned on by many SCA members. "We went into town in our garb to *freak the mundanes.*"

Fubba-Wubba *n.*   Fat Ugly Broad with a Bad Attitude. Not used by those of noble or gentle birth; as a sexist remark, it may require a challenge.

grrk *v.*   to disable or vanquish someone in a tournament. SCA combatants use wooden swords and wear up to sixty pounds of re-created armor. "I blocked his first shot, then *grrked* him with a shot on the head."

light *n.*   someone in war archery armor. "I am a heavy fighter, but my Lord is a *light.* That's him in the pretty green surcoat." Also, *adj.*   describes a blow that would not have killed anyone. "My Lord, your blow struck me in the body, but was *light,* and would have caused me no damage. I say we fight on."

mundane *n.*   anyone not part of the SCA. "We're going to a public park, so there will be many *mundanes* present." Also, *adj.*   modern or normal. "My *mundane* name is John Moloney. My *mundane* job is computer programmer."

parry dummy *n.*   an inexperienced fighter going against a knight. Syns. **fresh meat, human pell, walking pell.** (A "pell" is parchment; i.e., skin.)

portable hole *n.*   a metal stake with metal rings attached. It is pounded into the ground and a banner pole is inserted. "The *portable hole* was driven into a tree root and had to be pried out with a crowbar."

Port-a-Castle *n.*   toilet. "By the end of the event, the Port-a-Castles were somewhat fragrant." Syn. **biffy, House of Easy.**

porta-scribe *n.*   a typewriter. Also, a cassette recorder.

rhino *n.*   someone hard to "kill" in battle. Also, a mortal granted invulnerability. Rel. **demi-rhino:** a being who can only be injured by someone of higher rank; i.e., squire by knight, knight by duke, etc.

sand gollum *n.*   a computer.

stick jocks *n.*   heavy weapons fighters. *"Stick jocks* are big men or big women with big sticks, who will hurt you."

troll booth *n.*   a toll gate.

Valhalla *n.*   the hall in which Odin received the souls of slain heroes in Norse mythology. Also, a bar in Worcester, Massachusetts, where college drunks like to fence.

weeble *n.*   a fighter who does not acknowledge blows received. "Everyone knows that *weebles* wobble, but they don't fall down."

wire weenies *n.*   light weapons fighters. *"Wire weenies* enjoy fine liqueurs, while stick jocks are into cheap beer."

TATTOOED AND
BODY-PIERCED PEOPLE

ampallang *n.*   a piercing in which a small metal barbell passes horizontally through the glans of the penis. Rel **apadravya:** a piercing that passes vertically through the glans; **oompah-loompahlang:** a joke term used by women who are amused at trying to keep track of various penile piercings.

beeper *n.*   a piece of body jewelry that is big enough to set off airport metal detectors. "Damn, did you see the *beeper* on that guy's nipple?"

bodmods *n.*   human body modifications such as tattoos, pierces, brandings, and cuttings. "Visible *bodmods* aren't a good idea if you work in a bank."

cart *n.*   cartilage, usually in the ear; a pierce through cartilage. "I'm not sure what I'm going to do next; maybe another *cart* or two."

clicking *v.*   the sound that jewelry in a tongue piercing makes against one's teeth. "After she got pierced, it took her two weeks to learn to talk without *clicking.*"

Earl *n.*   a bridge-of-the-nose pierce.

flash *n.*   stock illustrations displayed on the walls at tattoo parlors; usually traditional images, such as skull-and-crossbones, roses, and so on. "Let's go down to Tattoo Mania and check out the *flash!*" Ant. **custom:** tattoo work done with a personalized design, usually brought in by the customer or created by the artist and customer together. "Wow—did you see that beautiful *custom* piece she had on her back?"

frenum *n.*   a piercing on the bottom of the penis, usually on the sensitive ridge along the bottom behind the glans. Rel. **lorum:** short for "lower frenum," a pierce located toward the lower penis area.

gun *n.*   a modern tattooing machine. "As a tattoo artist you'll use two kinds of *guns*—liners and shaders."

hafada *n.*   a piercing through the surface of the scrotal sac, at the side or center. Rel. **guiche:** a piercing between the scrotum and anus.

ink *n.*   a tattoo. "I'm considering getting some new *ink.* What do you think about a spider on my butt, sweetheart?"

labret *n.*   a pierce between the lower lip and chin. Also, the jewelry that goes in it. "The backs fall off a lot of people's *labret* studs."

Madison *n.*   a horizontal piercing at the base of the neck between the collarbones. Named for porn star Madison Stone, its first exponent. "Rumor has it Madonna got a *Madison.* Maybe she'll hang her keyring on it."

modern primitives *n.*   persons with pierces, tattoos, scarring, or branding. "He grew up on Park Avenue, but now only goes around with *modern primitives.*"

munch *n.*   an organized get-together, usually timed with events such as tattoo or body-piercing conventions. "Hey, let's organize a big *munch* this June in Chicago."

phallus full of malice *n.*   a penis that keeps an erection throughout a genital piercing.

piece *n.*   a tattoo. "I can't wait for you to see my new *piece.*"

Prince Albert *n.*   a piercing that enters through the urethra of a penis and exits under the glans. Syn. **PA.** Rel. **reverse PA** or **Cleopatra:** exits out the top of the glans.

prison tattoo *n.*   often a single tear near the eye, to signify time served.

quaker *n.*   a piercing client who is nervous to the point of quivering.

Queen Kristina *n.*   a horizontal piercing of the clitoral hood.

scratcher *n.*   an inept, self-taught tattooist, someone who has not properly apprenticed with an established artist. "Did you see the crap that *scratcher* did on my brother's arm?"

squick *v.*   to be grossed out, repulsed, disgusted. Being squicked has been characterized as "the sound your brain makes as it flees your skull in terror." "You should have seen the look on his face when I described in graphic detail how it felt when I got my nipple pierced. He was completely *squicked!*" Also, to disgust another person. "I really *squicked* out the girl at Burger King when she saw my tongue pierce." Also, *n.* "The other day I took off my shirt, so all my piercings and tattoos showed, and walked downtown, *squick* hunting."

SSS *n.*   Surgical Stainless Steel. "I have a twelve-gauge *SSS* captive bead ring in my PA."

stretch *v.*   to make a pierced hole bigger by putting in thicker jewelry. "I *stretched* my apadravya from fourteen to twelve gauge this weekend." Ant. **downsize:** to replace a piece of jewelry (usually a barbell in a tongue piercing or apadravya) with a shorter piece. "I got the barbell in my tongue *downsized* after the swelling went down."

temp tat *n.*   a temporary tattoo. "If you get a *temp tat,* people may call you a wimp. It's like taking your inflatable girlfriend to the prom: Nobody really wants to know you."

tribal *adj.*   a tattoo style involving geometric primitive designs, often from Pacific Islands. "I'd like to get *tribal* armbands, but none of the tattoo artists seem to know what they signify. I'd better do a little research first." Syn. **blackwork.**

twitchy *adj.*   describes a painful place to get tattooed. "Will it hurt to get ink there?" "Yeah, it's a *twitchy* spot."

VIDEO GAME PLAYERS

AccLAME *n.* refers to the company Acclaim, maker of "Mortal Kombat" and "NBA Jam" video games. In the eyes of some video game players, Acclaim has become money-grubbing, so "laim" becomes "lame."

boss *n.* a particularly challenging opponent who appears at the end of a level or game. Rel. **mid-boss:** boss who appears halfway through a level.

cheezy *adj.* refers to anything unfair in a video game.

cheezy victory *n.* a win that exploits a character's unfair advantages or flaws in the game's design. "In early versions of 'Mortal Kombat II,' a character named Sub-Zero could trap his opponent in the corner and continuously damage him until he died. Since the opponent could do nothing to stop it, I always thought a match won this way was a *cheezy victory.*"

cluck *n.* a person who does nothing but play games. "That *cluck* has been sitting there since noon playing 'Sonic and Knuckles.'"

combo *n.* a series of attack moves that prevent the victim from blocking in a fighting game. "Todd knows a vicious eight-hit *combo* that lets him wipe out half an opponent's hit points."

CPU *n.* a computer opponent in a fighting game. From Central Processing Unit. "The only way to beat the *CPU* on level six in 'Killer Instinct' is to sweat cheeze-whiz."

dummy *n.* when a company removes features from a game when translating it from one format to another. Also, *v.* "She knew some tips for the Japanese version, so it surprised her when she couldn't find the sword. It must have been *dummied* out of the American version."

Easter egg *n.* a hidden code or trick in a game, usually not stated in the manual. Many games have "cheat codes" that allow a player to become invincible, have more lives, or play the game as a hidden character. "He read gaming magazines to learn about *Easter eggs,* so he could beat the game more easily."

flap *v.* to play video games. Rel. **flapper** *n.* video gamer.

in the zone *adj.* when a player is on a roll and gets totally captivated by the game. "Check out Jimmy's little brother. He's *in the zone.*"

joystick *n.* the control unit used to manipulate characters in a game. It usually consists of two parts—a directional control for up, down, left, and right, and a set of buttons used to jump, kick, and so on.

lives *n.* the number of chances or turns one gets during a game.

newbie *n.* a newcomer still learning how to play a game.

1-up *n.* an extra life in a game. From Pac-Man, whose display screen would indicate the first player's turn as "1-Up."

pack-in *n.* a game that comes packaged with a system. " 'Donkey Kong Country' is a *pack-in* with certain Super Nintendo packages."

play control *n.* a measure of how easy or awkward it is to get a character to jump and perform other functions. "Rule of thumb: If you have to keep looking down at the joystick, then the *play control* is bad. Ideal play control is simple and intuitive."

programming guru *n.* a great designer of video games.

quarter muncher *n.* an arcade video game machine.

RAT *n.* a Reverse ATtack in "Mortal Kombat," a game in which you punch or kick other characters.

scrub *n.* an opposing player that gets completely demolished (the floor is "scrubbed" with him) in a fighting game. "I spent the morning playing 'Killer Instinct,' just toasting this newbie *scrub.*"

shooter *n.* a game based on shooting at attackers. The genre began with "Defender" and "Space Invaders."

Smegma *n.* a pejorative term for the Sega game system.

special move *n.* a sequence of button presses, usually in a fighting game, that allow a character to do additional or long-range damage. "I taught him some *special moves* for a dragon punch."

ten-button Aerosmith thing *n.*   a false rumor. Derived from a rumor that "Mortal Kombat III" would have ten buttons and that Steven Tyler of Aerosmith would be a secret character. By extension, if someone makes a statement about an upcoming game that doesn't sound plausible, one might ask, "Is this another *ten-button Aerosmith thing?*"

The Big N *n.*   the Nintendo company and game system.

translation *n.*   a game that is originally in arcades and is later programmed for a home system. "The *translation* of 'Mortal Kombat II' for the Super Nintendo was great." Rel. **port:** a direct copy of an arcade game; unlike a translation, it contains exactly the same elements with minimal or no loss in graphic quality, sound quality, or other elements of play.

vaporware *n.*   a new game system, piece of hardware, or software that does not exist except in company announcements and news articles. Usually implies that the product will never reach the market.

ZINE* READERS AND PUBLISHERS

anti-copyright *n.*   a statement that the publisher relinquishes ownership rights to the printed work, allowing others to reprint the material without prior permission.

DIY *n.*   Do It Yourself. A slogan used by punks, self-publishers, and others engaged in producing independent media.

editrix *n.*   editor dominatrix.

fanboy *n.*   an avid collector of comic books and related memorabilia. Often pejorative. "Buzz off, *fanboy.*"

fanzine *n.*   a zine produced by and for fans, focusing on such things as science fiction and pop music groups.

---

* Zines are handmade, amateur publications that are created from individual passion and rarely make a profit. These terms originally appeared in R. Seth Friedman's *Factsheet Five.*

Fortean *adj.* relating to the interests of Charles Fort, which include inexplicable phenomena such as rains of frogs, ridiculous weather, and objects in the sky.

furries *n.* comics and stories featuring anthropomorphized animals, often with strong erotic overtones.

Gemstone File *n.* a long conspiracy essay circulated through the underground, linking all the major political figures of the Kennedy and Watergate eras.

goth *n.* a person influenced by gothic fiction that emphasizes the grotesque or desolate. Such a person often adopts dark clothing and severe makeup.

HC *adj.* Hard Core. A style of punk music that is loud, fast, and often sounds angry.

homocore *adj.* homosexual hard-core punk culture.

indie *n.* an independent record, magazine, or other medium produced without support from large corporations.

jack chick *n.* a creator of miniature proselytizing comic books that feature ridiculous stories, fringe Christian ideology, and surprisingly precise art.

magalog *n.* a blend of magazine and catalog that features excerpts, original articles, or other materials beyond just a list of titles and prices.

mail art *n.* art circulated through the postal system; usually postcards, collages, or rubber stampings.

manga *n.* Japanese comics, cartoons, and models. Used primarily to describe comic anthologies as thick as telephone books.

MIB *n.* Men In Black. Legendary strange people said to dress in out-of-date clothes and intimidate UFO witnesses.

memes *n.* units of self-replicating information or ideas circulated by various means and media. Examples: musical tunes, ideas, catch phrases, faxed office jokes.

one-shot *n.* a single-edition zine.

otherstream *n.* a publication outside the mainstream.

perzine *n.* a personal zine, written by one person and typically detailing the publisher's daily life.

Riot Grrrl *n.* a movement of young women's political action, zines, and music.

samizdat *n.* Russian underground self-published newsletters that evaded governmental restrictions. Precursors to zines.

SF/F/H/M *n.* science fiction, fantasy, horror, mystery.

shitworkers *n.* people who help produce a zine by typing or collating, usually for little more reward than a mention in the zine, some pizza and beer, and the gratitude of the editor.

sXe *n.* straight edge, a movement within the punk community of people who have given up taking drugs and eating meat.

techno *n.* modern dance music similar to '70s disco, only faster, with a stronger beat and fewer words.

A SLANG MISCELLANY

Alaskans

bunny boots *n.*   heavy winter footgear made of white felt. "Sarah's *bunny boots* make her look like a giant snowshoe rabbit."

disco mushers *n.*   city slickers who go dogsledding in expensive, neon-colored ski suits.

family planning *n.*   two sled dogs mating during a pause in a race.

low bush moose *n.*   what a hunter says he shot when he misses the real thing and comes home with a rabbit.

outside *n.*   the rest of the world.

rocking chair money *n.*   one's unemployment check.

Aerobics Instructors

Chipmunk music *n.*   music played at a faster than normal tempo, to speed up the exercise pace.

shadow dancing *v.*   obsessively looking at oneself in the mirror throughout a workout. "The rest of us moved on to leg lifts, but the woman *shadow dancing* was still doing stretches."

sweat virgin *n.*   a person so far unsullied by the concept of working out.

Architects

puff 'n' powder *n.*   a remodel involving only cosmetic changes.

ranchburger *n.*   the typical rectangular, one-story ranch house with a low-pitched roof, found in Southern California housing tracts. "My sister bought a ranchburger, and now she wants me to *puff 'n' powder* it."

spinach *n.*   overdone embellishments and trim. "The lines of his residential designs are so clunky, it's no wonder he hangs *spinach* everywhere to cover them up."

Art Gallery Types

hors d'oeuvre circuit *n.*   a round of gallery openings, which often provide free snacks and drinks. "Ted apparently derives his entire minimum daily requirement of nutrition from the *hors d'oeuvre circuit*. He never misses an opening."

Last Supper *n.*   an opening where only about a dozen people show up.

lemmings *n.*   collectors with a follow-the-trend mentality regarding "hot" artists.

list lizard *n.*   a gallery patron who makes a showy request for the price list, but never makes a purchase. "That *list lizard* has come back twice with his girlfriend and his boss—I guess he's just showing off."

over-the-sofa painting *n.*   a work purchased not for its execution, subject, or style, but because it matches the customer's room decor or fills a blank spot on the wall.

Barbie Doll Collectors

Gay Parisienne and **Roman Holiday** *n.*   early Barbie outfits modeled on clothes in Audrey Hepburn movies.

Limited Edition and **Special Edition** *n.* Barbies of which Mattel makes only fifty thousand a year, compared to millions of the regular dolls. "Every Christmas I can't wait for the Holiday Barbie *Special Edition.*"

loose *adj.* out of the box.

mean greenies *n.* a condition of Barbie's skin, which may turn green where metal earrings attach. "All I found at the thrift store were two loose dolls, and one had quite a dose of the *green meanies.*"

#1 *n.* the oldest and rarest Barbie, made in 1959.

NRFB *adj.* Never Removed From Box. The best possible condition for a Barbie; mint. "I see where a #1 *NRFB* is selling above five thousand dollars."

PWH *adj.* Played With Hard. A Barbie that shows severe wear and probably damage.

1600s *n.* the Jackie Kennedy–style fashions that Barbie sported in the 1960s, such as pillbox hats and long, colored gloves. The "1600s" were Mattel's catalog numbers for these items.

Campaign Managers

affair *n.* a fund-raising event.

dump *n.* an affair at which many political contributors can be hit up for donations at a single stroke. "We've got a dinner *dump* planned for Wednesday the 24th."

gray ghost *n.* the chief staffer of a senator or congressman.

meet 'n' greet *n.* a social mixer with no pressure on guests to write checks. Syn. **mix 'n' mingle.**

war chest *n.* the coffers reserved for an incumbent's future campaigns.

CB Radio Users

DSOR *n.* Deathly Silence [was the] Only Reply. No response to a call.

foot warmer *n.* a linear amplifier, which boosts the power of a signal. So called because most amps have heat sinks whose fins get hot. Illegal but widely used on the CB band. Syns. **afterburner, boots, little helper.**

funny freqs *n.* the radio spectrum slightly above and below the CB band; reserved primarily for government use and legally off-limits to CBers. However, it is used by "freebanders," or para-hams without licenses. Syn. **extras.**

mud duck *n.* a weak station. Rel. **mud duckin'** *v.* broadcasting a weak signal.

readin' the mail *v.* listening to radio traffic. "You never know who's *readin' the mail,* so I can't say too much." Syn. **sandbagging.**

Cheerleaders

geek parade *n.* the school marching band.

M&M *n.* marching and maneuvering.

pinchpenny *n.* when cheerleaders stand so erect that they could grip a penny between their buttocks.

Child and School Photographers

gold mine *n.* a school with lots of students and thus potential sales.

luggage *n.* a child without animation before the camera. "You wouldn't believe the *luggage* this morning in the first grade at Emerson Elementary."

Weeping Willie *n.* a crying child. Also, **Weeping Wilma.**

Coin Collectors

ask *n.*   a coin's wholesale selling price. "What's *ask* on that 1856 Flying Eagle cent?" Ants. **bid, Mr. Bid:** wholesale buying price.

blazer *n.*   an uncirculated or proof coin with a desirably high sheen and radiance. Syns. **dazzler, Godzilla, killer, monster, moose, stone white headlight, wonder coin.**

California Special *n.*   a coin that's been polished to a gloss and otherwise doctored to enhance its appeal and value.

cartwheel *n.*   a silver dollar.

dog *n.*   a coin in terrible condition.

done *adj.*   describes a coin that's been doctored or cleaned. "I'll pass on that trade dollar. It's been *done.*"

hits *n.*   nicks on a coin's surface. "It's got some *hits,* so you can have it cheap."

park *v.*   to store away a coin in the hope that its value will go up. "Ed *parked* those Walking Liberty halves so long ago, he's forgotten he has them."

put it on a wall *v.*   to post a sales offer on the bulletin board at a coin shop. "Remember my Barber quarters? Maybe I should *put them on a wall* and get rid of them."

Construction Workers

headache! *exp.*   "Look out below!" Used when a worker drops something, such as a bucket of rivets, that may injure someone below.

Customs Agents

cold hit *n.*   when an agent ferrets out smuggled goods through a random search or lucky hunch.

Fred and Ethel *n.*   an older American husband and wife. "Let *Fred and Ethel* through. They have nothing to declare."

Fox Hunters

accounted for *adj.*   when a fox is killed or trapped by the hounds.

babbler *n.*   a hound that gives tongue constantly for no reason.

billet *n.*   fox dung.

chopped fox *n.*   a fox surprised and killed before it can leave its shelter.

give tongue *v.*   for a dog to vocalize. "Barking" is done by curs, never by hounds.

rat catcher *n.*   an informal riding outfit.

Garbage Collectors

motorized rice *n.*   maggots.

mungo *n.*   discarded items good enough for a garbageman to cull and keep. "The last *mungo* I got was a perfect set of golf clubs. I guess the owner must have played a really horrible round."

toss the salad *v.*   to throw garbage into the truck; to mechanically churn and compact the garbage.

Gardeners

beast *n.*   dog. "As we discovered when we weeded her back lawn, she has a *beast.*"

chunkmeister *n.*   a homeowner who makes great amounts of backyard compost.

cooked *adj.*   burned by the sun. "The begonias are totally *cooked*. Better rip them out."

deadhead *v.*   to pluck dead blossoms off a plant to improve its appearance and growth. *"Deadhead* all the geraniums, will you?"

involved *adj.*   covered with bugs. "Why don't you isolate that dwarf lemon. It's seriously *involved.*"

mow, blow, and go *v.*   to do a cursory job of garden maintenance. "Those guys at Sunshine Landscaping don't know diddly about planting or pruning. It's strictly *mow, blow, and go.*"

Hairdressers

crab meat *n.*   hair so damaged that it is stringy and limp.

cul-de-sac *n.*   a nearly bald male client. "I feel terrible charging twenty-five dollars to cut a *cul-de-sac*. It only takes five minutes."

nuked *adj.*   when hair has been chemically damaged by bleach, dye, or perming.

Headhunters

Don Quixote *n.*   a job hunter with a highly unrealistic idea of the type of position he is qualified for.

on the beach *adj.*   unemployed. "That art director has been *on the beach* since late last year. I don't think I can place him."

peacenix *n.*   defense industry workers who have been laid off.

stalking horses *n.*   fair-to-middling prospects sent to a company first, in order to make the top candidate an easy sell for the headhunter.

Librarians

eight o'clock *n.* a patron who shows up at the reference desk with a complicated question right before the library closes. "The number of bowling balls manufactured in the U.S. since 1900—that's what this *eight o'clock* wanted to know."

juvie *n.* the area of the library with books for children. "Ellen really enjoys working in *juvie,* but the moppets get to me after a few hours."

Maple Sugarers

doodlebug *n.* a homemade tractor, usually put together from old car and truck parts.

sugar bush *n.* an orchard of maple trees; may be cultivated for sap production.

sugar on snow *n.* an impromptu snowcone made of boiled maple syrup drizzled over packed wet snow.

Movie Ushers

Pepsi skating *v.* slipping and sliding on a floor drenched with spilled soft drinks.

picnickers *n.* movie patrons who pack their own snacks.

rip-and-grin *v.* to take tickets.

Mystery Fans

cozies *n.* genteel, usually British, mysteries in which a corpse seems to function more as a conversation piece than a cause for alarm.

had-I-but-known mysteries *n.* stories in which a distraught heroine is entangled with a villain who concealed his true colors from the beginning. Often these stories have gothic overtones and are first-person narratives.

Park Rangers

JDLR *n.* members of the public who Just Don't Look Right. "There's a herd of *JDLRs* in space 20 at Sequoia Campground. Keep an eye on them, will you?"

touron *n.* a park visitor who exhibits idiotic behavior. Combination of tourist and moron. "Two *tourons* came into the visitor center asking, 'What time do you turn off Yellowstone Falls at night?'"

Postal Workers

animals *n.* workers who do the heavy lifting of mail on the loading docks. Syn. **gorillas.**

baby buggy *n.* a steel-and-canvas trolley for moving letters and packages around the post office. Syn. **shopping carts.**

bomb *n.* an overwhelming load of mail to process. "It's Valentine's Day next month! Brace yourself for a *bomb.*"

nixie *n.* mail that is undeliverable, either because of an incomplete or nonexistent address or because of an incorrect zip code. "So many of those direct-mail pitches are *nixies.*"

pat the can *v.* to empty collection boxes.

zombie *n.* a graveyard shift worker.

Swimming Pool Cleaners

scum line *n.* the dirty green stain around the water line, created by algae and assorted muck.

shock *v.* to pour in lots of chlorine to prevent scum lines and general contamination. "I'd better *shock* the Davises' pool. It's starting to look like the Black Lagoon."

Taxi Drivers

black *adj.*   out of service.

bomb *n.*   a large fare, usually more than twenty dollars. Ant. **jerk:** a small fare for a brief trip.

dive *v.*   to wedge in front of other waiting taxis; to cut into a line. Syn. **boffing the line.**

dog pound *n.*   the Greyhound Bus station.

the farm *n.*   New York City's Kennedy Airport.

ice breaker *n.*   the day's first fare.

suspect *n.*   a late-night airport passenger without luggage.

Telephone Operators

didley *n.*   dial tone.

shoulder surfer *n.*   a thief who loiters near someone using a pay phone and surreptitiously steals the phone card number being used. "Grand Central Station is crawling with *shoulder surfers.* Five minutes after they get your card number, they're selling it on the street for ten bucks." Rel. **Montebello:** a card number that bypasses the phone company's fraud-detection system and, therefore, may be worth three thousand dollars on the street.

Tennis Players

bagel *n.*   beating someone 6-0, 6-0.

double Chrissie *n.*   a player with a double-handed backhand (like Chris Evert) and a double-handed forehand as well.

groundies *n.*   ground strokes. "My *groundies* sure could use some work."

paint the line *v.* to hit the line with a ball.

shank *v.* to miss a shot.

stick *n.* a tennis racket.

Tennis Teachers

screen door *n.* a student tennis racket with a very large face.

wake-up call *n.* when a student hits the ball into his doubles partner's back.

Transit Workers

Amshack *n.* a standard-issue modern Amtrak station.

foamer *n.* a rail fan who figuratively foams at the mouth over trains.

freight *n.* passengers. Rel. **standing freight:** passengers or commuters jammed onto a train.

mule *n.* a bus.

off the iron *adj.* derailed.

ride the cushions *v.* to take a bus, when you're a bus driver.

taking the scenic route *v.* when a bus driver gets lost.

Veterinarians

blue-plate special *n.* all of a pet's shots given at one appointment.

finger painter *n.* a dog that poops on the floor and then walks through it, making tracks.

land shark *n.* a biting dog.

Weather Forecasters

BICO *exp.*   Baby, It's Cold Outside.

positive vorticity advective *n.*   rain is expected.

Whitewater Rafters

hydraulics *n.*   wave action during high water. "By the end of summer, the *hydraulics* on the river have pretty much died down."

maytagged *v.*   to be churned under a powerful current. "We got *maytagged* on the Middle Fork of the Salmon."

swimmer *n.*   person overboard. "What a trip—I had two *swimmers* the first morning."

teacup *v.*   to spin the raft continuously, in the manner of the whirling teacup ride at Disney World.

ACKNOWLEDGMENTS

Barnaby Conrad, head of the Santa Barbara Writers Conference, generously gave me the idea for this book. A suggestion from "my lovely and talented wife, Merry," led to the title. In addition to her help on the project, she handled household duties during my long work days. (Thank you!) Among other major helpers and supporters are Christopher Reynolds of the *Los Angeles Times,* Colin Campbell, Karen Bloomquist, the Munzig family, Frances Atkeson, and John Nuñez. My tireless and charming literary agent, Alice Martell, worked double overtime. Editor Cynthia Vartan at Henry Holt and Company was a joy, giving me insightful suggestions and cordial support, and Felecia Monroe was the excellent copyeditor.

More than seven hundred people contributed slang to *Idiom Savant.* Many thanks to all of them:

Kal Abu-Shalback/volleyball
Justene Adamec/lawyers
George Adams-Day/pilots
Edwin Aguilar/fly fishing
John Alexander/Harley riders
Rhonda Alterson/nurses
The Amazing Sling/jugglers
Mark Ambrose/pilots
Gary Anderson/fishing
Justin Anderson/skating
Kevin Anderson/ice skating
Whit Andrews/bird watchers
Joe Arkin/volleyball
Paul Asente/roller coasters
Dan Asimov/crosswords
Paul Aughey/cavers

Nancy Augustine/nurses
Mike Aukslong/surfers
Don Baccus/bird watchers
Hazel Baden/science fiction
Barry Bakalor/jugglers
Dave Baker/tattoos, pierces
Steve Baker/darts
Doug Baldwin/truckers
Loren Bandiera/wrestlers
Ade Barkah/pilots
Steve Barnard/tennis
Victor J. Barry, D.D.S./dentists
Less Bartel/cavers
Hubert Bartels/comics
Luis Barthel-Rosa/skiers
Jeff Bartlett/truckers

Luke Barton/mountain bikes
Peter Baum/gamblers
Bob Baxter/nurses
Bill Beaman/baseball cards
James Beauregard/gamblers
Christina Beck/ice skating
Jeff Beckham/skydivers
Adam M. Bell/mountain bikes
Peter Bellwood/screenwriters
Noam Ben-Ami/audiophiles
Mark Bentkower/gamblers
David L. Bergart/Harley riders
Torsten Berger/volleyball
Jake Bergmann/crosswords
Ron Berry/nurses
Skip Bertsch/karaoke
Rachel Beyer/skydivers
Rob Bigg/pot smokers
Rendell Bird/roller coasters
Rob Bird/nurses
Karen Bloomquist/dentists
Tom Blue/gambling cheaters
Eric Bockstahler/truckers
Dave Boll/bowlers
Jim Bolus/horseracing
William Bond/inline skating
Albert G. Boulanger/ice skating
Mike Bourk/darts
Bill Bowers/magicians
Melissa Bowman/ice skating
Cliff Boxer/pilots
Casey Boyce/climbers
Regis Boyle/FBI
Kelly Bradley/video games
Seth Breidbart/science fiction
Don Brocha/pilots
Joel Brodsky/mountain bikes
Jimmy Brokaw/jugglers
A. Bromley/hockey
Lew Brooks/gamblers
Dave Brown/boating
Dennis Brown/volleyball

Marcus Brown/wrestlers
Paul R. Brown/mountain bikes
Rich Brown/science fiction
Barry Brumitt/skydivers
Eric W. Bryant/mountain bikes
Tom Buchanan/skydivers
Harold Buchman/animators
Bryan C. Buckley/snowboards
Erika Buky/climbers
Al Bundy/bowlers
Skip Burrell/skiers
Brent Burton/mountain bikes
Bill Burton/Harley riders
Margaret Burwell/ice skating
Tim Bushko/truckers
Jeffery Butler/climbers
Jonathan Byrd/mountain bikes
Ken Byrd/cavers
Scott Callantine/pilots
Colin Campbell/baseball, football
Andreas Caranti/mountain bikes
Lisa Carlson/funeral directors
Ray Carpenter/table tennis
Thom Carpenter/nurses
Avedon Carol/science fiction
Michael Carmack/video games
Gerry Caron/pilots
Chuck Cartwright/football
Joseph W. Casey/science fiction
Allen Chan/horseracing
Bobby Chan/mountain bikes
Girard Chandler/mountain bikes
Richard Chandler/pilots
Ray Chapa/fly fishing
Alex F. Charles/basketball
Eric "T-Rex" Chastain/comics
Chad Childers/science fiction
Jeff Chiou/weight lifters
Steve Ciccarelli/mountain bikes
Carol M. Ciliberti/climbers
Bruce Cleveland/jugglers
Dave Cloutier/surfers

Cara Cocking/skateboarders
Bram Cohen/jugglers
Ken Colburn/truckers
Niki Coleman/volleyball
L. Conant/Harley riders
Barnaby Conrad/bullfighters
Reid Conti/mountain bikes
Andrew John Conway/jugglers
Mike Corman/boating
Marc Cormier/nurses
Nic Cornell/boating
Robert Corns/animation
Bill Couturié/mob
Fred Cox/boating
Michael A. Cramer/SCA
Jon Crane/skateboarders
Karen J. Cravens/science fiction
John Crawford/nurses
Scott R. Crawford/fishing
David Cray/baseball players
Mark Cronan/lawyers
Shaun Crouch/weight lifters
Chris Croughton/science fiction
Butch Curry/weight lifters
J. M. Curry/climbers
Simon Cushing/basketball
Marcia Cutler/bird watching
Charlie Dancey/jugglers
Philip Darbyshire/nurses
Carl Davis/horseracing
Donald Davis/cavers
John Davis/climbers
Rob Davis/CB radio users
Paul Davison/pilots
Ted Dasher/skydivers
Alan Davenport/pilots
Tom Dawes-Gamble/pilots
Shawn Dawson/comics
Pat Deane/bowlers
Robbie De Arras/video games
Rolf A. de By/bird watchers
Michael DeChaine/cavers

Garth deCocq/wrestlers
William C. Dedes/lawyers
Harrison Dekker/climbers
Nev Delap/skydivers
Michel Denber/ice skating
Matt Dick/tennis
Jeff Dilcher/cavers
Daniel Dillon/mountain bikes
Madelyn Dinnerstein/jugglers
Dan Dionne/mountain bikes
Patrick Penzias Dirks/pilots
Chris Dixon/surfers
Jeff Dodd/Harley riders
Nick Doelman/wrestlers
Larry Doering/pilots
Thomas Donalek/climbers
Dana Dorsett/skiers
Mark Dougherty/cavers
Rod Downey/surfers
Brian Drake/comics
Ed Dravecky III/science fiction
Mark Ducati/comics
Ray Duffy/wrestlers
Jim Duhl/pilots
Mark Dursin/wrestlers
Bonnie Dutile/skydivers
Rob Dyson/snowboarders
Sam Eaton/lawyers
Mark Eckenwiler/lawyers
Tom Eblen/fly fishing
Jon A. Egger/nurses
John Eckert/fishing
William Edews/horseracing
Egyptoid/science fiction
Jay R. Eick/skydivers
Lewis S. Eisen/weight lifters
Al Eisner/bird watchers
Darren Eley/pot smokers
Steven Elinson/mountain bikes
Tim Elliott/skydivers
Erin Endom/ice skating
Louis Epstein/ice skating

Jon Ernst/fly fishing
Peter Errico/fishing
Steve Fafel/mountain bikes
Orval R. Fairbairn/pilots
Falcon/pot smokers
Andrew Falconer/mountain bikes
Mike Falkner/game shows
Wendy Faulkner/skydivers
Francis Favorini/jugglers
Ben Feen/tattoos
Kassim M. Ferris/skiers
Alan Fetters/jugglers
Ed Figuli/pilots
Seth Finkelstein/comics
Eric Fischer/tattoos, pierces
Mike "Fish" Fischer/climbers
Matt Fisher/darts
Rick Fletcher/fly fishing
Ned Foley/waiters
Rob Follo/wrestlers
Stephanie Folse/SCA
Wayne R. Foote/lawyers
Maurice Forrester/wrestlers
John S. Fowler/pilots
Dave Fox/nurses
Kurt Fox/bird watchers
Bill Franz/cavers
Mark Frattarola/skydivers
John Freas/pilots
Leny Freeman/fishing
Molly Freeman/hockey
N. Freeman/climbers
Dana Friedman/standup
    comedians
Eric Friedman/table tennis
Neal Friedman/karaoke
R. Seth Friedman/zines, science
    fiction
Michael Fuhrer/mountain bikes
Guy Fuller/fishing
David E. Gabbard/nurses
Steven Gale/climbers

Ted Gallop/pilots
Tom Galloway/comics
Andy Gamache/skydivers
Maxwell Garrison/SCA
Roy Gathercoal/SCA
Gay-Mart/gays and lesbians
Derek Gee/roller coasters
John Gerard/roller coasters
Joe Gerardin/computers
Michael Gerlek/jugglers
Erik Gibbons/skiers
Klein Gilhousen/pilots
Darrell Gilleland/nurses
Brad Gillies/pilots
Dwight Ginn/bird watchers
Martin Ginsburg/nurses
Keith Glasscock/pilots
Emily Rose Glick/snowboarders
J. Michael Glynn/tabloid reporters
Jason Goertz/pilots
Lynn Gold/science fiction
Brian Golden/skydivers
Alan Goldman/mountain bikes
Jeff Goldsmith/ice skating
Ray Gompf/truckers
Darrin Jamie Granter/wrestling
Russell Granzow/fashion
Matt Gross/skateboarders
Michael Grossman/fishing
Zack Grossman/climbers
Tom Grotenhuis/wrestlers
Ann Grusin/ice skating
Joe Leon Guerrero/volleyball
Helge Gundersen/audiophiles
Tom Gwilym/pilots
Gene Haas/pilots
Stella Hackell/mountain bikes
David Hall/baseball cards
Randy Hall/volleyball
Paul Halter/jugglers
Jay J. Hamacek/fishing
Ray Hamel/crosswords

Aaron T. Hamilton/pool players
Marshall Hance/mountain bikes
Rob Hanson/science fiction
Frank Hardy/pilots
Nick Hardy/golf
Rob Harper/cavers
Tim Harrison/cavers
Rob Hawkes/mountain bikes
Jane Hawkins/science fiction
Patrick N. Hayden/science fiction
Sonny Hays-Eberts/hockey
Dave Hearn/volleyball
Candace Heath/pilots
Catherine Heggtveit/mountain
   bikes
Gary J. Heidenreich/basketball
Russell Heithoff/skiers
Gregg Henderson/golf
Jay Hendrickson/Harley riders
Malcolm Herbert/cavers
George Herbig II/wrestlers
Marc Hershon/comedians
Paul Herzog/wrestlers
Gregory Hill/climbers
James Hill/skiers
Janet Swan Hill/ice skating
Kit Hill/surfers
Bill Hilton/fishing
Phaedra Hise/pilots
Dana Hlusko/nurses
Christina M. Hoffman/nurses
Eric Holma/wrestlers
Chris Holmes/pilots
Geoff Holroyd/bird watchers
Gary Hoo/animators
Nathan Hoover/jugglers
Vince Horan/pilots
John Horton/nurses
Mike Hovan/pilots
Warren Hovland/pilots
Michael Howden/jugglers
Bob Hoye/nurses

Jeremy Hoyland/boating
Rhonda Hoyle/ice skating
Bruce Hoylman/mountain bikes
Bill Huang/golf
Patricia Spencer Huczko/nurses
Richard Hudson/game shows
Robert Huizinga/nurses
Martha Hulley-Jones/nurses
Mark Hullinger/bird watchers
Emily Hunter/ice skating
Brent "Bubba" Hurd/Harley
   riders
M. Huret/crosswords
Barry Hurwitz/antiques dealers
Kent Huth/snowboarders
Taneli Huuskonen/jugglers
Nelson Ing/volleyball
Jerry Irish/truckers
Jeff Jackson/inline skating
Alan Jaffray/pool
Loren Janes/stunt doubles
James Jay/jugglers
Eric Jego/volleyball
Chris Jenkins/lawyers
Steve Jensen/nurses
Reverend Joe/boating
Ed Johnson/baseball players
Jeff Johnson/volleyball
Paul Johnson/roller coasters
Rich Johnson/fishing
Wade Johnson/basketball
Patrick Jordan/crosswords
Chris Jung/SCA
Richard Kalk/police officers
James Kalyn/wrestlers
Paul Kamen/fishing
Mark Kaminsky/pilots
Tom Karner/skiers
Joseph Keefhaver/auctioneers
Marilyn Weyman Kegg/skiers
Bill Keith/weight lifters
Gary Keizur/skiers

Mark Kelly/fishing
Timothy Kelly/karaoke
Berry Kercheval/pilots
John Kessel/volleyball
Warren Kidd/skydivers
William Kiene/fishing
Skip King/skiers
Kevin R. Kirtley/pilots
Henry Kisor/pilots
Joshua Knapton/tattoos
Knut Olaf Knutsen/mountain bikes
Andrew Koenig/pilots
Joyce Kolb/comics
Barb Konopka/nurses
Herb Kraft/wrestlers
Stephen J. Kramer/mountain bikes
John Krawczuk/horseracing
John F. Krenz/bowlers
Jennifer Kretschmer/ice skating
Amy Kriston/bird watchers
Carl B. Kuck/skiers
Herb Kunze/wrestlers
David Kurensky/mountain bikes
Bruce Kvam/volleyball
Doc Laing/karaoke
Joseph Lalor/pilots
Karen Landau/nurses
James Landess/mountain bikes
Geoffrey A. Landis/science fiction
Michael Lang/volleyball
Tony Langdon/CB radio users
Bill Langley/basketball
Chris LaReau/jugglers
Steve Lau/trucking
Blackie Lawless/nurses
David Lawrence/boating
Joel Laws/cavers
Lori Leary/nurses
Nancy Lebovitz/science fiction
Brian Lee/mountain bikes

Caron Leff/table tennis
Tish and Jeff Lehman/antiques dealers
Janell Lehmann/jugglers
Chris Lesher/climbers
Fred Levy-Haskell/science fiction
Arthur Lewbel/jugglers
Brian Lewis/pilots
James Lewis/magicians, con artists
Jordan Lewis/gamblers
Douglas Limmer/comics
Dave Linton/cavers
Michael Lipman/animators
Keith Lipski/snowboarders
Jerry L. Logsdon/mountain bikes
Michael E. Lovell/fly fishing
Sloane Y. Lucas/comedians
Todd Ludwig/baseball players
Barney Lum/pilots
Chad Lundgren/science fiction
Alan MacDonald/jugglers
Gregg P. Machacz/mountain bikes
Don Mack/golf
Gail Mackiernan/bird watchers
R.J.P. MacKinnon/mountain bikes
Leslie Madeo/nurses
Liz Madigan/nurses
Lee Mahan/nurses
Marc Majka/pilots
Terry Mankus/hockey
Laurie Mann/science fiction
Shirley Mann/volleyball
Lesley Manning/theater
Scott W. Manzi/boating
Ben Marks/car salesmen
Amanda Marmie/tattoos
Trudi Marrapodi/ice skating
Dave Marshall/gamblers
Dave Martin/pilots
Susan Martin/nurses
J. Mason/boating
Kent Matthewson/weight lifters

Maciej M. Matyjas/skateboarders
Phil Maurer/volleyball
Rich Maxson/antiques dealers
Joe Mazza/pilots
Dan McCauley/mountain bikes
Todd McClary/crosswords
Chip McDaniel/darts
Patrick McDonough/basketball
Brad McGee/wrestlers
Charlie McGee/nurses
Steve McIntosh/computers
Cameron McKeel/mountain
  bikers
Gordie McKinnon/bird watchers
Tim McMichael/skydivers
Cullen McMorrow/inline skating
Gil Meacham/boating
Josh Mehlman/ice skating
Geoff Melnychuk/skiers
Robert L. Meredith/Harley riders
Barbara Metzler/antiques dealers
Jack Michaud/snowboarders
Brian N. Miller/jugglers
Doug Milliken/mountain bikes
Mark Minton/cavers
Mike Mitchell/mountain bikes
Jeff Moersch/pilots
Fraser Moffatt/mountain bikes
Joel Monleon/bowlers
Laura Montagano/antiques
  dealers
Jamie Montgomery/fly fishing
Mike Morefield/weight lifters
James Morgan/gamblers
Matt Morse/fly fishing
Tom Moss/cavers
Thomas Mueller/pilots
Joe Mugnier/gambling
Rich Muller/weight lifters
Dan Murphy/basketball
Michael L. Murphy/pilots
Tom Murphy/boaters

Tana J. Murrah/skiers
Shaun C. Murray/mountain bikes
Kristen Mustad/fishing
Larry Nash/fly fishing
Ron Natalie/pilots
John Nations/jugglers
Jay Lloyd Neal/animators
Sean Neeley/mountain bikes
Ken Neely/climbers
Clayton Neff/football
Mark Nevins/comics
Louise Newness/nurses
Chris Nickel/science fiction
Jimmy Nguyen/snowboarders
Vanchau Nguyen/volleyball
Eileen Noel/skiers
Peter Norquist/climbers
Manny Nosowsky/crosswords
Jason Nugent/mountain bikes
Kevin O'Brien/fly fishing
Trish O'Brien/ice skating
Tom Obszanski/roller coasters
Chad O'Hara/mountain bikes
Jim Olsen/cavers
Erik Olson/skiers
Rob Olson/volleyball
Darryl Ong/audiophiles
Rick Osgood/darts
David Oshinsky/mountain bikes
Greg Ostravich/jugglers
David Ottenstein/pool
Will Outlaw/pilots
J. Chris Pace/baseball
Howard G. Page/pilots
Tom Pardue/nurses
Gregg Park/fishing
Nick Parker/climbers
Simon Elliott Parker/climbers
Dan Patnode/antiques dealers
Chris Patterson/mountain bikes
George Patterson/pilots
Greg Pavlov/fly fishing

Ben Pearlman/gamblers
Bernard Peek/science fiction
Mark Pemburn/mountain bikes
Marti Penn/horse racing
P. J. Perdue/skydivers
Sarah H. Perry/nurses
James Phillips/fishing
Daniel Pierce/audiophiles
Cindy Pierson/horseracing
Jeff Pikor/airlines
Mitch Pinard/inline skaters
David Pinzino/skydivers
Jeff Piroozshad/bowlers
Ken Pitts/golf
Craig Poff/fly fishing
K. A. Pohjola/tattoos
Tom Poindexter/pilots
Paul Polak/hockey
Jake Pooler/skateboarders
Whitney Potter/climbers, theater
Mike Powers/bird watchers
Penny Powers/Harley riders
Ram Prasad/jugglers
Brian Prendota/wrestling
Dave Pretz/volleyball
Lee Price/truckers
Irwin Prince/lawyers
Mike Pritchard/darts
Graham Proudlove/cavers
Stephen Prouse/nurses
Tom Purvis/mountain bikes
W. T. Rabe/stone skipping
Darrell Ralston/firefighters
Tom Rankin/volleyball
Chris Rasley/pilots
Katie Rathslag/science fiction
Robert Reagan/roller coasters
Sharon Reagan/roller coasters
Frank Reid/cavers
Jim Rehrer/fishing
Joyce Reis/nurses
P. J. Remner/mountain bikes

James Rice/animation
Gerome Rich/skydivers
Jim Ricks/truckers
Nonie Rider/science fiction
Jim Riley/waiters
Bert Robbins/skydivers
James Robertson/climbers
Scott Robertson/snowboards
Rich Robinson/mountain bikes
Chris Rockwell/golf
Dan Roddick/Frisbee players
Jay Rogoff/baseball players
David Romm/science fiction
Phil Rose/crosswords
Mel Rosen/crosswords
Chris Rotelli/volleyball
Ahti Eric Rovainen/football
Dave Rowland/climbers
Pete Ruckelshaus/mountain bikes
Lee Ann Rucker/ice skating
Matt Ruddy/skiers
Simon Rundell/nurses
Sheila Russell/nurses
Ryber/tattoos, pierces
Sabrina from San Diego/
     basketball
Steve "Doc" Salberg/jugglers
Shaun Salter/Harley riders
Daan Sandee/bird watchers
Dan Savage/standup comedians
Aaron Sawchuk/baseball cards
Dottie Schaefer/nurses
Dirk Schaeffer/ice skating
Cathy Schenck/horseracing
John Schultz/fishing
Larry Shilkoff/pilots
Mike Shirer/fishing
Patrick Schlagel/magicians
Harvey Schlesinger/antiques
     dealers
Robert B. Schmunk/inline skating
Mike Schneider/volleyball

Rita Schreiber/nurses
David Schriber/snowboards
Joseph Schuld/bowlers
Bill Scott/truckers
Chris Scott/mountain bikes
Roy SeGuine/table tennis
Ken Seiss/fishing
Dave Selin/nurses
Keith Shackleford/surfers
Eiran Shalev/weight lifters
Mike Shaver/video games
Steven Sheffield/mountain bikes
Julia E. Shields/bird watchers
John S. Shipley/football
Al Sigman/hockey
Brian Silverman/jugglers
Eric T. Simon/roller coasters
Mark Sinkovic/skateboarders
Brad Sinrod/fly fishing
Tom Sito/animation
Max Slover/truckers
Justin Smith/golf
Mike Smedley/darts
Dave Smith/pilots
David Smith/nurses
Greg Robin Smith/SCA
Josh Smith/snowboarders
Leah Zeldes Smith/science fiction
Mark Smith/skydivers
Mike Smith/bird watchers
Mark Sondeen/mountain bikes
Vello Sork/truckers
Steve Sosensky/bird watchers
Jeff Souza/wrestlers
"Spectral Image"/pot smokers
The Spook/video games
Duane Starcher/jugglers
Jon Steckelberg/wrestlers
Bill Steel/cavers
Steve Stein/baseball players
Adam Stein-Sapir/weight lifters
Mark Stephen/mountain bikes

Brian Stern/bird watchers
Ilana Stern/climbers
Carl Stevens/pilots
Bob Stewart/nurses
Alexis G. Stobbe/pilots
Whitney Stocker/bird watchers
Ted Stodgell/mountain bikes
Jeremy Storteboom/snowboarders
George A. Strain/jugglers
Kurt Strain/audiophiles
Jeffrey Strang/audiophiles
D. Stringer/nurses
Marc E. Strohwig/mountain bikes
Garrett C. Stumb/pilots
Erik Stumph/wrestlers
Connie Swaim/antiques dealers
Steve Tatham/comedians
Lance Taylor/fly fishing
Julie Teater/nurses
Mary Terhaar/nurses
Lani Teshima-Miller/tattoos
Ryan Thieme/hockey
James Thom/nurses
Linda Thomas/bowlers
Phil Thomas/jugglers
Tom Tobszanski/roller coasters
M. D. Troll/Harley riders
Richard Tucker/roller coasters
William D. Turcotte/pilots
Marie Turock/skateboarders
Eric Twardzicki/video games
Michael T. Tyler/bowlers
Pat Tyler/car salesmen
William Tyler/fishing
Judy Leedom Tyrer/ice skating
Tom Unger/climbers
Scott VanArtsdalen/pilots
John Vance/mountain bikes
Rob Vancko/jugglers
Jean-Yves Vanier/bowlers
Jim Verran/hockey

Carlos Javier Vergara/inline skating
Tony Verhulst/pilots
Robin Vernell/animators
Alan Villiers/nurses
Mark Vinsel/fly fishing
John M. Vogel/nurses
Bill Von Novak/skydivers
Andy Waddington/cavers
Nathan Waddoups/inline skating
Ray Wagner/mountain bikes
Christopher Wahl/mountain bikes
Chris Wajciechowski/weight lifters
Bill Walker/skiers
Ed Walker/science fiction
Lynn Wallace/volleyball
Tom L. Wallace/mountain bikes
Ann Waller/horseracing
Brent Ware/climbers
Andy Warner/skiers
Terri Watson/pilots
Rick Wayne/pilots
Brian Wayson/nurses
Ron Webb/nurses
Bud Webster/science fiction
Jay Weinberg/volleyball
Pauline Welby/jugglers

Roger Wells/science fiction
Ryan White/video games
Thomas White/baseball cards
Mark Whitson/Harley riders
Adrian Wible/pool
Peggy Williams/nurses
Robin Williams/computers
Cheyenne Wills/climbers
Nicholas Winton/hockey
Bob Wise/television folk
Eric Witherspoon/pilots
Jim Wolper/pilots
Tony Woltermann/comics
Clark Woolstenhulme/table tennis
Daniel "Skid" Wroe/pilots
Annette Wysocki/nurses
Xiaocun Xu/volleyball
Rusty Yarnall/mountain bikes
Jim Yeager/pilots
Curt Yee/skiers
YoRelles/skiers
Nancy Zee/nurses
Dick Zeitlin/pilots
R. C. Zimmerman/skydivers
Kevin E. Zsenak/roller coasters
Ben Zuhl/science fiction